Adobe
FrameMaker 8.0

**A Hands-On Guide to
Creating DITA Compliant Documents™**

BrightPath
<Solutions/>

www.brightpathsolutions.com

About the Authors

BERNARD ASCHWANDEN

Bernard Aschwanden, Director of Technology and Publishing Architecture with Bright Path Solutions, is a recognized publishing technologies expert. He is an Adobe Certified Expert, a Certified Technical Trainer and the author of numerous articles on XML-based publishing and single sourcing. He presents at conferences and events across Europe and North America. A dynamic and entertaining speaker, he tailors his presentations to the audience and welcomes participation.

JACQUIE HEYS

Jacquie Heys, Senior Information Developer and Technical Editor with Bright Path Solutions, is an accomplished technical writer and editor. She graduated from York University with a Bachelor of Arts degree in English and acquired an M.A. in English Literature from the University of Toronto before receiving a certificate in Technical Writing from Seneca College.

CHRISTY JACKSON

Christy Jackson, Information Architect and Technical Trainer with Bright Path Solutions is an accomplished developer and trainer. She has extensive experience working with FrameMaker and XMetaL. In addition to her training experience, she is a knowledgeable industry expert and regularly presents at a client sites and conferences across North America.

Preface

This book is about DITA and Adobe FrameMaker 8.0. If you are working with a different version of FrameMaker, some procedures or settings shown in this text may differ from what you see on your screen.

DITA is a technology buzzword and a format that definitely offers opportunities. Companies that are generating content for publishing, enterprise systems, catalogs, or the Web are looking for a way to make the content more reusable. Some companies are also interested in ways to get their information out in multiple formats to their clients. Adobe noticed this interest and has been developing their FrameMaker software to become a "DITA publishing solution."

FrameMaker round-trip DITA capability means that, in addition to the technical publishing groups that have been using FrameMaker for years, DITA producers and information managers can publish using this and other tools. Fitting nicely into an enterprise workflow, FrameMaker allows users to bring in their raw DITA to create documents, help content, PDF, and HTML using the DITA Open Toolkit. It also permits extraction of DITA, allowing users to make changes and then ship the DITA based XML content wherever they need it.

DITA can be difficult to work with. FrameMaker is high-end and requires a moderate level of technical skill to use properly. Combine these two difficulties and you have a puzzle. This book serves to help you piece together that puzzle by taking an applied approach to both DITA and FrameMaker.

Introduction

In order to get the most value from this book it is suggested that you have an understanding of the Darwin Information Typing Architecture (DITA). If you are not familiar with DITA, then you should first read Appendix A: DITA Primer to familiarize yourself with general concepts related to DITA. Information on "DITA Primer" can be found on page 161.

Once you have a familiarity with DITA it is suggested that you alternate between the chapters and the related tutorial. The chapters outline ideas and procedures in a general fashion. The tutorials provide a structured set of exercises related to these ideas with specific examples.

When working with either a chapter or a tutorial it is in your best interest to first read the entire content and then review the ideas a second time before moving to a tutorial. Once in a tutorial it is best to review the steps and the expected results before attempting any tutorial.

Contents

Chapter 1: Application overview

Understanding the Adobe FrameMaker 8.0 conceptual model   1

Getting started   2

Topic management   3

Application interface   5

Document View   12

Setting user and compatibility preferences   14

Setting viewing preferences   17

Associating the .xml extension with FrameMaker   20

Chapter 2: File edits

Selecting and deselecting text   23

Editing text   24

Clearing, cutting, copying, and pasting text   25

Word processing tools   25

Undoing and redoing   28

Chapter 3: Structuring basics

Element terms and definitions   30

Element Catalog   33

Structure View   36

Chapter 4: Developing topics

Considerations in topic-based writing   39

Topics and specializations in DITA   40

Create a new topic   43

Chapter 5: Developing concepts

Basic concept example   45

Commonly used elements in a concept   46

Detailed concept sample   52

Create a new concept   52

Chapter 6: Prolog elements

Purpose of prolog elements (metadata)   53

Commonly used elements in a prolog   54

Working with metadata (prolog) information   54

Chapter 7: Publishing

Publishing formats   57

Generating PDF   59

Chapter 8: Paragraphs and notes

Paragraph types   61

Working with paragraphs, notes, and quotations   62

Chapter 9: Lists

Lists and list parts   65

Working with lists   67

Working with list items   67

Working with definition lists   69

Chapter 10: Working with domains

Domain element overview   71

Typographical elements   72

Programing elements   72

Software elements   73

User interface   74

Chapter 11: Footnotes

Footnote element overview   75

Working with footnotes   76

Chapter 12: Indexes

Guideline for indexing   77

Working with index entries   78

Chapter 13: Attributes

Purpose of attributes   81

Attributes and the Structure View   82

Attributes dialog   82

Types of attributes   83

Working with attributes   84

Attributes and new elements   86

Chapter 14: Tables

Understanding table components   87

Table types   88

Working with tables   89

Moving within tables   90

Selecting and deselecting table content   90

Adding, moving or deleting columns or rows   91

Table properties   92

Merging or splitting cell content   93

Chapter 15: Images

Anchored frames   95

Supported formats   96

Inserting images   96

Manipulating images in frames   99

Chapter 16: Developing references

Basic reference example   101

Commonly used elements in a reference   102

Detailed reference example   104

Create a new reference   104

Chapter 17: Sections and examples

Comparing sections and examples with nested topics   105

Commonly used elements in a section or example   107

Working with section and example elements   108

Chapter 18: Developing tasks

Basic task example   109

Commonly used elements in a task   110

Detailed task example   112

Create a new task   113

Chapter 19: Track text edits

Tracking text edits   115

Track text edits display   116

Working with track text edits   117

Chapter 20: Validation

Understanding valid versus invalid documents   119

Checking validity   120

Allowing or ignoring errors   121

Fixing invalid documents   122

Chapter 21: Linking in topics

Types of links   125

Working with links   126

Chapter 22: Reusing content

About reuse   133

Conditional content   134

Filter by attribute   135

Working with content references   139

Working with variables   141

Chapter 23: Maps

Introduction to maps   143

Attributes and maps   144

Attributes and topicrefs   146

Working with maps   147

Publish a map   148

Adding content to a map   149

Organizing maps   150

Modifying relationships between map or topicref elements   152

Chapter 24: Relationship tables

Introduction to relationship tables   155

Working with relationship tables   156

Add a topicref to a relationship table   158

Organizing relationship tables   158

Working with topicref attributes and reltables   159

Appendix A: DITA Primer

DITA defined   161

Origin of DITA   162

Benefits of working with DITA   162

Difficulties in working with DITA   162

Key information types   163

Commonly used elements   167

Linking in DITA   189

Domain elements   191

Prolog elements   198

Common attributes and values   201

Map elements   204

Relationship table   206

Publishing from DITA   208

Tutorial 1: Get started with FrameMaker

Tutorial overview   215

Create a new concept   216

Display and configure the Structure View   218

Display and configure the Element Catalog   219

Work with document views   220

Setting user and compatibility preferences   220

Close the file   220

Exit the application   221

Tutorial 2: Work with basic content

Tutorial overview   223

Opening a previously created DITA concept   223

Save files to a new location   225

Set up the Structure View and Element Catalog   226

Add a short description   227

Insert the concept body   227

Add a new paragraph   228

Add an unordered list   229

Tutorial 3: Work with structure

Tutorial overview   231

Opening a previously created DITA concept   232

Save the file   232

Convert an unordered list to an ordered list   233

Add a new paragraph   234

Wrap content in tags   234

Remove tags   235

Change a paragraph to a note   236

Delete an element   237

Convert an unordered list to an ordered list   237

Tutorial 4: Work with topics

Tutorial overview   239

Create a new topic   240

Close a topic   241

Tutorial 5: Work with concepts

Tutorial overview   243

Create a new concept   244

Develop the short description   244

Modify content, change views, save and close   245

Tutorial 6: Work with metadata

Tutorial overview   247

Opening a previously created DITA concept   247

Save the concept   248

Adding initial metadata information   249

Adding additional metadata information   253

Tutorial 7: Publish topics

Tutorial overview   255

Opening a previously created DITA concept   255

Save the concept   256

Publish a topic to HTML   257

Publish a topic to PDF   257

Tutorial 8: Work with paragraphs

Tutorial overview   259

Create a new concept   260

Develop the short description   260

Develop initial paragraph content   261

Insert notes   262

Insert quotations   263

Modify an existing paragraph   264

Tutorial 9: Work with lists

Tutorial overview   265

Opening a previously created DITA concept   266

Save the concept   267

Insert an ordered list   267

Work with an unordered list   268

Work with an ordered list   268

Work with list items   269

Work with a definition list   270

Tutorial 10: Work with domains

Tutorial overview   273

Opening a previously created DITA topic   274

Save the topic   275

Work with typographic formats   275

Work with code phrase and codeblock   276

Work with software elements   278

Work with user interface elements   278

Tutorial 11: Work with footnotes

Tutorial overview   281

Opening a previously created DITA topic   281

Save the topic   282

Work with footnotes   283

Tutorial 12: Work with indices

Tutorial overview   285

Opening a previously created DITA topic   285

Save the topic   286

Work with single-level index entries   287

Generate a standalone index   288

Modify existing index entries   289

Tutorial 13: Work with attributes

Tutorial overview   291

Opening a previously created DITA topic   291

Save the topic   292

Work with attributes   293

Change the note type   294

Tutorial 14: Work with tables

Tutorial overview   297

Opening a previously created DITA topic   298

Save the topic   299

Insert a basic table   299

Add, move and delete content in a table   300

Modify table properties   302

Modify column widths   303

Modify cell properties   304

Merge and split cell content   305

Tutorial 15: Work with images

Tutorial overview   307

Opening a previously created DITA topic   307

Save the topic   308

Insert an image   309

Modify image properties   309

Insert an image with a title   310

Tutorial 16: Work with references

Tutorial overview   313

Create a new reference   313

Tutorial 17: Work with sections and examples

Tutorial overview   315

Create a new reference   316

Add a section   317

Insert a properties table   317

Update content and develop another section   319

Create and save a new concept   320

Add and develop section content   320

Add and develop example content   321

Complete the concept with sections and examples   322

Tutorial 18: Work with tasks

Tutorial overview   323

Create a new task   323

Develop the cmd and stepresult   324

Add a prerequisite   325

Create a detailed task   327

Tutorial 19: Work with track changes

Tutorial overview   329

Open a sample file   330

Add content to a document while tracking changes   330

Modify content in a document while tracking changes   331

Delete content in a document while tracking changes   333

Modify the structure in a document while tracking changes   333

Accept or reject changes in a document   334

Tutorial 20: Work with validation

Tutorial overview   337

Open a sample file   338

Perform a basic validation check   338

Invalidate content   339

Open content with missing elements   339

Open content with invalid element names   341

Tutorial 21: Work with links

Tutorial overview   343

Insert a FrameMaker cross-reference link   344

Insert inline internal xrefs links   345

Insert inline external xref links to DITA files   347

Insert inline external xref links to non-DITA files   350

Insert inline web links   350

Insert related links to topics   351

Insert related links to web pages   353

Insert related links to files   353

Tutorial 22: Work with content reuse

Tutorial overview   355

Apply conditional content markup   356

Create filter by attribute settings   358

Configure output for conditional content   359

Remove conditional content markup   360

Reference other topics   361

Modify a content reference in another topic   363

Create a reusable component   364

Insert a reusable component   365

Modify a reusable component   366

Tutorial 23: Work with maps

Tutorial overview   367

Open and publish an existing map   368

Create a map   369

Add DITA topics to a map   370

Adding non-DITA content to a map   371

Reorganize map content   373

Group map content   375

Inserting maps within maps   377

Implement multiple changes to a ditamap   378

Tutorial 24: Work with relationship tables

Tutorial overview   381

Open and publish an existing map   382

Insert a basic relationship table   383

Add content to a relationship table   384

Nest entries in a relationship tables   386

Working with topicref attributes and reltables   389

Create a collection-type   395

Chapter 1

Application overview

Overview

This topic teaches you the basics of using the application and how the interface works.

The following topics are covered:

- *Understanding the Adobe FrameMaker 8.0 conceptual model*
- *Getting started*
- *Topic management*
- *Application interface*
- *Document View*
- *Setting user and compatibility preferences*
- *Setting viewing preferences*
- *Associating the .xml extension with FrameMaker*

Understanding the Adobe FrameMaker 8.0 conceptual model

The software is used to create various XML documents that adhere to the DITA specification, including DITA map, topic, concept, reference, and task elements. These documents may be composed of a variety of elements. Each element has unique content (usually entered by the user of the software—the author). Element content may include graphics, text, tables, or any combination of this and other material.

Formatting is attached to the page content using stylesheets. The end result is a very visually rich and easy-to-use document that may be delivered in print, on-line as an HTML, XML, PDF or other document, or any combination thereof.

Using word processing capabilities

You can create the types of documents traditionally associated with DITA, such as DITA maps, topics, concepts, references, tasks, and more, using word processing features such as:

- Text editing capabilities
- Spell checking and thesaurus
- Search capabilities
- Templates for standardized appearances
- Tables with a variety of formatting
- Revision management

Publishing features

The software has features unique to XML-based publishing systems. These allow you to create complex manuals such as software user guides, hardware maintenance manuals, service and revision reports, and other DITA-specific content including topics, references, concepts, tasks, and maps through the use of functionality such as:

- Flexible output design
- Table formatting
- Graphic and text object layout
- DITA map building
- Information links (hypertext)
- Automatic hypertext links

Integrating with the DITA Open Toolkit

Users can create HTML, XHTML, Eclipse Help, or PDF files quickly from DITA-compliant files using the DITA Open Toolkit. Very little control over the output is available. For full control over the output, as well as the ability to create your own templates, you need to modify or develop files that are included in the DITA Open Toolkit. This utility must be installed independently of FrameMaker.

HTML, XML, and PDF formats can be created from FrameMaker 8 using tools like Adobe Acrobat and Adobe RoboHelp.

Getting started

To start, first launch the software and then create a new basic topic.

Launch the software

This task teaches you how to launch the software after it has been installed.

1. Click Start.

2. Select Programs > Adobe > FrameMaker 8 > Adobe FrameMaker 8.

   The software launches and the workspace displays.

©2008 Bright Path Solutions—Contents are copyrighted. Do not photocopy or distribute.

> **Note**
>
> These steps are based on standard installation settings on a Windows®-based system.

Exit FrameMaker

Exit the software before you turn off your computer. If you simply turn your computer off instead of exiting properly, errors may occur.

1. Select File > Exit.

   If there is an open file that has not been saved, you are prompted to save the topic.

Create a new DITA topic

When you create a new topic, start by choosing one of the four DITA templates. Each template contains some basic elements and placeholder text to get you started. You can type over the placeholder text in the existing elements and add new elements as needed.

1. Select DITA > New DITA File.

2. Select New <topic> or choose the task, reference, or concept if desired.

3. Select a location and name the file.

4. Click Select.

5. Modify the document as required.

Topic management

Topic management includes a variety of topic-specific commands.

Saving topics

You have multiple options to choose from when saving topics: Save, Save As, Save As PDF, and Save As XML. When an existing topic is to be saved with a new name, use the Save As menu option. Once a topic has been created and saved, the Save option replaces the original topics with any changes you made to the material, effectively deleting the older versions of the topic. Therefore, if you want to keep the original version of a topic, use the Save As command to save new material under a different name.

The topic naming convention has specific rules about topic and folder names for DITA. Therefore, ensure that names have no spaces and use no special characters.

Save a new topic

The Save As option allows you to specify a path and name for a topic.

1. Select File > Save As.

   The Save Document dialog box displays.

2. Specify the server, drive, or folder to save the topic to.

3. Name the topic.

4. Click Save .

Save an existing topic

The Save option saves your current topic.

1. Select File > Save.

Save an existing topic under a new name

The Save As option allows you to specify a path and name for a topic.

1. Select File > Save As.

   The Save Document dialog box displays.

2. Specify the server, drive, or folder to save the topic to.

3. Under Save As Type, select an extension if required.

4. Name the topic.

5. Click Save .

Closing topics

When closing topics, you may be prompted to save a topic if you have not already done so. If you choose to save the topic, FrameMaker displays the Save Document dialog box or simply saves the topic if a name and path already exist.

Close the current topic

The Close option allows you to close your current open topic.

1. Select File > Close.

   You are prompted to save the topic if changes have been made without saving.

Open a single topic

Topics that have been saved may be opened for editing, printing, and so on.

The Open option allows you to browse to a topic location and select one or more topics to open.

1. Select File > Open.

2. Specify the server, drive, or folder to open the topic from.

3. Select the topic to open.

4. Click [Open] .

5. If required, select the Structured Application to use.

    By default this is usually named DITA-Topic-FM.

Managing multiple open topics

When you are working with several open topics at once, there are some options available to make it easier to manage them.

Move between open topics

If multiple topics are open you can move from one to the other as required.

1. Select the desired topic from the tabs beneath the tool bar.

    The bold topic is your current topic.

Display all topic headers

The Cascading view displays all the topic headers of your open topics, making it easy to click on a header and display that topic.

1. Select Window > Cascade.

Display all open topics vertically

The Tiling view splits the topic window so that you can see a small section of every open topic at the same time.

1. Select Window > Tile.

Application interface

The application interface contains a variety of visual components to identify and manage content, simplify tasks like inserting elements or modifying attributes, provide quick access to commonly used features, and provide an authoring environment to support the creation of DITA-compliant content.

Default appearance

The default appearance depends on the configuration of the application when it is first installed, the way the application is configured within your organization, and the way the application is configured by you, the user, when you last worked with it. Therefore, a variety of appearances may be considered the default. In most cases though, the default appearance has several toolbars displayed, specific content visible in a topic, and tools available to simplify writing content.

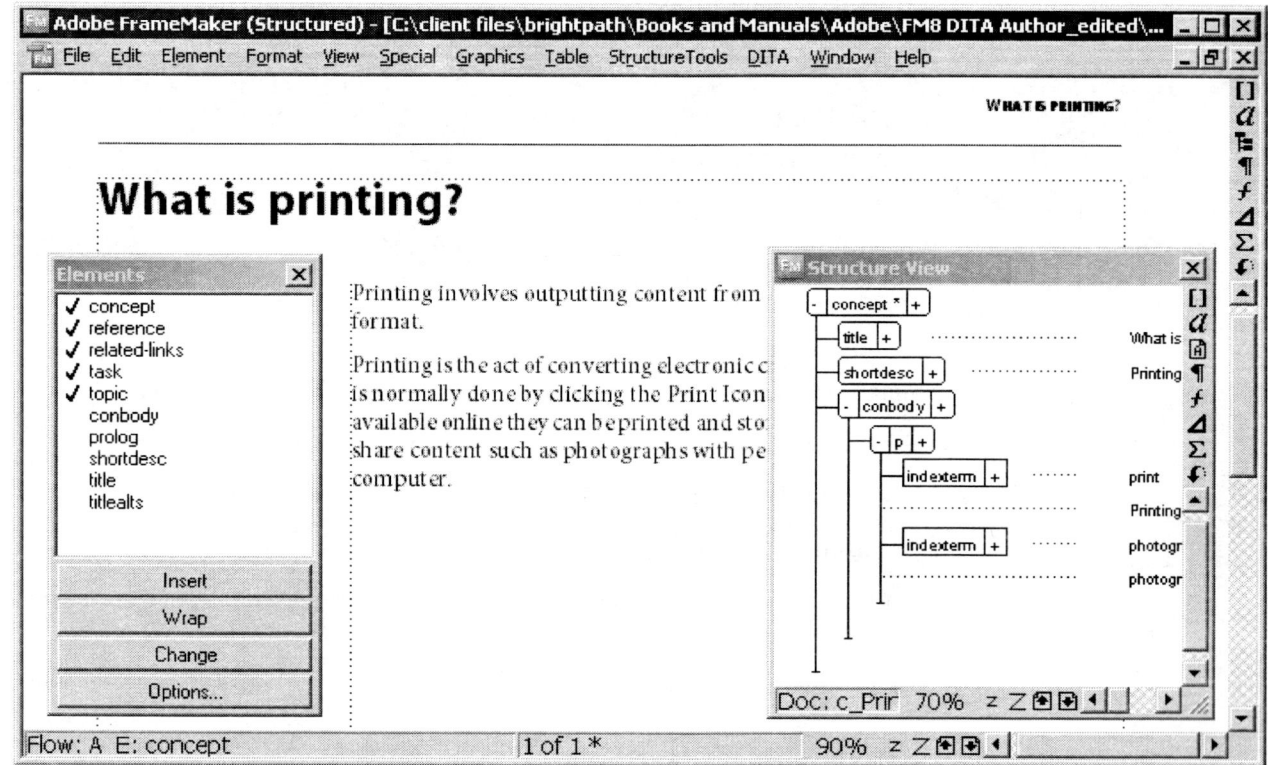

Customizing the display

The application interface is fully and easily customizable to allow displaying and moving catalogs, configuring and placing toolbars, and more.

The application is composed of several key components. In the sample above are menus and toolbars, the Element Catalog, the Structure View, and the body pages (which contain scroll bars and have view icons and the context bar at the bottom).

Additional palettes or menus may be visible depending on the topics that are open and the user options that you specify.

Menu   The menu contains File, Edit, Element, Format, View, Special, Graphics, Table, StructureTools, Window, and Help.

Toolbars   Numerous toolbars are available.

QuickAccess toolbar

This toolbar includes icons for common tasks such as saving, opening, or printing.

QuickAccess toolbar extensions

This toolbar includes four sets of extensions. To toggle between extension click the blue triangular icons to move to the next or previous toolbar.

Formatting toolbar

This toolbar includes icons for applying common formats such as centered text, tabs, line spacing, symbols, and font options.

Track Text Edit toolbar

This toolbar includes icons for making and managing text edits.

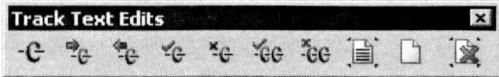

Tabbed toolbar

This toolbar gives you a tabbed view of any open topics and maps.

Configuring toolbars   The various toolbars in FrameMaker can be configured as required.

Show or hide toolbars

Toolbars can be shown or hidden as required.

1. Select View.

   Any toolbars with a check mark are already displayed.

2. Select the toolbars to show or hide.

Move QuickAccess toolbar

The QuickAccess toolbar can be moved to customize the appearance of the application.

1. Click [icon] to undock the QuickAccess toolbar and display it in a vertical layout.

   The QuickAccess toolbar can now be moved to any location.

Dock QuickAccess toolbar

The QuickAccess toolbar can be docked (or anchored) to its original location.

1. Click ▯ to dock the QuickAccess toolbar.

Structure View

The Structure View is primarily used to see a visual representation of the structure of the elements in a topic.

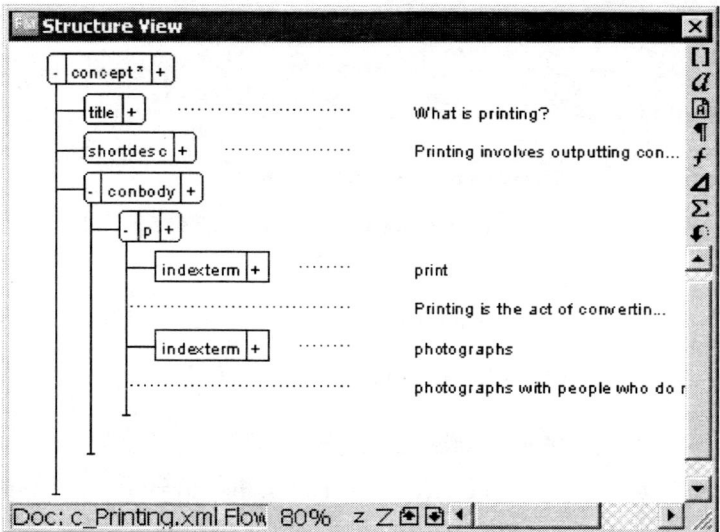

1. Select 🖿 from the sidebar.

Attributes Editor   The Attributes Editor is used to see and modify attribute options and values related to the selected element.

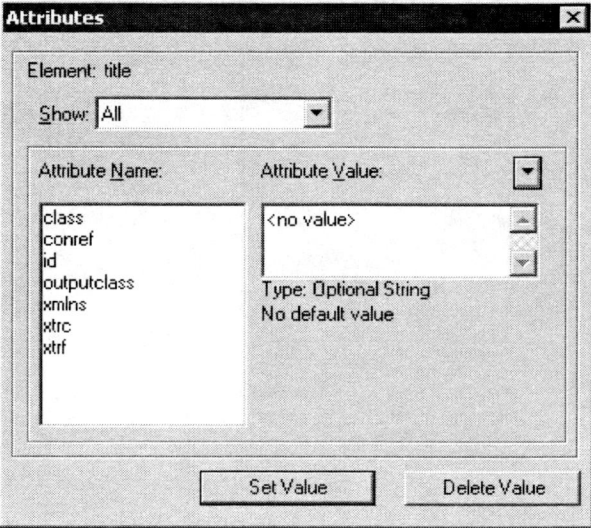

Show or hide the Attributes Editor

The Attributes Editor can be shown or hidden as required.

1. Select *a* on the sidebar to display the Attributes Editor.

    Close the editor to hide it again.

Customize the Attributes Editor

The Attributes Editor can show required and specified attributes, all attributes (default), or no attributes. Setting this option to required and specified attributes is recommended.

1. Select View > Attribute Display Options.

2. Select one of the options.

3. Click Set .

Element Catalog

The Element Catalog is primarily used to display a list of element tags that can be inserted at the current location or that can be changed from the current element.

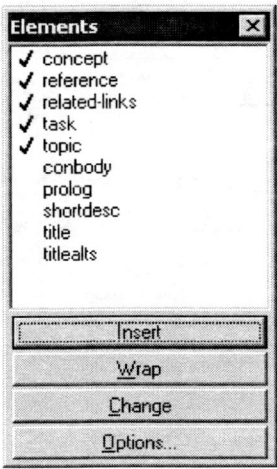

1. Click **[]** in the sidebar.

   Hide the Element Catalog again by closing it.

Document View

The Document View can be displayed in four primary modes.

The Document View panel contains the primary work location for authors. This panel can be configured to display in a variety of ways. Changing the Document View may result in other panels displaying or hiding automatically.

Element Boundaries (as Tags)

The Element Boundaries (as Tags) view shows content as well as the XML tags that wrap it. The current location of the insertion point displays at the bottom of the window.

Depending on your configuration, the Element Boundaries (as Tags) may restrict your ability to select content. The boundaries are also displayed in print output. This view is generally only recommended for reviewing structure or if the tags need to be displayed in the print or PDF version of your content.

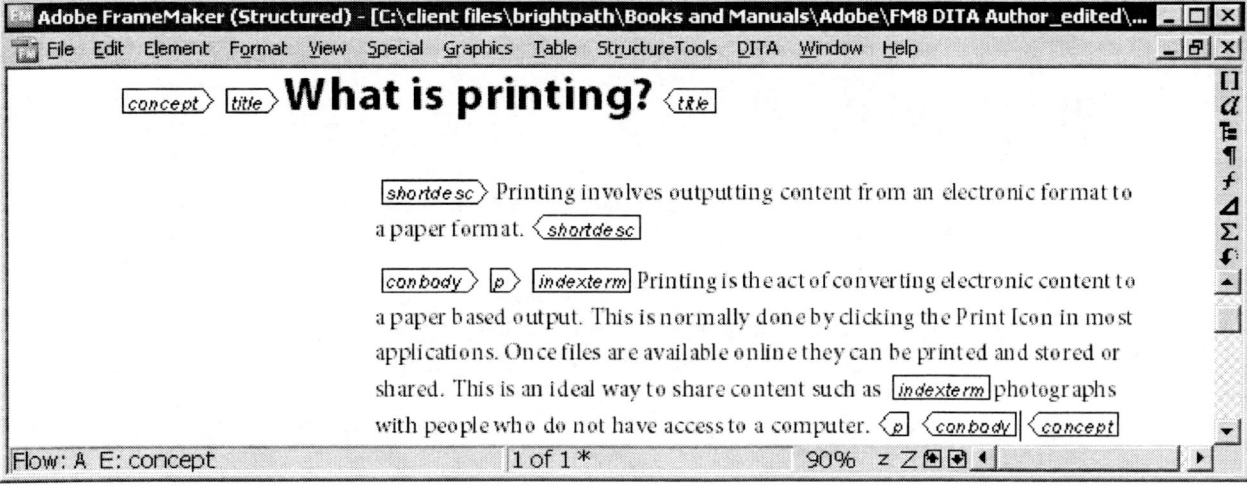

1.   Select View > Element Boundaries (as Tags).

Element Boundaries   The Element Boundaries view shows content as well as markup to indicate the start and end of an element that wrap it. The current location of the insertion point displays at the bottom of the window. The boundaries are also displayed in print output. This view is generally only recommended for reviewing structure or if the tags need to be displayed in the print or PDF version of your content.

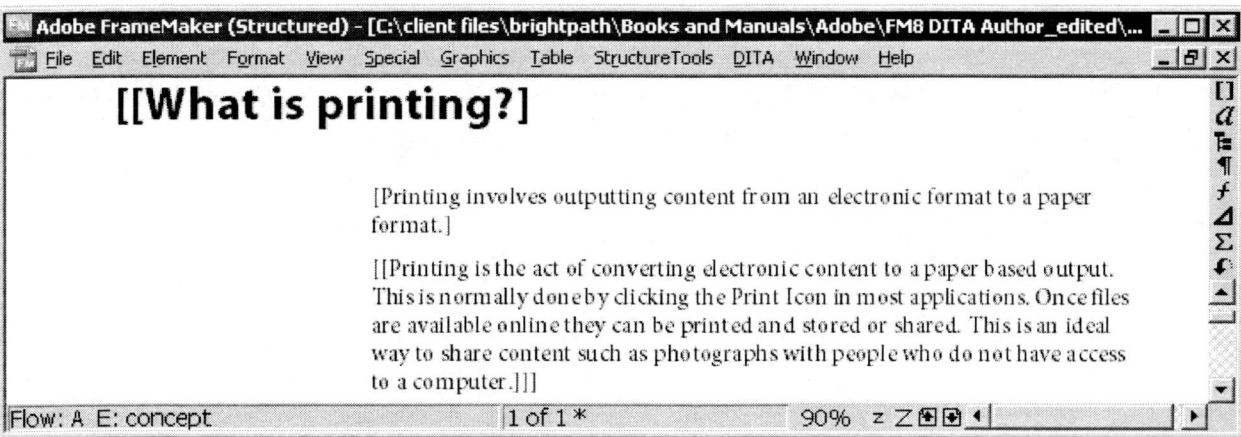

1.   Select View > Element Boundaries.

Normal View The normal view shows content but hides the tags that wrap it. The current location of the insertion point displays at the bottom of the window.

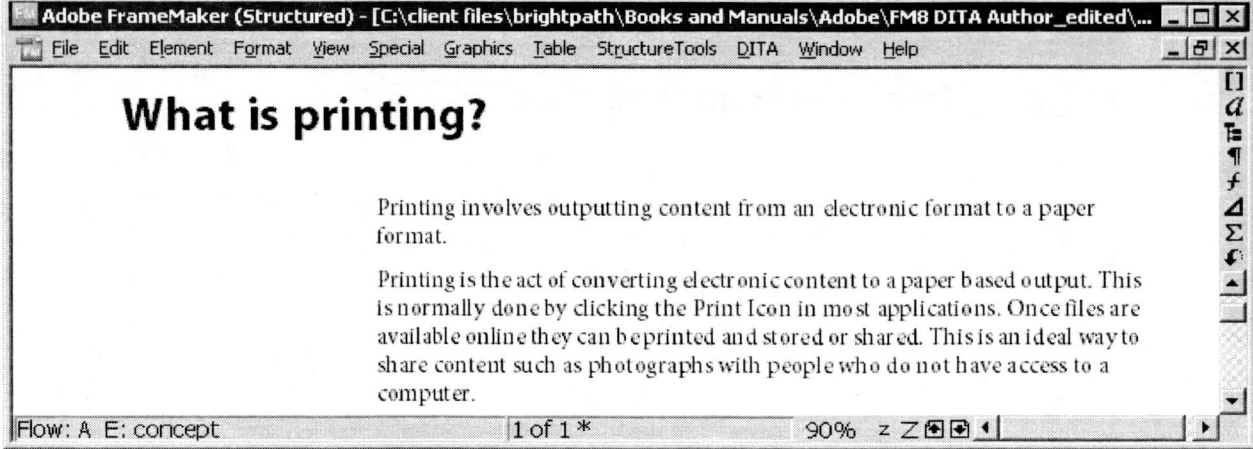

1. Select View.

2. Deselect either Element Boundaries or Element Boundaries (as Tags).

Setting user and compatibility preferences

This topic explains how to change some of the options in the application.

There are a variety of preferences that may be set in FrameMaker. Preferences are specific to the computer system on which they are set, and are not a part of a document's properties. Therefore, your settings are unique to your computer and do not impact documents sent by others. In the same way, FrameMaker does not overwrite your preferences when opening another user's files.

1.   Select File > Preferences > General.

The Preferences dialog displays.

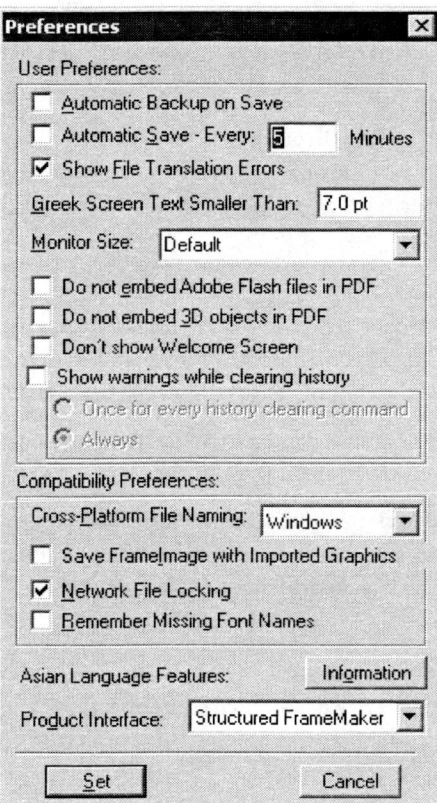

2.   Specify user preferences as required.

3.   Click Set .

Automatic backups   When saving your FrameMaker file, the automatic backup creates a duplicate copy of the previous version of a file. This allows you to have a duplicate file that can be used to recover content or act as a source for document comparison.

The automatic backup file is assigned a default name based on your filename. The extension backup.fm is added by FrameMaker to the file. Therefore, if you are working with a document named Overview.fm, the automatic backup would be Overview.backup.fm.

Each time a file is updated and saved, the backup is replaced with the previously saved version.

Automatic saves

Autosave allows you to automatically save a file at a regular specified interval. This file can then be opened in the event of a system error, allowing you to restore a document up to the time of the last autosave. When the document is saved manually, the autosave file is deleted automatically.

The autosave file is assigned a default name based on your filename. The extension auto.fm is added by FrameMaker to the file. Therefore, if you are working with a document named Overview.fm, the autosave file is Overview.auto.fm.

File translation errors

If active, this setting displays a list of errors encountered by the software when opening files. The most common error is related to missing fonts, but other messages can display. For more information on these errors, and resolutions to them, review the FrameMaker documentation.

File locking

When a document created by FrameMaker is opened (usually over a network), a lock file can be created. This file notifies a user who tries to open it that another user is already accessing the document. This temporary file is deleted when you exit the program.

If FrameMaker crashes and a lock file exists, you may be prompted that the file is in use. In this situation, you need to reset the lock.

The lock file is assigned a default name based on your filename. The extension .lck is added by FrameMaker to the file. Therefore, if you are working with a document named Overview.fm, the locked filename is Overview.lck.

Greek text

Selecting this option enables FrameMaker to display text quickly, by changing the onscreen appearance of text. All content smaller than a set threshold displays as a bar rather than individual characters. This bar acts as a placeholder for content and is not representing each character.

Changing the product interface

Changing interfaces lets you switch between Unstructured and Structured FrameMaker.

When changing interfaces, the preferences reset. For example, if you decide to turn off Automatic Backup on Save and set the Network File Locking, you must reset them when you switch the interface.

1. Select File > Preferences > General.

2. Select, under Product Interface, either FrameMaker or Structured FrameMaker.

3. Click   Set   .

The FrameMaker dialog displays to prompt you to restart FrameMaker before the changes are applied.

4. Click   OK

5. Close and relaunch FrameMaker.

Setting viewing preferences

This topic explains how to change some of the viewing options.

Borders, text symbols, rulers, and gridlines   Borders, text symbols, rulers, and gridlines are displayed by default in most new documents. If these objects are not visible, you may display them. If you do not want them displayed, you can hide them.

- Borders display around graphics, tables, and frames.
- Text symbols include characters such as tab symbols, end of text flow markers, and paragraph markers.
- Rulers display paragraph indents, tab stops, and object positions.
- Gridlines are useful when working with graphics, tables, frames, or other objects that need to be accurately positioned on screen.

To display or hide any of these objects, do the following:

1. Select View > Borders, or View > Text Symbols, or View > Rulers, or View > Gridlines.

Setting multiple viewing options

The Option selection allows you to set up many of the viewing preferences in a single dialog box.

1. Select View > Options.

   Once the View Options dialog box displays, several options are available.

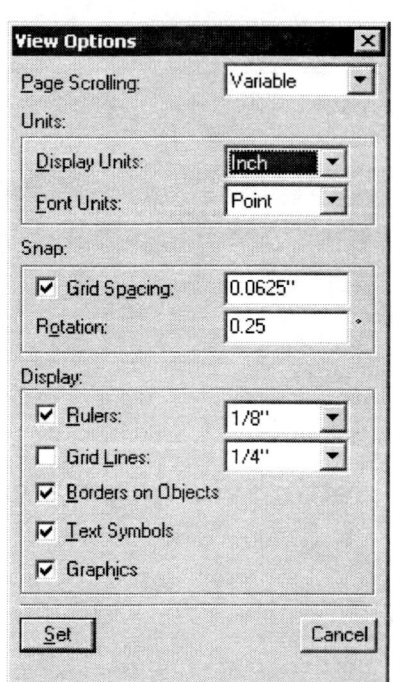

2. Under Page Scrolling, specify the type of scrolling

   - Vertical displays pages stacked one on top of the other.
   - Horizontal displays pages in side by side layout.
   - Facing Pages arranges pages so left and right sheets are next to each other.
   - Variable alternates between all three as required to accommodate the best view.

3. Select the preferred unit of measurement for Display Units and Font Units under Units.

   - Display Units can be in Centimeters (cm), Millimeters (mm), Inch, Pica, Point, Didot or Cicero.
   - Font Units may be either Point or Q.

4. Set Grid Spacing and Rotation under Snap.

   - Grid Spacing is the distance used by default when objects are moved on the page as a fixed grid to which objects align.
   - Rotation specifies the percentage of a degree to which rotated objects align.

5. Set values for the rulers markings and distance between grid lines.

   These values are based on the Display Units specified under Units.

   - Rulers settings determine how often markings display on the rulers.
   - Grid Lines value determines how far apart gridlines are, when displayed.

6. Select or de-select Borders On Objects, Text Symbols, and Graphics.

   - Borders and text symbols are displayed by default in most new documents.
   - De-selecting Graphics hides all graphics in the document, increasing the speed of both online display and printing.

7. Click [Set] to save your changes.

Zooming the document

The zoom setting of a document may be increased (to show more detail of a smaller portion of the page) or decreased (to show less detail and more layout in relationship to the page). The zoom settings are specified on a per document basis. The minimum setting for a zoom is 25% and the maximum is 1600%.

Decrease or increase the zoom

These buttons, located in the bottom right of the document window, increase or decrease the current zoom.

1.   Click Zoom Out 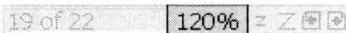 or Zoom In .

Zoom to a preset value

1.   Click the Zoom popup.

     This popup, located in the bottom right of the document window, displays the current zoom.

2.   Click on a value from the pop-up menu.

Setting zoom values

FrameMaker allows you to configure individual files with unique zoom settings. These values may range between 25 and 1600 percent. Additionally, the document window and the current page may be resized in various ways.

1.   Click the Zoom button.

     This button, located near the bottom middle of the document window, displays the current zoom setting in percentage.

2.   Click Set from the pop-up menu.

     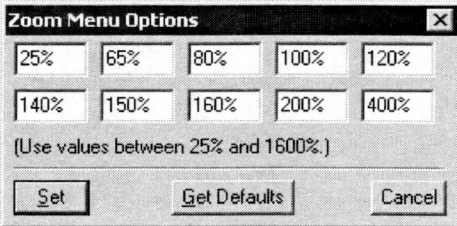

3.   Enter new values as required.

     Click Get Defaults to change the values back to original settings specified for the document.

4.   Click Set .

Associating the .xml extension with FrameMaker

By default, a variety of software tools may be associated with the .xml extension.

For example, if an XML topic is double clicked, it may open with tools such as Internet Explorer, Notepad, or other XML-enabled software tools.

Windows may be configured to associated the XML extension with a variety of software tools, including FrameMaker.

Configure file associations

The default association of an XML file can be modified in Windows to automatically be associated with the application.

1. Launch a Windows Explorer session.

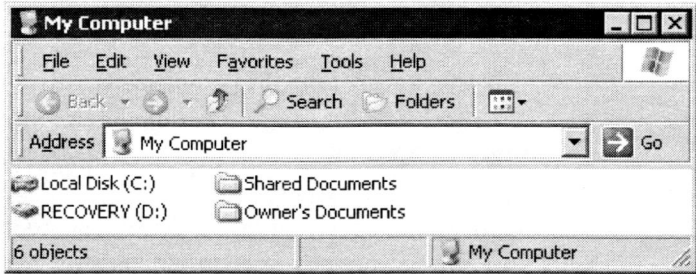

2. Select Tools > Folder Options.

3. Select the File Types tab.

4. Under Registered File Types, select XML.

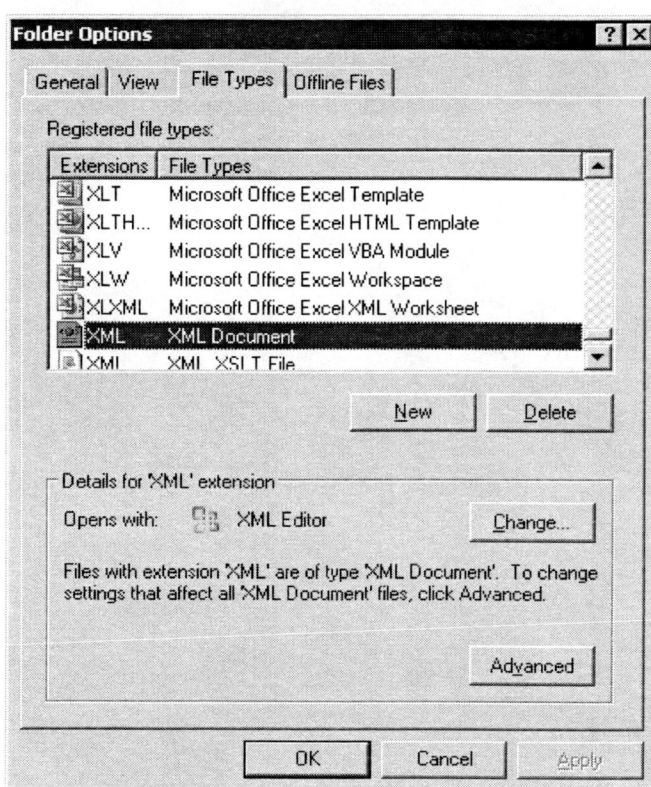

5. Click Change... .

6. Under Programs, if available, select Adobe FrameMaker 8.0 and click OK .

   At this point the file association is complete and XML files open using FrameMaker. However, if the required option is not available proceed to the next step.

7. If the program is not available by default, click Browse... .

8. Navigate to the FrameMaker installation folder.

   This folder is located, by default, in C:\Program Files\Adobe\Adobe FrameMaker 8.

9. Select the FrameMaker.exe file.

10. Click OK to return to the Open With dialog.

11. Click OK .

 **Note**

Only perform this task from the current step onwards if you were unable to select the correct program in the previous step.

Chapter 2

File edits

Overview

This topic teaches you how to create and manage text content in a structured document. The following topics are covered:

- *Selecting and deselecting text*
- *Editing text*
- *Clearing, cutting, copying, and pasting text*
- *Word processing tools*
- *Undoing and redoing*

Selecting and deselecting text

This topic explains how to select text so that you can work with it.

To select text, you need to highlight it, and there are several ways to do this. Using the mouse or the keyboard, you can select text character by character, word by word, paragraph by paragraph, or select your whole document at once.

Select characters

1. Use the mouse to position the insertion point at the beginning of the letter you want to select.

2. Click and drag to the opposite end of the letter to highlight it.

    To select multiple letters, click once and continue to hold down the mouse button while dragging across multiple letters.

Select words	1.	Double click the word to select.
		To select multiple words in the normal view and Element Boundaries view, double click and continue to hold down the mouse button while dragging across multiple words.
Select paragraphs	1.	Use the mouse to position the insertion point at the beginning of the paragraph you want to select.
	2.	Click and drag to the opposite end of the paragraph to highlight it.
		To select multiple paragraphs, click once and continue to hold down the mouse button while dragging across multiple paragraphs.
Select the whole document	1.	Click in the document view.
	2.	Press *Ctrl+a*.
Deselect text		In order to deselect any text simply click in a different location within your document view. Clicking within text places the insertion point in a new location.

Editing text

This topic explains how to edit text in an FrameMaker document by deleting or modifying existing text.

Delete text		Text that has been added to a document may be deleted. Ensure that you select only the content that is to be removed.
	1.	Select text to delete and press *Delete*.
Modify text		Text in a document may be modified in any number of ways. The most common change made to text in a document is to change content by replacing one phrase, sentence, or paragraph with another.
	1.	Select the text to change and type the new content.
		Old content is deleted at the first keystroke and new content replaces the previous data.

Clearing, cutting, copying, and pasting text

Clear text   Clearing text removes it from the document and does not store it for pasting elsewhere.

1. Highlight the content to clear.

2. Press *Delete*.

Cut text   Cutting text removes it from the document and stores it on the system clipboard so that it can be pasted elsewhere.

1. Highlight the content to cut.

2. Select Edit > Cut.

Copy text   Copying text does not remove it from its current location, but still stores it on the system clipboard so that it can be pasted elsewhere.

1. Highlight the content to copy.

2. Select Edit > Copy.

Paste text   Pasting inserts the text that was last cut or copied to the system clipboard.

If you paste non-XML content from another application, you need to wrap it in valid elements in FrameMaker.

1. Position the insertion point at the approximate place you want to paste content.

2. Select Edit > Paste.

Word processing tools

A variety of tools exist to perform word processing functions.

Spell check

1. Select Edit > Spelling Checker.

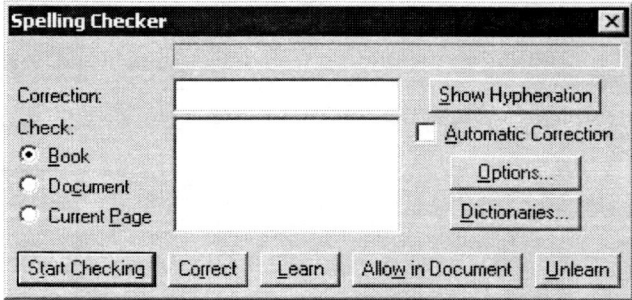

2. Select Start Checking.

3. Navigate the document and correct spelling errors as required.

Thesaurus

1. Select a word to look up in the thesaurus.

2. Select Edit > Thesaurus.

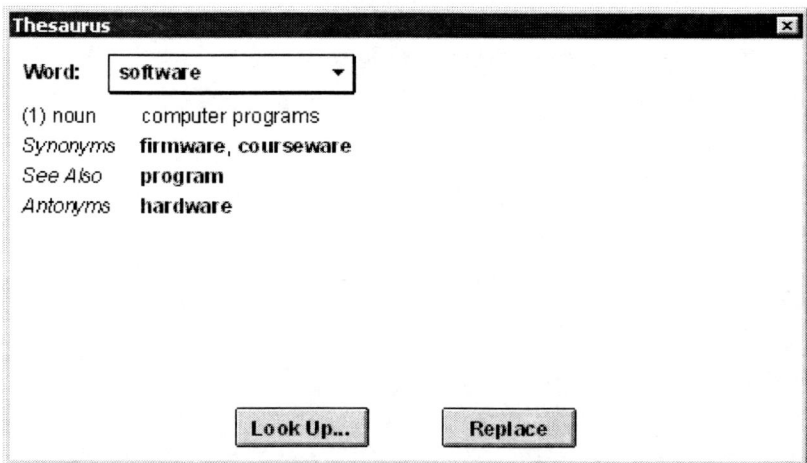

3. Click Look Up... .

4. Click Replace to change the word in the document.

Find and replace

Content can be found and changed. The type of content you can search for includes text, elements, attributes, marker text, variable text, as well as the existence of markers, variables, and anchored frames, for example. Additionally, the find and replace feature can be limited to only find and change text within specific elements.

Using Find and Replace

1. Select Edit > Find/Change.

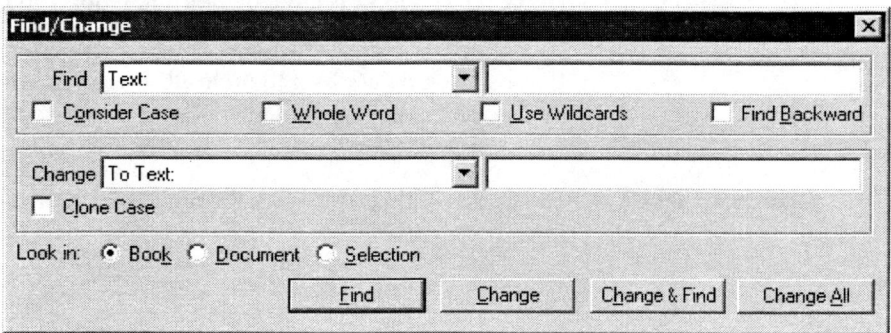

2. Select what type of construct you want followed by the text, marker type, or element you want.

3. Under Change, select what type of construct you want to change it to, followed by the text, marker type, or element you want to change it to.

-   Click **Find** to find the next instance.
-   Click **Change...** to replace the current instance.
-   Click **Change & Find** to replace the current instance and find the next instance.
-   Click **Change All** to replace all instances.

Options in Find and Replace

-   Select Consider case to only find an instance that matches the upper or lower case you typed in.
-   Select Whole word to only find an instance that matches the entire word you typed in.
-   Select Use wildcards to let you search for character patterns and for text that displays at the beginning or end of a line.
-   Select Find backward to search upwards instead of downwards through the document.
-   Select Clone case when replacing text with the same upper or lower case that existed in the text being replaced.
-   Select Look in: Book to search an entire book or map.
-   Select Look in: Document to search the current open document.
-   Select Look in: Selection to search the current selected content.

Undoing and redoing

FrameMaker supports limited undo and redo. If you perform actions and then save the document, you cannot undo any changes before the save.

However, you do not have to undo all changes in order. You can view the history of your changes and select one to undo or redo.

Undo an action

The Undo command reverses the previous action taken by a user.

1. Select Edit > Undo.

Redo an action

The Redo command reverses the previous undo.

1. Select Edit > Redo.

View history of actions

The History window allows you to select an action to undo or redo from a list.

1. Select Edit > History.

Chapter 3

Structuring basics

Overview

This topic teaches you how to create and manage valid structure by inserting and modifying structural elements.

The following topics are covered:

- *Element terms and definitions*
- *Element Catalog*
- *Structure View*

Element terms and definitions

This topic explains the key terms that apply when working with XML. Refer to the following image when reading terms and their definitions below.

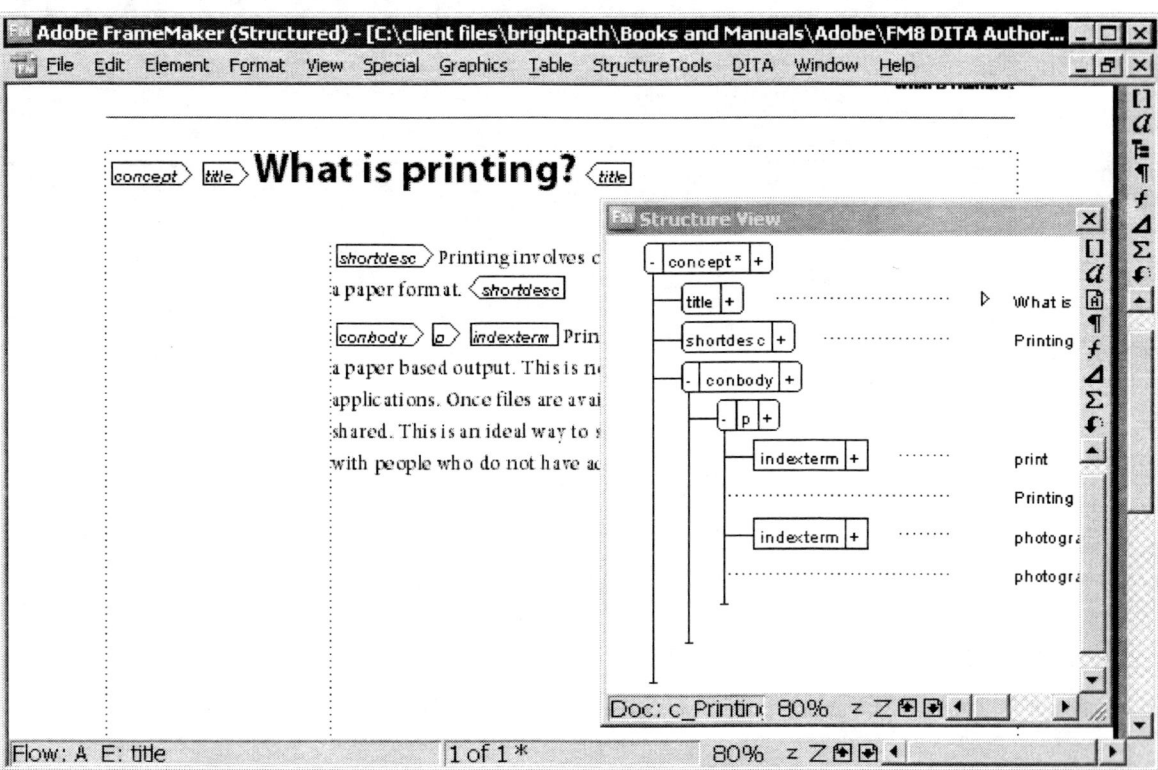

Ancestor   An ancestor is any element that contains another element.

In the element example, <concept> is the ancestor of all other elements in this example, including <title>, <shortdesc>, <conbody>, <p>, and <indexterm>. The element <conbody> is an ancestor to only two different elements; <p>, and <indexterm>.

Attribute   An attribute is any additional information used to describe an element; an attribute has both a name and a value.

Attributes are displayed in the Attributes Editor. In this example, the <title> element has an *id* attribute. The value of the id attribute is *concept_about_printing*.

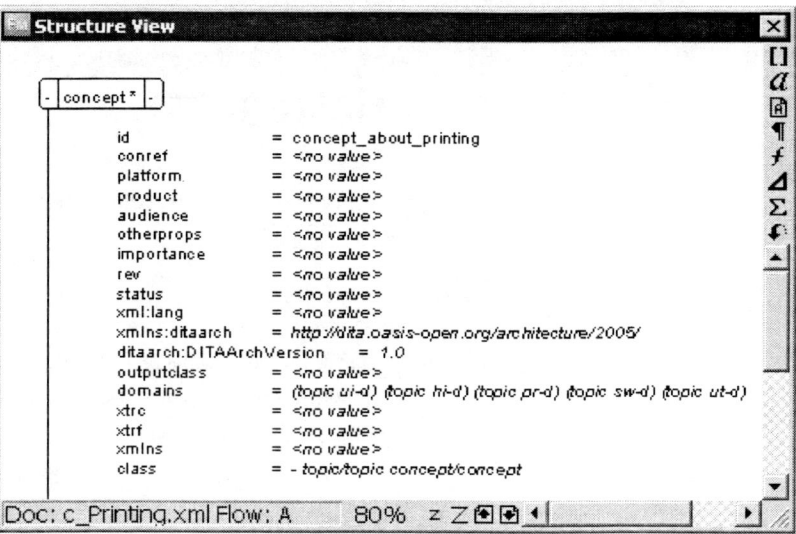

Child　A child is any element that is immediately subordinate to another element. In the element example, most elements are children.

In the element example, <title> is a child of <concept>. The elements <shortdesc> and <conbody> are also children of <concept>. This relationship is only one level in depth. Therefore, <p>, and <indexterm> are not considered children (or grandchildren) of <concept>. They are, however, descendants of <concept>.

Descendant　A descendant is any element that is contained by another element. In the above image, most elements are descendants. The exception is <concept>.

Element　An element is any single structural component in a structured document.

In the element example, <concept>, <title>, <shortdesc>, <conbody>, <p>, and <indexterm> are all elements. Elements may be reused if the document rules allow it.

Element tag　An element tag is any markup used to describe the start or end of an element.

In the element example, <concept>, <title>, <shortdesc>, <conbody>, <p>, and <indexterm> are all elements. Named tags surround these elements. In the Element

Boundaries (as Tags) view, you can see your elements surrounded by the element tags that markup the content.

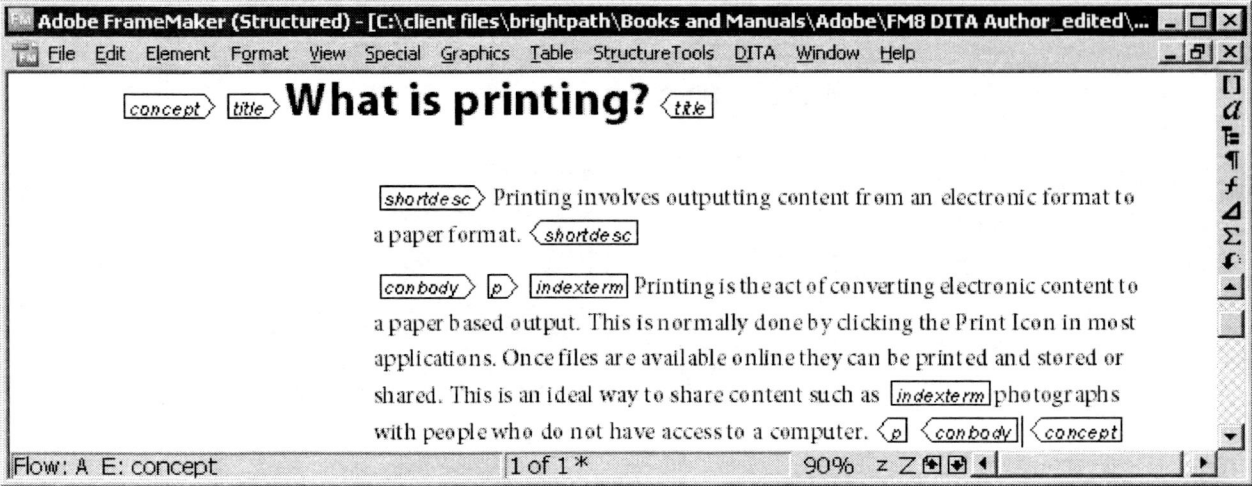

Element Catalog

The Element Catalog is a list of elements that can be added to the document. By default, this list displays only the elements that are valid at your current insertion point.

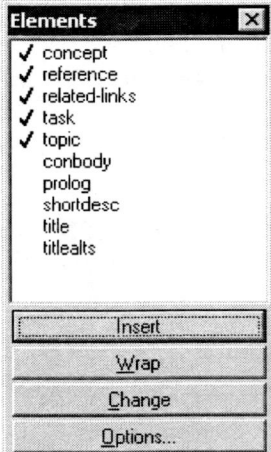

Hierarchy

Hierarchy is the relationship between elements that are defined as ancestors, children, descendants, parents, or siblings.

Parent

A parent is any element that has immediate subordinates.

In the element example, <concept> is the parent of <title>, <shortdesc>, and <conbody>. This relationship is only one level in depth. Therefore, <concept> is not considered to be the parent (or grandparent) of <p>, and <indexterm>. The element <concept> is, however, the ancestor of these elements.

Sibling

A sibling is any element that shares a parent with another element.

In the above example, <concept> has no siblings. The elements <title>, <shortdesc>, and <conbody> are siblings to each other.

Valid and invalid documents

XML documents can be valid and meet the rules of DITA. However, in some cases an XML document can be invalid because it does not meet the rules. For example, if a required title is not included, a document is invalid.

Element Catalog

In FrameMaker, you can insert and modify elements in a number of ways. Some users prefer using the menus, some prefer the Element Catalog, and others prefer the keyboard. You also have a choice of document views to work in. When you first start working with FrameMaker, we recommend that you try all of the different ways to work with elements and choose the one or ones that you feel most comfortable with.

When there is more than one way to accomplish a task, we usually describe how to use either the Element Catalog or the menus.

The Element Catalog gives you the most control when working with elements, but also requires a more detailed knowledge of DITA and the elements. By default, the Element Catalog displays only the elements that are valid at your current insertion point.

Display the Element Catalog

1. Select Element > Element Catalog.

2. If required, in the Element Catalog, click [Options...] to modify the available elements.

Element Catalog symbols

The Element Catalog uses various symbols to display elements that are valid, invalid or structurally incomplete if inserted at a current location.

Symbol	Purpose
Heavy Check	Allowable at this location. Valid structure.

Symbol	Purpose
Light Check	Allowable at this location. Invalidates structure prior to the new element.
Question Mark	Allowable at this location. Invalidates structure after the new element.
No Symbol	Not allowable at this location. Invalidates structure if inserted.

Element Catalog display options

The Element Catalog can be configured to display various combinations of elements, depending on your preferences.

A dialog of options related to the available elements can be displayed.

Tip

Consider leaving the default of seeing only valid elements in the Element Catalog when first working with the application. This will speed up your ability to learn what elements are valid in each location.

1. Click [Options...] in the Element Catalog.

   The Set Available Elements dialog displays.

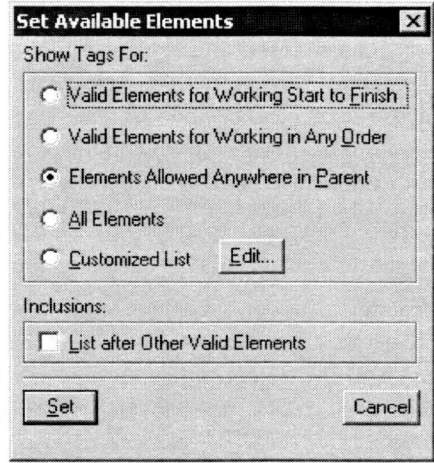

Valid elements for working from start to finish

Used to display only elements that may be inserted at the current location. With the exception of the highest level element, elements are shown if they only if they may be inserted as an immediate child of a parent.

1. Display the Set Available Elements dialog.

2. Select Valid Elements for Working Start to Finish.

3. Click [Set].

Valid elements for working in any order

Used to display only elements that may be inserted at the current location. All elements that are children are shown, even if the current location does not allow their insertion as valid children.

1.   Display the Set Available Elements dialog.

2.   Select Valid Elements for Working in Any Order.

3.   Click Set .

Elements allowed anywhere in the parent

Used to display all elements that are allowed in the parent element. All elements that are allowed as valid children in the parent are displayed.

1.   Display the Set Available Elements dialog.

2.   Select Elements Allowed Anywhere in Parent.

3.   Click Set .

All elements

If required, all elements that are available in a structured document can be displayed in the Element Catalog.

1.   Display the Set Available Elements dialog.

2.   Select All Elements.

3.   Click Set .

Customized lists of elements

Should a specific set of elements be required, the Element Catalog can be customized to display only specific elements, regardless of structural rules.

1.   Display the Set Available Elements dialog.

2.   Select Customized List.

3. Click Edit... to modify the list of elements displayed.

The Customize List of Available Elements dialog displays. It has a Show and a Don't Show pane that list elements.

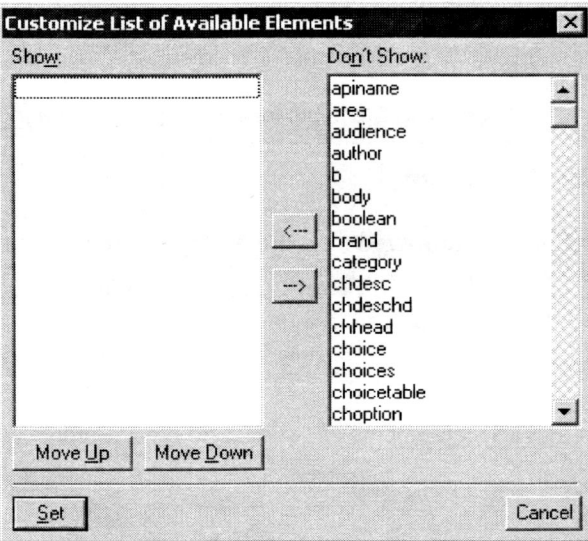

- Click <--- or ---> to move elements from one side of the dialog to the other.
- Double click an element to toggle it from one side of the dialog to the other.
- Press and hold *Shift*, click <--- or ---> to move all elements from one side of the dialog to the other. Then release *Shift*.
- Elements that are in under Show in the dialog can be rearranged by selecting the element name and clicking Move Up or Move Down as required.

4. Click Set .

Structure View

The Structure View provides a tree-like hierarchy to display the elements and the relationship between elements. It can be used to select elements, move elements, and insert elements as well as allowing for some selection of content.

Insert elements at the insertion point

Elements may be inserted in a variety of ways depending on the location of the insertion point and specific requirements of the author.

DITA documents have set rules governing where elements can be used. By default, the Element Catalog displays only the elements that are valid at your current insertion point.

1. Position the insertion point where you want to insert a new element.

2. Select Element > Element Catalog.

3. Double-click an element in the Element Catalog.

   FrameMaker inserts the element into the document.

Modifying elements

Elements can be modified in a variety of ways by selecting them and then changing or removing elements or their content.

Select elements

When you select an element, you also select all of its descendents.

1. In the structured view, click the element name you want.

Change elements

The Insert Element Catalog displays only elements that are valid at the insertion point.

1. With the element you want to change selected in the Structure View, display the Element Catalog.

2. Select an element from the Element Catalog and click Change... .

   FrameMaker replaces the selected element with the new element.

Expand and collapse content displays

In the Structure View, the elements and the first few words of their content can be expanded or collapsed as required.

1. In Structure View, click the + or the - sign in the element name.

   The element and its content are expanded or collapsed.

Remove tags from elements

Removing the tags from an element clears the structural tags, but leaves the element content (for example, text) intact. This is most useful if content has been tagged as bold, italic, or underlined and the tags need to be cleared.

1. Select the element you want to remove the tags from.

2. Right-click and select Unwrap.

   The tag is cleared but the element content remains in the document and is now wrapped in the parent element of the element you just removed.

Delete elements

When deleting elements that contain text or other elements, you delete all text and other elements it contains.

1. Display the Structure View.

2. Click on the name an element to delete.

3. Press *Delete* on your keyboard.

Chapter 4

Developing topics

Overview

This topic teaches you how to create and develop the <topic> element.

The following topics are covered:

- *Considerations in topic-based writing*
- *Topics and specializations in DITA*
- *Create a new topic*

Considerations in topic-based writing

A variety of issues should be considered before topic-based writing is undertaken. These may include detailed reviews of legacy content, analysis of the audience that the content is geared towards, and more. However, there are also many simple considerations that can save dozens or even hundreds of hours over the course of a documentation project.

Single topic content

When writing in a topic-based environment, each topic should be written as a standalone piece of information with no specific dependency on another topic. Each should therefore make sense on its own. Concepts, tasks, and references can be combined and nested within a topic as required, but, generally, maps are a better approach to building hierarchies.

Creating new topics

When first creating new topics, it is advisable to plan the documentation that needs to be created, and develop titles for tasks, concepts, and references. Create appropriate short descriptions for each of the primary topics.

Linking within topics   Identify the methods you want to use for linking between topics. These include inline cross-references, related links managed within topics, or relationship tables. Relationship tables, because they are applied to a map rather than being part of the topic, are a best practice for linking.

Topics and specializations in DITA

Three types of specialized topics already exist in DITA. These are the concept, the task, and the reference topics. While similar to the <topic> element, each is specialized to a degree allowing for more finite control over content.

Topic <topic>   The element <topic> is used as a container for a single-subject topic. It should be short enough to give users answers to a question without breaking away from the problem they are trying to solve. It should be long enough to make sense as a standalone unit of information. Other more content-specific top-level elements include concept, task, and reference.

Concept <concept>   The element <concept> is used as a container for an answer to a "what is" question. It provides background information that a user must know to successfully work with a product.

A concept explains and teaches ideas to help users build on experience and knowledge they may already have before using a product or performing a task. In this capacity, they are one of the first information types a user is exposed to.

The concept introduces the system, solution, process, or characteristics, and provides background information the user should know before starting a task or exploring a reference. Features and benefits of the product would be described in the concept; concepts can also have detailed information about how something works.

A concept is focused on providing information on the technology, user concerns, decisions that may need to be made, background information, product overview, or relationships between products.

The concept contains a variety of elements including a single title, an optional short description, one or more paragraphs, index entries, lists, tables, figures or images, sections and examples, and more.

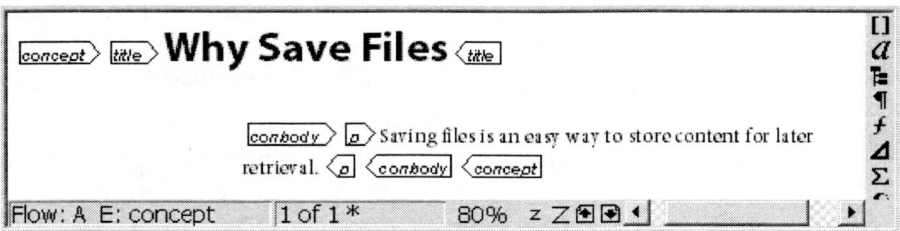

Reference
<reference>

The element <reference> is used as a container for facts or information that needs to be looked up and for technical information that is not conceptual. This element is usually built by creating specific sections and populating them with concise information.

A reference is generally only read by a user when specific technical information is required, usually while doing a specific job. The reference provides the facts without background information or procedural steps. Any reference may be heavily linked to other related reference materials.

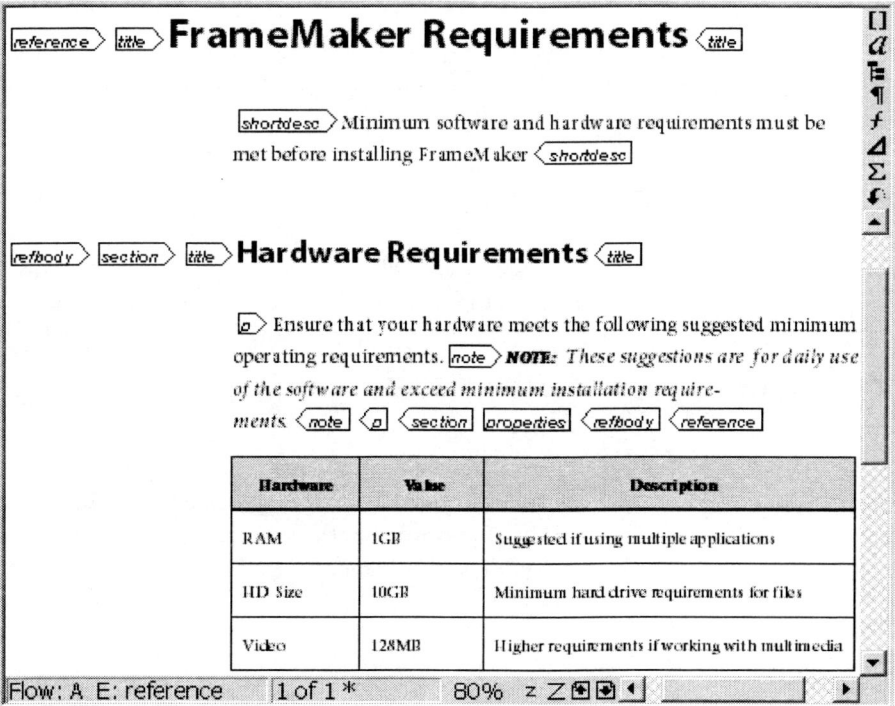

Task <task>
The element <task> is used as a container for the elements of a procedure. This element provides instructions related to addressing how to do a specific thing and the order of steps to follow.

The purpose of a task is to tell the user how to accomplish a specific set of procedures to achieve a goal. It is often read while a user is performing a specific task and should provide enough information to guide the user to a logical conclusion.

Tasks provide detailed, step-by-step instructions and provide context and examples as required. They may have explicit prerequisites or postrequisites that must be performed by the user. Within the task, there are usually multiple single-step procedures to follow. Each step may be made up of a variety of information including an explicit command (a call to action) and related supporting information.

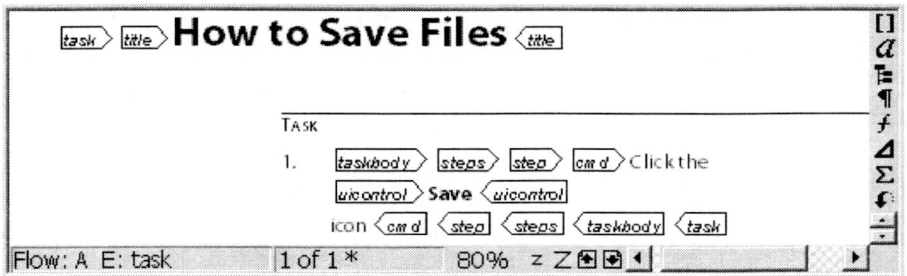

Other common elements in topics
A topic contains a variety of elements including a single title, an optional short description, one or more paragraphs, and more. However, one of the more common ways that the topic is used is to group together tasks, concepts, and references. This provides a single topic that contains numerous information types in a single collected deliverable.

Some content management system (CMS) tools do not properly support nesting topics within topics. A best practice is to manage nested topics using DITA maps.

Topics and maps
The element <map> is used to provide information about the relationships between topics.

The relationships in the map can be represented as navigational for tables of contents or for the purpose of developing related links. Because topics are written as standalone units of information, they need a way to be added to a larger deliverable for true functionality of content.

A map is a simple XML file. This XML file contains references to specific topics and instructions that are used when processing the map for output. The topics can be pulled into a map in a hierarchy. For example, three tasks can be nested under a concept.

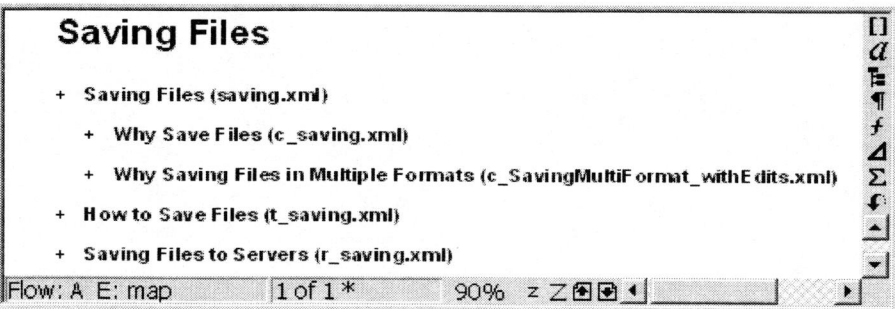

Create a new topic

A new topic can be created as needed.

1. Select DITA > New DITA File.

2. Select New <topic>.

3. Select a location and name the file.

4. Click [Select] .

5. Modify the document as required.

Chapter 5

Developing concepts

This topic teaches you how to create and develop the <concept> element.

The following topics are covered:

- *Basic concept example*
- *Commonly used elements in a concept*
- *Detailed concept sample*
- *Create a new concept*

Basic concept example

The element <concept> is used as a container for an answer to a "what is" question. It provides background information that a user must know to successfully work with a product.

A concept explains and teaches ideas to help users build on experience and knowledge they may already have before using a product or performing a task. In this capacity, they are one of the first information types a user is exposed to.

The concept introduces the system, solution, process, or characteristics, and provides background information the user should know before starting a task or exploring a reference. Features and benefits of the product would be described in the concept; concepts can also have detailed information about how something works.

A concept is focused on providing information on the technology, user concerns, decisions that may need to be made, background information, product overview, or relationships between products.

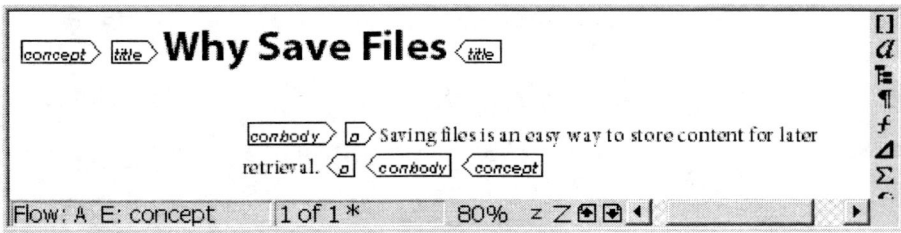

This basic sample contains a title and a single paragraph of content.

Commonly used elements in a concept

This topic provides a detailed list of commonly used elements in a DITA concept.

The concept contains a variety of elements including a single title, an optional short description, one or more paragraphs, index entries, lists, tables, figures or images, sections and examples, and more.

Title <title>

The element <title> is used as a heading or label for a variety of elements including topic, concept, reference, task, section, example, table, and so on.

Short Description <shortdesc>

The element <shortdesc> is used to represent the purpose of the content that follows. It may also be used as a link preview and in search results.

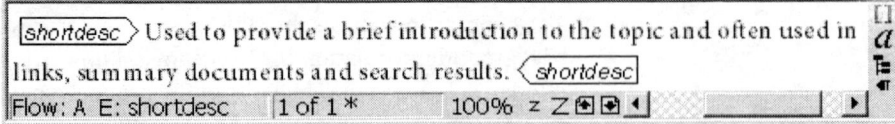

Paragraph <p>   The element <p> is used to identify a string of text that has a single main idea.

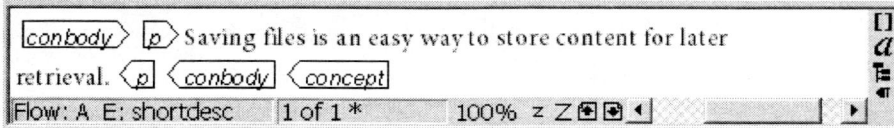

Index entries   The element <indexterm> is used to represent content that is not displayed in the
<indexterm>   specific topic, but rather in a generated, sorted document.

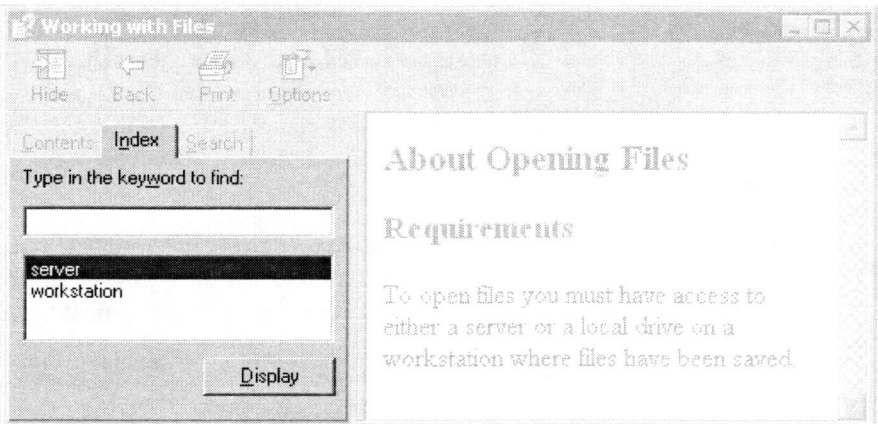

Unordered List <ul>   The element <ul> is used to identify a collection of items in which the order is not
relevant.

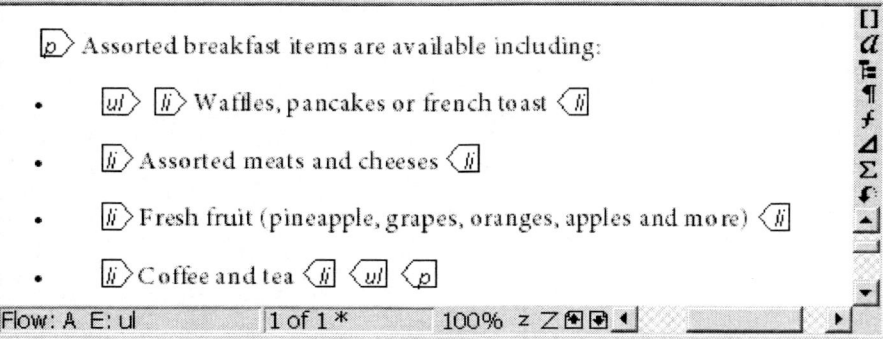

Ordered List <ol>   The element <ol> is used to identify a collection of items in which the order is relevant.

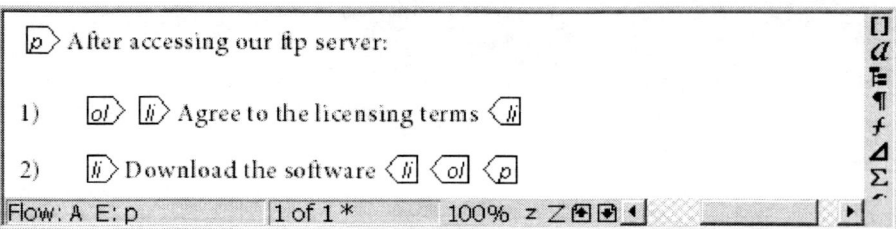

List Item <li>   The element <li> is used to contain content that composes a single main idea within a list. If <li> is contained in an <ol> element, the <li> element is usually displayed as a numbered list item (using traditional numbering, roman numerals, or alphabetical characters in order). If <li> is contained in a <ul> element, the <li> element is usually displayed as a bullet or dash.

Table <table>   The element <table> is used to organize a set of information into tabular constructs. This allows the representation to be displayed in a grid-like fashion with content spanning rows or columns. An optional title can be included to further identify the table.

A table is made up of one or more elements including:

- Column specifications <colspec>
- Table group <tgroup>
- Table header <thead>
- Table body <tbody>
- Table row <trow>

- Table entry or table cell <entry>

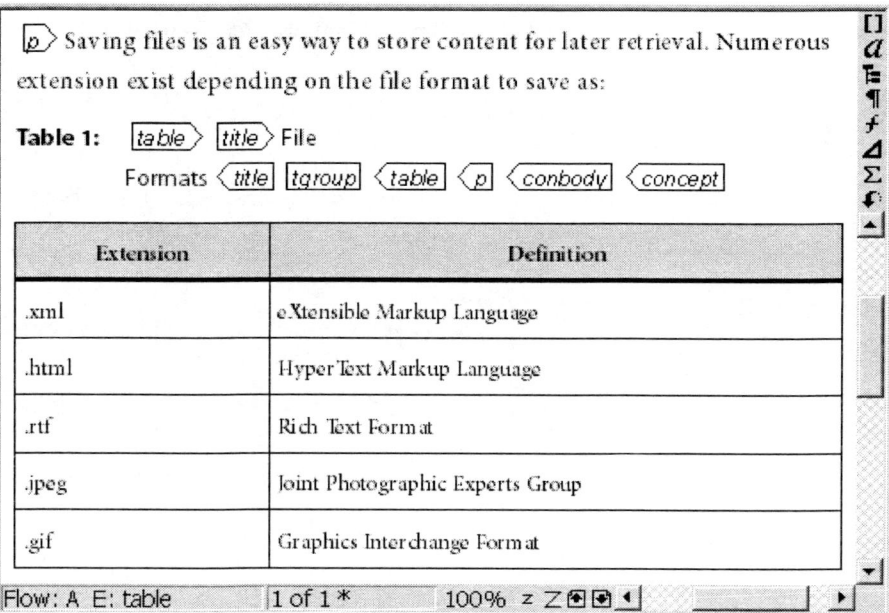

Figure <fig>   The element <figure> is used as a container for an image and an optional title, which acts as a figure caption.

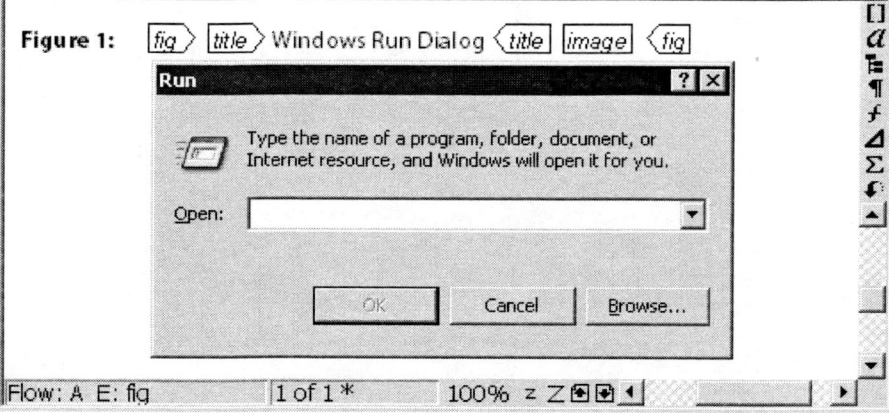

Image <image>   The element <image> is used to display an image and may be displayed on its own line (often the default for large images) or inline (often the default for an icon or button).

Section \<section\>

The element \<section\> is used to represent a collection of organized information. They represent subsets of content that are related to a larger topic and are treated as siblings to each other. An optional title may be used.

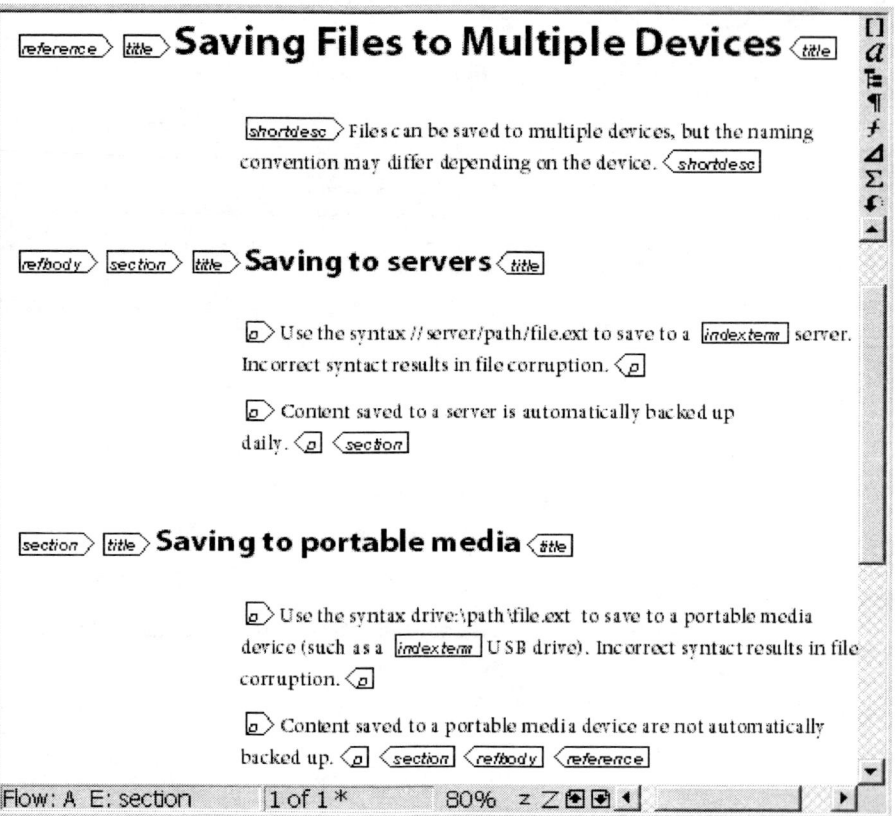

Example <example>   The element <example> is used to represent a sample to further illustrate a topic. An example is otherwise identical to a <section> element.

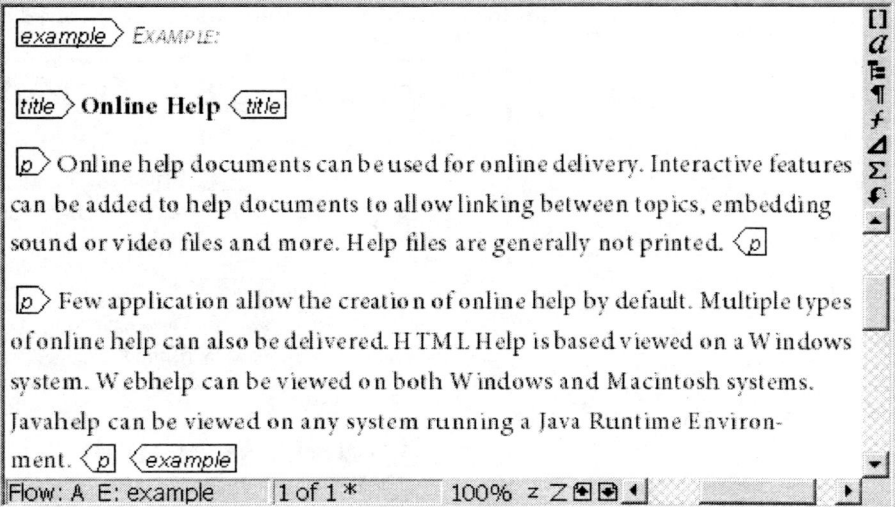

Detailed concept sample

This topic provides an example of a more involved concept and elements it may contain.

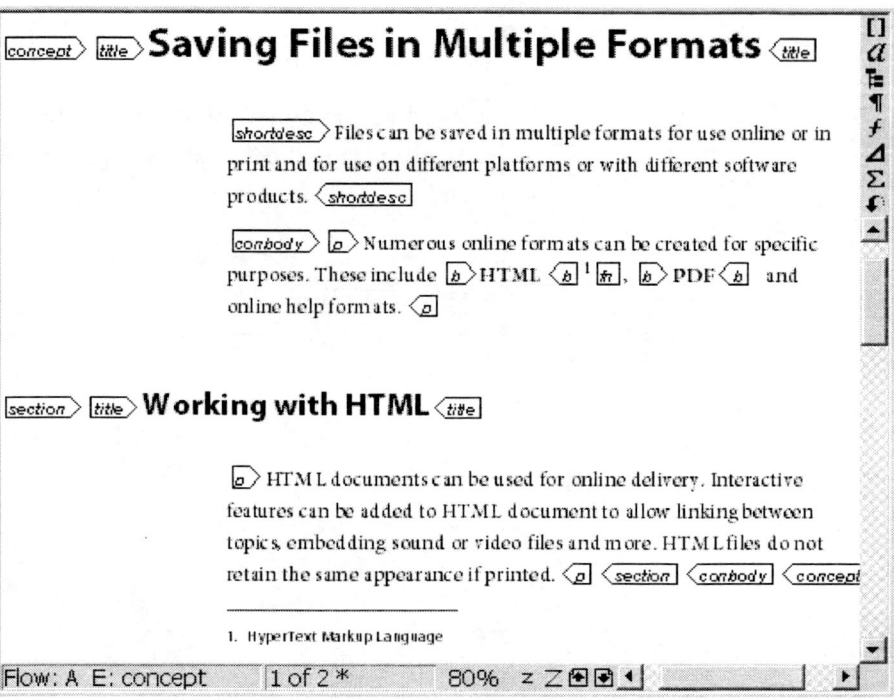

Create a new concept

A new concept can be created as needed.

1. Select DITA > New DITA File.

2. Select New <concept>.

3. Select a location and name the file.

4. Click Select .

5. Modify the document as required.

Chapter 6

Prolog elements

Overview

This topic teaches you how to create and manage the <prolog> element to provide information about a topic.

The following topics are covered:

- *Purpose of prolog elements (metadata)*
- *Commonly used elements in a prolog*
- *Working with metadata (prolog) information*

Purpose of prolog elements (metadata)

The <prolog> element contains information about a topic or a map that is generally not included in the output, but can be used to generate indexes, links, or custom navigation.

Document-level metadata

The elements related to <prolog> are used to add information to the document being created. This information is generally not displayed in generated output. The metadata is generally used for publishing purposes to identify content that may or may not be published. It may also be used to build a navigation system, customize the index entries, or even to automatically include or exclude specific topics in the published version depending on the permissions granted.

Map-level metadata

The metadata information may also be included in DITA maps as part of the <topicmeta> element. Use this element to override content such as titles and short descriptions of a topic or to build additional index entries (using the keywords element).

Commonly used elements in a prolog

This topic provides a detailed list of commonly used elements in a prolog.

Author <author>

The element <author> is used to provide information about the person or persons who wrote the topic.

Publisher <publisher>

The element <publisher> is used to provide information about the company or person who is responsible for publishing the topic.

Copyright <copyright>

The element <copyright> is used to provide information about a single copyright entry including copyright years and copyright holder.

Critical dates <critdates>

The element <critdates> is used to provide information such as creation date and revision dates.

Working with metadata (prolog) information

Adobe FrameMaker 8.0 manages the topic prolog information as a mix of topic metadata and content that displays in the document by default. Due to the wide number of options that are available, it is better to work with the structure view to initially define the prolog topic metadata. Content that is added to a topic should be done by having an information architect assess the metadata requirements for an organization and then specify options that are best suited to the organization's implementation.

By doing so, an organization can be selective about how the metadata is viewed and managed. This helps avoid confusion caused by providing choices that may not be applicable or by having authors define the same information in a variety of ways.

View metadata information

If topic metadata is already inserted in a document it may be viewed using the Structure View. This is the suggested method to use when working with metadata.

1. Display the Structure View.

   The elements display, with a + after each name.

2. In the structure, after the <title> and optional <shortdesc> but before the <body>, review any <prolog> content.

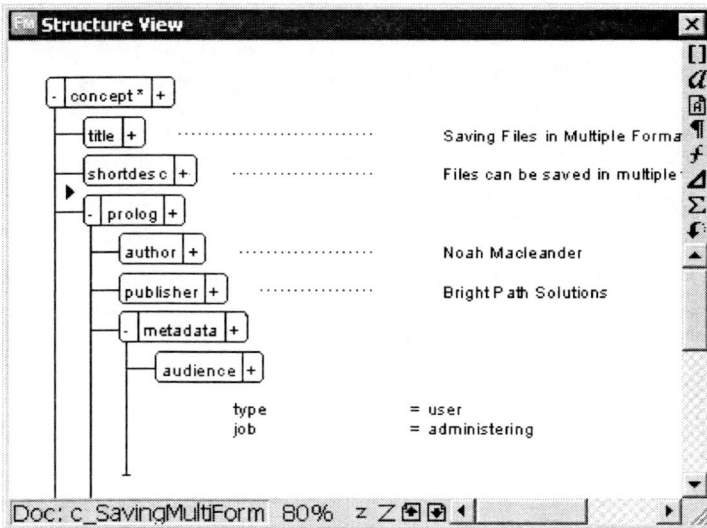

3. If required, click the + after any element name again to see all metadata, required and optional.

Modify metadata information

All metadata information is stored in the XML code of the file and only visible through the Attributes dialog or using the Structure View.

1. Display the Structure View.

1. If required, insert the prolog element.

2. Add additional elements as required.

3. Modify attributes as required.

Chapter 7

Publishing

Overview

This topic teaches you how to use standalone topics to create finished, published output for online or print delivery.

The following topics are covered:

- *Publishing formats*
- *Generating PDF*

Publishing formats

Outside of FrameMaker you can use the DITA Open Toolkit to transform XML content into an output deliverable. The DITA Open Toolkit is installed independently of FrameMaker.

In the toolkit, there are a set of pre-configured output types you can use to produce output. You can modify these output types and set up new ones specific to a document or project. Once an output type has been customized, it is available every time content is published. However, modifying them requires knowledge of XML, FO, and XSLT.

As an alternate, you can publish documents in a variety of preconfigured formats in FrameMaker. The following output types are related to the toolkit with FrameMaker options detailed where available. For example, the toolkit can create PDF as can FrameMaker. Therefore, the PDF topic is further detailed with information about the way that FrameMaker can be used to create PDF.

XHTML   Primarily a Web-based format that meets both the HTML and XML specifications. Basically XHTML is HTML that is also valid XML content.

PDF	Primarily a format that can be delivered for print. PDF displays information in a way that can be viewed using the free Adobe Reader to view and print content.
	FrameMaker source files can be used to create PDF. By using the Save As PDF feature, a document can be converted and will retain all layout, hyperlinks, formats, header/footer information and more in the resulting PDF. Additionally, by using FrameMaker to create PDF you can first preview a file that has been converted from DITA-compliant XML to an intermediary format. This allows you to create manual overrides where required to create content keeptogethers (ensuring that specific paragraph stay on the same page), force page breaks (to ensure that specific content is forced to start at the top of the page) and so on. This generally cannot be done using the default conversions provided by the DITA toolkit.
RTF	Primarily a format that can be modified using standard desktop authoring tools such as Microsoft Word.
	FrameMaker source files can be used to create RTF. By using the Save As RTF features, a document can be converted to RTF using default conversion functions provided by FrameMaker.
TROFF	Primarily a format to designate fonts, spacing, paragraphs, margins, footnotes, and more for specific print environments.
Help formats: HTML Help (CHM), JavaHelp, Eclipse Help	Primarily a format that is used to deliver standard types of help content for distribution with an application.
	FrameMaker source files can be used with tools like Adobe RoboHelp, Quadralay WebWorks ePublisher, and MIF2Go to create various help formats. Each of these third-party tools must be purchased and installed independently of FrameMaker.
Eclipse Content	Primarily used for creation of Eclipse help, an XML-based help system.
XML for use with other tools	Primarily used to create XML content for further processing. With this option, the system does the work of assembling topic files into an XML document, but does not do the work of converting it into an output format. You can use other XML tools to convert the resulting files into a custom output format.
	FrameMaker source files can be used to create other XML outputs. To do so, an application file and associated read/write rules, DTD, and more must be created.

Generating PDF

When generating output, a set of predefined PDF options are used. These can be changed, if required, using the Adobe Acrobat Distiller. The process to do so is not detailed here. If required, review the Adobe Acrobat Distiller help documentation.

1. Open a topic to publish.

2. Select File > **Save As PDF**.

3. Under Deliverable type, select the type of output to generate.

4. If required, browse to specify the server, drive, or folder to save the file to.

5. Name the file.

6. Click [Save].

   The PDF Setup dialog displays.

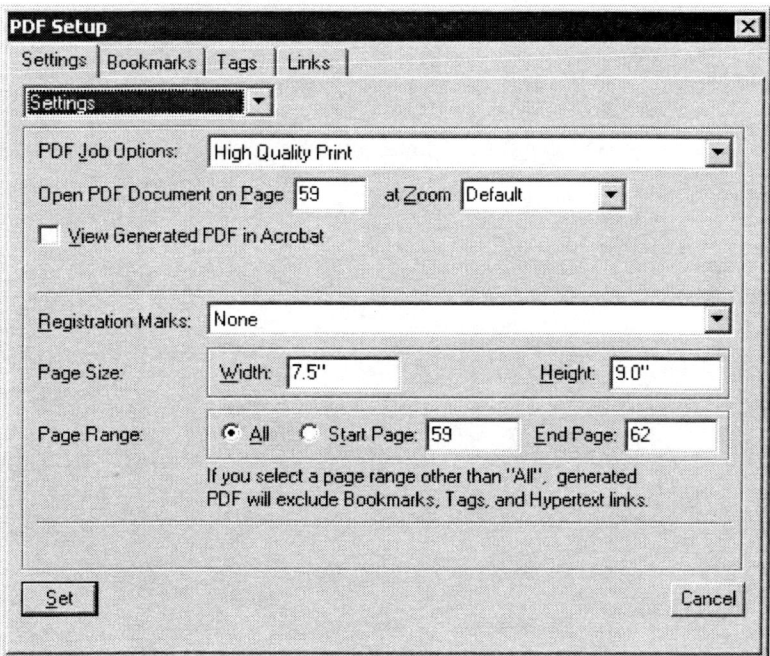

7. Configure PDF options as required.

8. Click [Set].

   FrameMaker generates the file.

Chapter 8

Paragraphs and notes

Overview

This topic teaches you how to create and manage paragraphs and notes.

The following topics are covered:

- *Paragraph types*
- *Working with paragraphs, notes, and quotations*

Paragraph types

There are several primary paragraph types that can be used:

- *Paragraph <p>*
- *Note <note>*
- *Long quotation <lq>*

Paragraph <p> The element <p> is used to identify a paragraph.

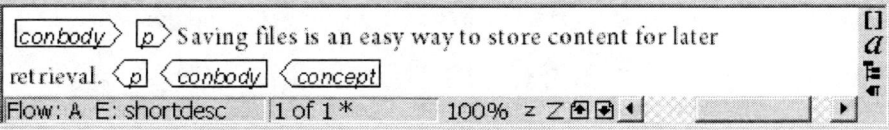

Note <note>

The element <note> is used to identify content that displays in a different format from the default of a document and draws attention to a point.

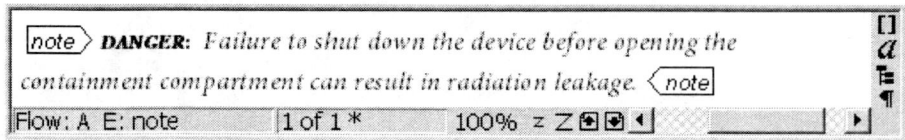

Long quotation <lq>

The element <lq> is used to identify a longer string of text that is a quotation from another source and is usually treated as a standalone element, similar to a paragraph.

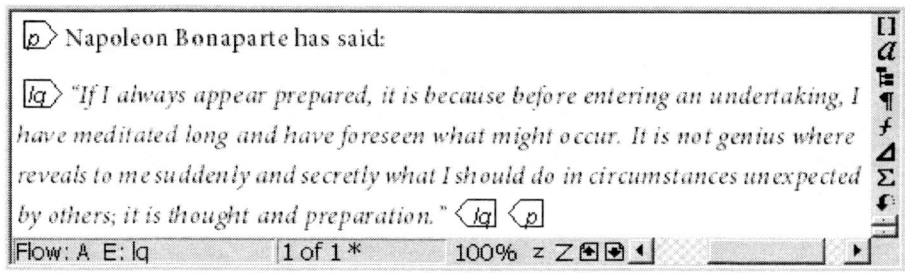

Working with paragraphs, notes, and quotations

This topic explains how to insert text elements.

Insert paragraphs at the insertion point

In most cases, a new paragraph can be inserted by simply pressing *Enter* at the end of an existing paragraph.

Insert paragraphs via the Insert menu

1. Position the insertion point at the location you want to insert a new paragraph. This is usually at the end of a paragraph or other element.

2. Open the Element Catalog and double-click the paragraph element.

Insert notes

1. Position the insertion point at the approximate place you want to insert a new paragraph.

2. Open the Element Catalog and double-click the note element.
   The note and paragraph elements are added to make the note text valid.

Insert quotations

1. Position the insertion point at the approximate place you want to insert a new quotation.

2. Open the Element Catalog and double-click the <lq> element.

   The quotation and paragraph elements are added to make the quotation text valid.

Change paragraphs

The default paragraph type, using the <p> element can be changed to other element types.

1. In the Structure View, select the paragraph to change.

2. With the Element Catalog, select a new element.

3. Click Change... .

Change note types

1. In the Structure View, expand the attributes for the note element to change.

2. Double-click Type.

3. Click ▾.

   A list of note types display.

4. Select a new note type.

5. Click Set Value .

Chapter 9

Lists

Overview

This topic teaches you how to create and manage various types of lists.

This topic contains the following topics:

- *Lists and list parts*
- *Working with lists*
- *Working with list items*
- *Working with definition lists*

Lists and list parts

While DITA provides numerous list-related elements, this topic addresses only some of the common elements that a new user should initially be aware of. For more detailed information, review the documentation included with the DITA Open Toolkit.

Note that lists are not the same as procedures in a task. There is a specific purpose of a list, different from the specific purpose of a task. Lists should only be inserted as required and in the correct context. If the information that is presented is a numerical list then the list element can be used. However, if it is procedural then use a task element instead.

Unordered list \<ul\>	The element \<ul\> is used to identify a collection of items in which the order is not relevant.

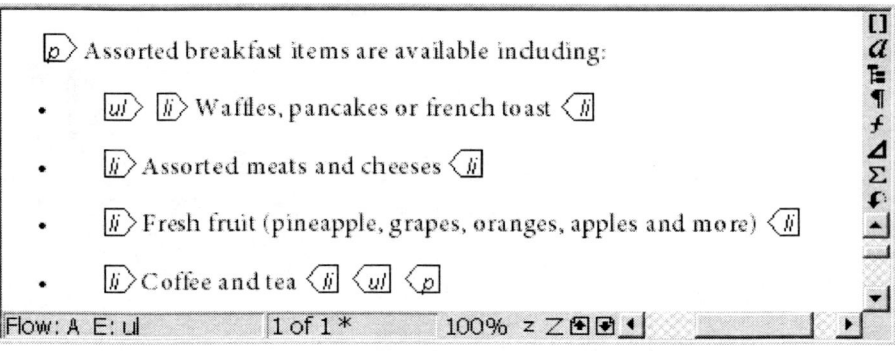

Ordered list \<ol\>	The element \<ol\> is used to identify a collection of items in which the order is relevant.

An ordered list is a sequential collection of information or content that is listed in order of priority, but is not a task and should contain no procedural information.

Tip

A task has far more specific requirements and optional choices than an ordered list.

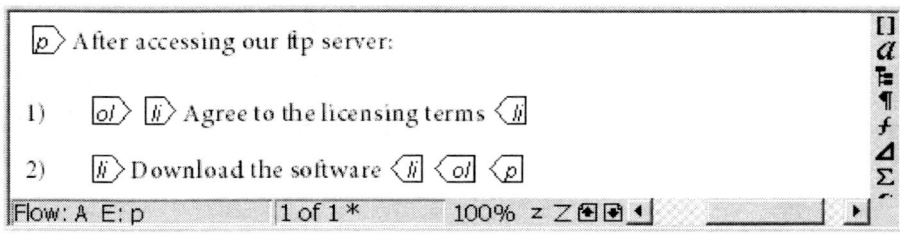

List item \<li\>	The element \<li\> is used to contain content that has a single main idea within a list. If \<li\> is contained in an \<ol\> element, the \<li\> element is usually displayed as a numbered list item (using traditional numbering, roman numerals, or alphabetical characters in order). If \<li\> is contained in a \<ul\> element, the \<li\> element is usually displayed as a bullet or dash.

Definition lists   The element <dl> is used to build a list of terms and definitions.

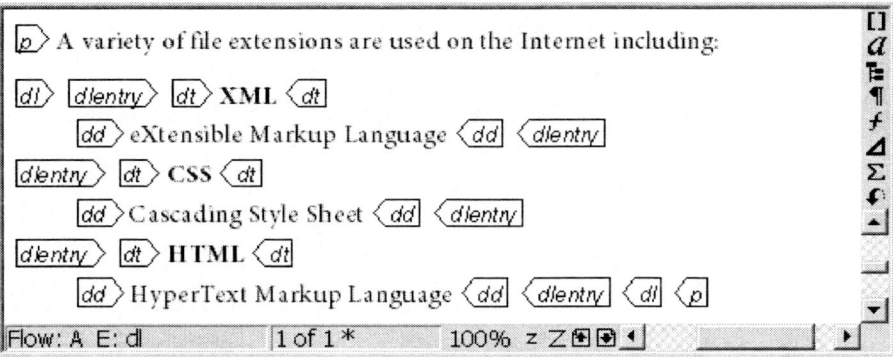

Working with lists

This topic explains how to create a new list.

Insert an unordered list

1. Select a valid location for the list.

2. Open the Element Catalog and double-click the <ul> element.
    The first <li> and <p> elements are added automatically to make the list text valid.

Insert an ordered list

1. Select a valid location for the list.

2. Open the Element Catalog and double-click the <ol> element.
    The first <li> and <p> elements are added automatically to make the list text valid.

Working with list items

This topic explains how to work with list items.

The list item can contain a wide range of other elements. It is important to plan the list item carefully and decide what information is within an item. If it is a single string of text or only one paragraph, then a self-contained list item works well. However, if more than one piece of information is contained—for example, a note or additional paragraphs of text—other procedures may be required.

A complex item in a list may also contain subordinate elements. If this is the case, consider grouping information within a collection of paragraphs or other elements within the list item.

Add list items

This topic explains one of the several methods available to add list items to an existing list.

1. Open the Structure View.

2. Click just to the right of an existing list item element.

   That is, click on the line of the element <li>.

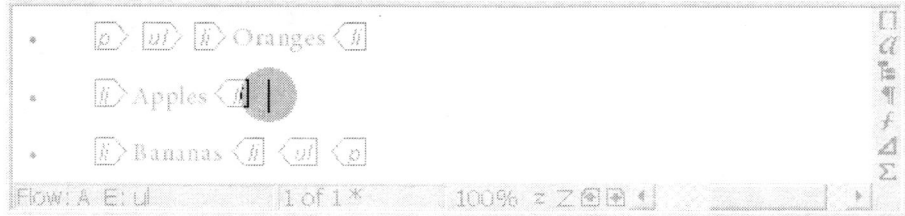

3. Press *Enter*.

Rearrange list items

This topic explains how to rearrange items in an existing list.

1. Open the Structure View.

2. Drag and drop a list item to a new location.

   All related content is moved with the list item.

Add elements to list items

This topic explains how to add additional elements to items in an existing list.

1. Open the Structure View.

2. Position the insertion point before the end tag of an existing list item.

   That is, click after the last text or element in the list item, but before the closing tag.

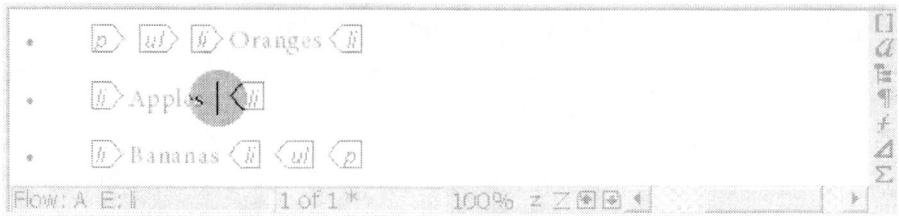

3. Using the Element Catalog, add additional elements.

Delete list items   This topic explains how to remove items from an existing list.

1. Open the Structure View.

2. Select the list item to remove.

3. Press *Delete*.
    All related content is removed with the list item.

Change list types   This topic explains how to convert from one basic list type to another.

1. Using the Structure View, select the <ul> or <ol> element.

2. Using the Element Catalog, select the list type you want.

3. Click ⬚ Change... .
    The list type is changed.

Working with definition lists

This topic explains how to create and populate a definition list.

Insert a definition list   1. Using the Structure View, select the location for the definition list.

2. From the Element Catalog, double-click <dl>.

    A new list is inserted at the location you specified. The elements <dlentry> and <dt> are added automatically. The element <dd> is required as well to make the list valid.

Add definition entries

This topic explains one of the several methods available to add list items to an existing list.

1. Display the Structure View.

2. Position the insertion point between the <dl> and <dlentry> elements.

3. Press *Enter*.
   A new entry is inserted.

4. Add the <dt> and <dd> elements.

Rearrange definition list entries

This topic explains how to rearrange items in an existing list.

1. Display the Structure View.

2. Drag and drop a definition list entry to a new location.
   All related content is moved with the list item.

Add elements to definition descriptions

This topic explains how to add additional elements to items in an existing list.

1. In the document, highlight the text you want to wrap in a new element.

2. Using the Element Catalog, double-click the desired new element.
   The text is now wrapped in the new element.

Delete definition entries

This topic explains how to remove definitions from an existing definition list.

1. Display the Structure View.

2. Select the definition list entry to remove.

3. Press *Delete*.
   All related content is removed with the definition list.

Chapter 10

Working with domains

Overview

This topic teaches you how to create and manage typographical, programing, software, and user interface domains that contain a variety of special elements.

This topic contains the following topics:

- *Domain element overview*
- *Typographical elements*
- *Programing elements*
- *Software elements*
- *User interface*

Domain element overview

Purpose of domains

Domain elements support a richer and more functional variety of terms that relate to programing, software, and user interface-specific writing. Additionally, they also support conventions related to common typographical conventions such as bold and italic.

Most (but not all) domain elements are used to create ranges of structure that are transformed into the equivalent of character range formats or treated as a related block of information (such as a string of code or even an entire block of code).

DITA domains are groups of elements that are useful to certain industries or types of documents, but are not needed by everyone. For example, elements in the Programing domain are mostly useful for documenting computer programs.

While DITA provides numerous domain-related elements, this topic addresses only some of the common elements that a new user should initially be aware of. For more detailed information, review the ditaref-book.chm that is included with the DITA Toolkit.

Comparing semantic and typographic markup

While the DITA specification supports a variety of elements that can be used to apply typographical markup, it should generally be avoided. Semantic markup provides a far more meaningful set of tags for content.

For example, by simply applying bold or italic to a range of words, no additional information is imparted. If, instead, the markup implies user input or a system response, the usability (and the reuse) of the content is greatly enhanced.

Typographical elements

This topic explains how to work with typographical elements.

Generally avoid bold, italic, and underline as they apply typographical, style-based formats. Normally, apply the element to text for meaningful or purpose-driven semantic formatting. If no semantic markup is applicable, then the typographical elements and style-based formats may apply.

Bold

1. Select the text to modify.

2. From the Element Catalog, double-click b.
   The content displays as bolded text.

Italic

1. Select the text to modify.

2. From the Element Catalog, double-click i.
   The content displays as italicized text.

Underline

1. Select the text to modify.

2. From the Element Catalog, double-click u.
   The content displays as underlined text.

Programing elements

This topic explains how to work with programing elements.

Code phrase   The representation of a code phrase is usually inline as a text range.

1. Select the location to insert a code phrase.

2. From the Element Catalog, double-click codeph.

3. Type content as required.

Code block   The representation of a code block is usually a multiple line string.

1. Select the location to insert a code block.

2. From the Element Catalog, double-click codeblock.

3. Type content as required.

Software elements

This topic explains how to work with software elements.

User input
1. Select the location to insert user input.

2. From the Element Catalog, double-click userinput.

3. Type content as required.

System output
1. Select the location to insert a system output.

2. From the Element Catalog, double-click systemoutput.

3. Type content as required.

Message phrase
1. Select the location to insert a message phrase.

2. From the Element Catalog, double-click msgph.

3. Type content as required.

File path
1. Select the location to insert a filepath.

2. From the Element Catalog, double-click filepath.

3. Type content as required.

User interface

This topic explains how to work with user interface elements.

User interface control

1. Select the location to insert a user interface control.

2. From the Element Catalog, double-click uicontrol.

3. Type content as required.

Menu cascade

1. In the Structure View, select two or more <uicontrol> elements you want for a menu cascade.
   Press Ctrl while clicking to select multiple elements.

2. From the Element Catalog, double-click menucascade.

Window title

1. Select the location to insert a window title.

2. From the Element Catalog, double-click wintitle.

3. Type content as required.

Chapter 11

Footnotes

Overview

This topic teaches you how to create and manage footnotes.

This topic contains the following topics:

- *Footnote element overview*
- *Working with footnotes*

Footnote element overview

Footnotes in Document view

When you create a footnote, you get an <fn> footnote element.

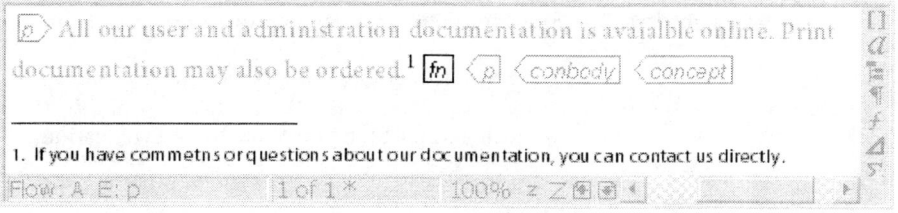

Footnotes in output

Depending on the configuration of the output, the footnote is automatically numbered and positioned. For example, when the topic is converted to a CHM file, a number displays where the footnote was inserted. This number links to the footnote text, which is now placed at the bottom of the page.

Working with footnotes

Insert a document footnote

1. Position the insertion point at the end of the word(s) you want to footnote.

2. Using the Element Catalog, double click <fn>.

    A footnote displays at the bottom of the page.

3. Type the text for the footnote.

Insert a table footnote

1. Position the insertion point in a table cell at the end of the word(s) you want to footnote.

2. Using the Element Catalog, double click <fn>.

    A footnote displays at the bottom of the page.

3. Type the text for the footnote.

Edit a footnote

This topic explains how to edit the text in a footnote.

The most common change made to text in a footnote is to change content by replacing one phrase or sentence with another.

1. Select the text to change and type the new content.

    Old content is deleted at the first keystroke and new content replaces the previous data.

Move a footnote

This topic explains how to move a footnote from one location to another.

1. Select the <fn> element to move.

2. Cut and paste the footnote to a new location.

Delete a footnote

This topic explains how to remove a footnote from a structured document.

1. Select the <fn> element to delete.

2. Press *Delete*.

Chapter 12

Indexes

Overview

This topic teaches you how to create and manage index entries.

The following topics are covered:

- *Guideline for indexing*
- *Working with index entries*

Guideline for indexing

Purpose of an index

An index generally creates an alphabetical list of content to assist a user in finding information that a simple search may not find. However, simply creating a collection of words that are already in the document is not a good practice for indexing. Instead, indexing should allow content to be logically grouped and sorted. Content can also be marked up using words that are not found in your documentation.

For example, while a document about sound files may have entries such as *recording sound* and *modifying sound*, a user may search for information in a different way. If users search for *audio*, no results would be returned (because the word *sound* was used in a standard index). By developing an index and finding content that includes audio content, a user can more effectively find answers. In the same way, a group of entries on *sound* with *recording* and *modifying* as subtopics may be more useful.

Index samples

A single-level index entry has no subordinate content. That is, the entry is usually a self-contained entry such as, for example, *server* or *workstation*. The index may generate two primary entries for this sample. One entry under *server* and another under *workstation*.

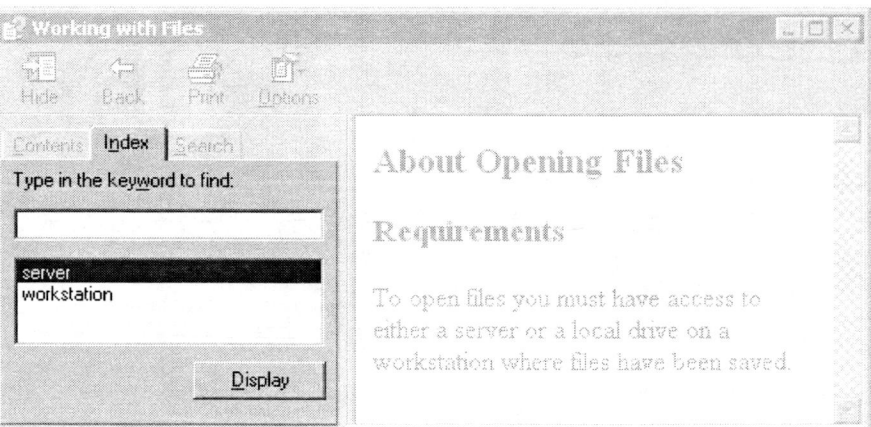

A subordinate level index entry has parent content. That is, the entry is usually a child contained by another entry such as, for example, *hardware* with two subordinates of *server* and *workstation*. The index may generate one primary entry with two subordinate entries for this sample: one primary entry under *hardware* and two immediate subordinates of *server* and *workstation*.

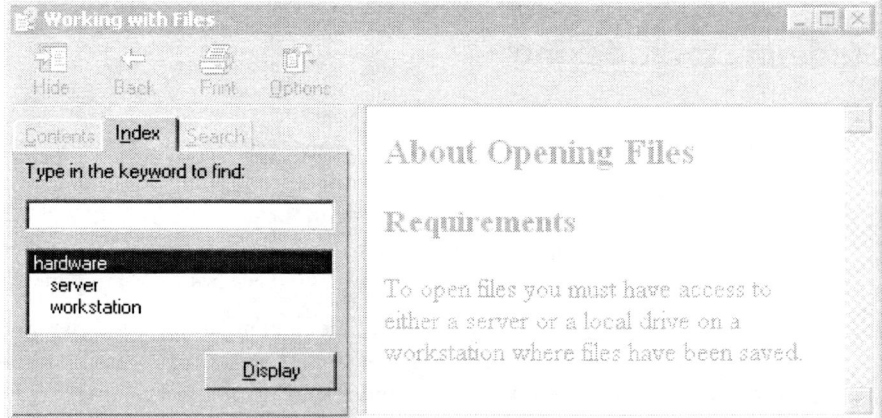

Working with index entries

When creating index entries, elements are added to a topic. The publishing system (i.e. the DITA Open Toolkit) determines what page in the output is associated with each index entry, and compiles to create an index.

Create a single-level index entry

1. Position the insertion point where you want an index entry.

2. Using the Element Catalog, double click <indexterm>.

   The Insert Marker dialog displays. There may be default text from earlier index terms that needs to be deleted.

Tip

Create a subentry by using a colon. For example, the entry *hardware:server* creates a primary entry for *hardware* and a subordinate entry for *server*.

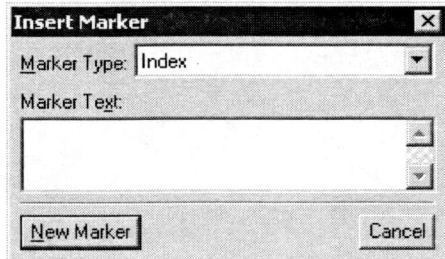

3. Under Element Tag, select indexterm.

4. Under **Market Text**, type the text of the index entry.

5. Click New Marker .

Modify index entries

1. In the Structure View, select the indexterm element to modify.

2. Select **Special** > **Marker**.

   The existing marker text displays in the Marker dialog.

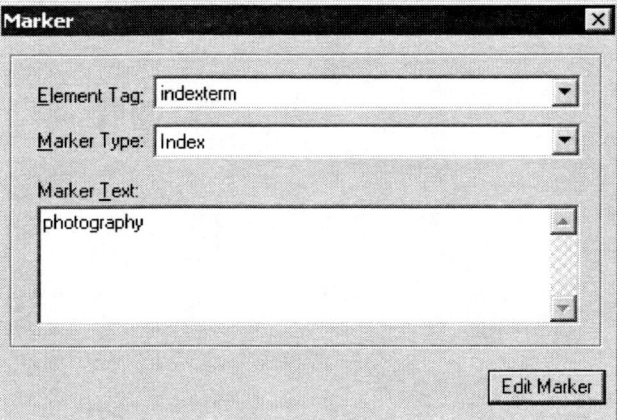

3. Make the changes required.

4. Click Edit Marker .

Delete index entries   This topic explains how to remove index entries.

1. Using the Structure View, select the index entry to delete.

2. Press *Delete*.

    Only the element has been deleted. The content in any generated output is not removed until the index is regenerated.

Chapter 13

Attributes

Overview

This topic teaches you how to work with attributes to add and modify descriptive information about elements.

The following topics are covered:

- *Purpose of attributes*
- *Attributes and the Structure View*
- *Attributes dialog*
- *Types of attributes*
- *Working with attributes*
- *Attributes and new elements*

Purpose of attributes

Purpose in XML

Attributes help to further define elements by adding information to the element. Additional information used to describe an element is usually stored in an attribute and is composed of both the attribute name and the attribute value.

Purpose in publishing

Attributes are used to assist tools to understand the purpose of the element. This can determine how content displays when published, what unique named values are assigned to an element to make it distinct, additional information about an element for security purposes, and more.

Attributes and the Structure View

Collapse or expand attributes

Any attribute value may be collapsed or expanded.

 Tip

To collapse or expand all sibling elements' attributes, press and hold **Shift** prior to clicking the - or the + at the end of the element bubble.

1. Click the - or the + at the end of the element bubble to collapse or expand an attribute.

    The first plus sign indicates that required or set attributes can be displayed, the second instance indicates that all attributes will be displayed and the minus sign will collapse the attribute display.

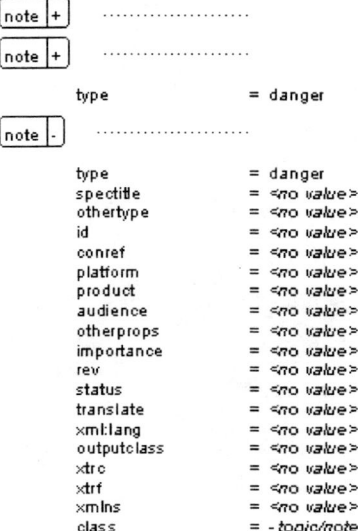

Select attributes in the Structure View

Clicking anywhere in an element that has attributes selects the element and automatically also selects all attributes associated with the element.

Attributes dialog

The Attributes dialog displays the name of the current element and the name and value of the attributes of the current element. It also allows attribute values to be changed, set, or deleted.

The Attributes dialog allows you to view information about attributes related to the current element.

1. Select Element > Edit Attributes.

   FrameMaker displays the Attributes dialog.

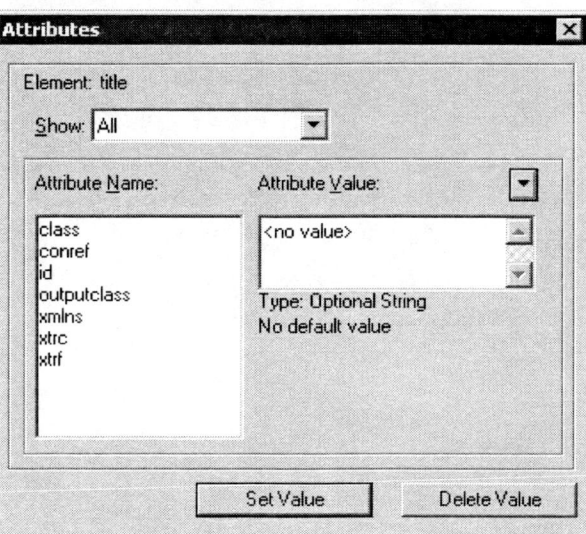

Types of attributes

This topic discusses the numerous types of attributes that are available in structured documents.

Required versus optional

Attributes may be optional or required. This is set by the developer of the structure. Required attributes must be inserted and have valid content or the document is considered invalid. Optional attributes are not mandatory and can be inserted if desired.

Choice

Choice attributes allow you to choose from a predefined list of attribute values for a given element.

Numeric values

Two types of numeric values can be set. These are integer(s) and real(s).

An integer is a whole number that can be positive or negative or zero. The set of integers is generally defined as {… -3, -2, -1, 0, 1, 2, 3, …}.

Real numbers include all integer values as well as all rational and irrational numbers. These include decimal values, fractions, exponential values, and other sets of numbers.

References References are either a reference to something or an identifier that is unique and used to define a location.

href

href attributes are generally a link to a unique named destination in a structured document. They are most often used to link to an ID or a destination such as an email address or a weblink.

id

An id is generally a named destination in a structured document. They are often used to identify the location that a cross reference or related link goes to.

String and strings String or strings are attributes that allow a variety of characters to be entered. These include most characters and numbers.

Working with attributes

When working with attributes, there are numerous options available. Generally, it is easiest to use feature-specific dialogs to work with attributes.

Add content to attributes Interactive dialogs guide the author through the required and optional attributes and assist in selecting the correct values.

Attribute content can be added using the Attributes dialog or before inserting a new element.

Changing attribute values The value of an attribute can be modified.

Choice

Select a choice from the available list of elements. Invalid choices result in structurally invalid documents.

1. In the Structure View, select the element that you want to modify the attributes for.

2. Display the Attributes dialog.

3. Double-click the attribute name that has choices available.

4. Click ▾ to view the available choices.

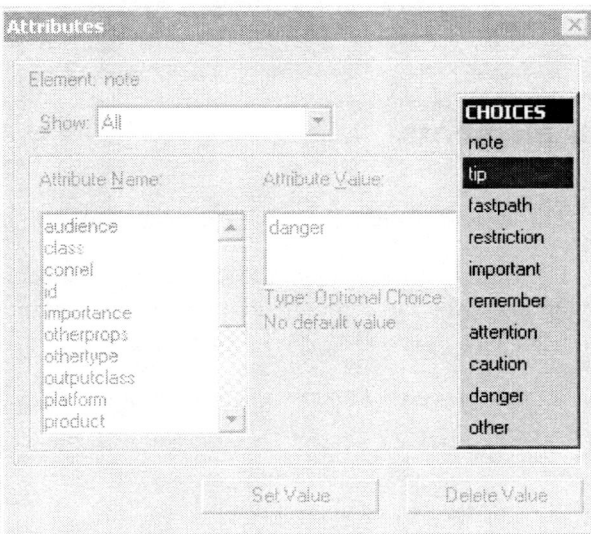

5. Select one of the choices.

6. Click [Set Value].

References

In many cases, the id and href values are automatically managed by FrameMaker. Technically, it is possible for an author to modify the content. However, use caution when doing this, because changing these attributes can break links to images or to other topics.

String and strings

1. In the Structure View, select the element that you want to modify the attributes for.

2. Display the Attributes dialog.

3. Select an attribute that has a string.

4. Enter a value for the string.

5. Click [Set Value].

Delete attribute values

1. In the Structure View, select the element that you want to modify the attributes for.

2. Display the Attributes dialog.

3. Select the attribute that has a value that is to be deleted.

4. Click Delete Value .

The attribute value is deleted.

Attributes and new elements

 **Note**

The selection you make has no bearing on the validity of the document. It only sets when, and if, you are prompted for attributes. Therefore, attributes that you do not insert can still impact the structural validity of the document.

This topic explains how to work with attributes when new elements are inserted.

Depending on the setup of the structured document attributes may be required or optional. You can configure FrameMaker to prompt you as the types of attributes that need to be inserted.

1. Select View > Attribute Display Options.

The Attribute Display Options dialog displays.

- Select **Required and Specified Attributes** to be prompted for attributes that must be inserted or are already defined.
- Select **All Attributes** to be prompted for any attribute associated with an element.
- Select **No Attributes** to avoid being prompted for attributes.

Chapter 14

Tables

Overview

This topic teaches you how to work with tables and table-related elements to create, edit, and modify content in a variety of table types.

The following topics are covered:

- *Understanding table components*
- *Table types*
- *Working with tables*
- *Moving within tables*
- *Selecting and deselecting table content*
- *Adding, moving or deleting columns or rows*
- *Table properties*
- *Merging or splitting cell content*

Understanding table components

This topic explains the different components of a table.

The table is composed of several optional or required components. Tables are made up of four types of content. These are the table title, heading rows, body rows, and footing rows. The three types of rows contain cells.

Table titles

A table contains an optional title.

Table headings

The table heading is optional, and consists of one or more rows.

Table body	Tables must contain a table body, which must contain at least one row with at least one cell.
Table rows	Each row in a table is made up of one or more table cells.
Table cells	Content appearing in the body of the table is contained in a cell that is contained within a row. Text content only displays within a table title or a table cell.

Table types

DITA supports a variety of table types. Some can only be used in specific contexts.

Not all types of tables support all properties and options.

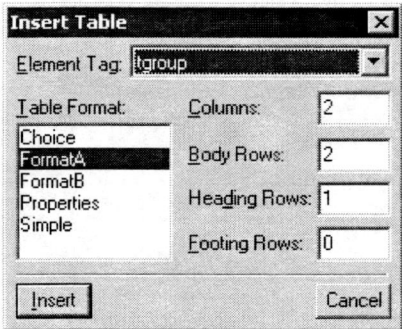

Format A table	The FormatA table inserts a traditional-styled table with row, columns, and cells.
Properties (reference topics)	The properties table inserts a table representation of properties by displaying three default columns. The fact that this displays in a table format is for convenience. The DITA specification does not explicitly call for properties to be represented by a table.
Simple table	The simple table inserts a very basic row and column layout with minimal structure.

Working with tables

Table toolbar The Table toolbar provides additional functionality and ease-of-use features.

1. Ensure the QuickAccess toolbar displays.

2. Click the toolbar extension icons until you reach the table toolbar.

Insert tables This topic explains how to insert a table into a document.

Default values are used when tables are inserted. If required, you can specify the number of columns, body rows, heading rows, and footing rows and override the default settings. When tables are inserted, an anchor is created at the insertion point. This anchor ensures that the table moves with the text instead of anchoring itself to a set place on the page.

1. Position the insertion point at a valid location the table is to be inserted.

2. Using the Element Catalog, double click <table>.

The Insert Table dialog displays.

Tip

DITA tables do not support Footing Rows. Therefore, leave the value at 0.

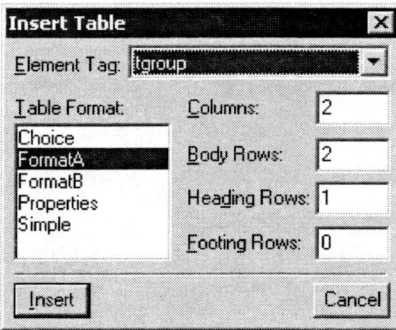

3. Under Table Format, select the type of table to insert.

4. In Columns, specify the number of columns.

5. In Body Rows, specify the number of rows in the body of the table.

6. In Heading Rows, specify the number of heading rows in the table.

7. Click Insert .

The table is inserted. A variety of additional elements may also be inserted within the various cells of the table.

Moving within tables

This topic explains how to move within a table.

Not all types of tables support all properties and options.

Navigate between cells with the mouse

1. To move from one cell to another, click in a cell.

Navigate between cells with the keyboard

1. Use the arrow keys to move up, down, left, or right.

To select	Windows	Unix
Next cell	Tab	Tab
Previous cell	Shift-Tab	Shift-tab
Cell below	Alt-Control-Tab	Meta-n
Cell above	Alt-Control-Shift-Tab	Meta-p

Selecting and deselecting table content

This topic explains how to select table content in order to work with it.

Tables are made up of text in cells. These cells are parts of rows and the rows are in the footer, header, or body of the table. Tables may also contain titles. Therefore, selecting table content is dependent on the type of content that you wish to select.

Not all types of tables support all properties and options.

Select text in tables

To select text in a table, simply follow the instructions related to selecting text anywhere else in the document. That is, single click or double click text. The keyboard method of selecting (using the *Shift* key and the directional arrows) also works within tables.

Select individual cells

1. Click at the end of a text range in a cell.

2. Press and hold *Shift*.

3. Press the arrow key to the right.

4. Release the *Shift* key.

Selecting individual rows

1. Click and drag from the first cell to the last cell in a row.

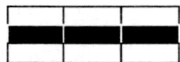

Select individual columns

1. Click and drag from the first cell to the last cell in a column.

Select table content

In order to deselect cells, rows, columns, table titles, or entire tables, simply click in a different location.

Adding, moving or deleting columns or rows

This topic explains how to work with tables to add, move or delete columns and rows.

Add columns or rows

Empty columns or rows may be added to a table using the following method.

1. Select the location within a table to add next to or above/below.

2. Select Table > Add Rows or Columns.

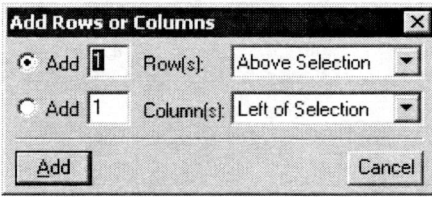

3. Select one of the options to insert rows or columns.

4. If required, specify the number of rows to add.

5. Click Add .

Delete columns or rows

1. Select entire row(s) or columns(s).

2. Press *Delete*.

   The Clear Table Cells dialog box displays.

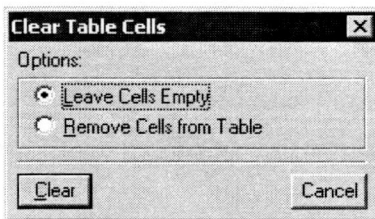

3. Select either Leave Cells Empty or Remove Cells from Table.

4. Click Clear

Table properties

This topic explains how to make columns wider or narrower.

Table column widths may be resized manually or to exact values by using a detailed dialog box.

Manually resize table columns

When manually resizing tables a single cell may be selected and resized. This forces the entire column to resize. FrameMaker does not allow an individual cell to be sized to a different setting than the rest of the column containing it.

1. Select one or more cells in column(s) to be resized.

2. Drag the resize handle appearing on the right border of the selected cells.

   Column(s) width changes by amount you drag. As cells are resized, the remainder of the table moves to accommodate the new width.

 **Tip**

To change a column's width without changing the table width press and hold *Shift* while dragging the resize handle.

**Change column width
to defined values**

Rather than resizing tables manually by dragging resize handles, you may resize column(s) to an exact value based on various factors.

1. Select one or more cells in column(s) to be resized.

2. Select Table > Resize Columns.

   The Resize Selected Columns dialog box displays.

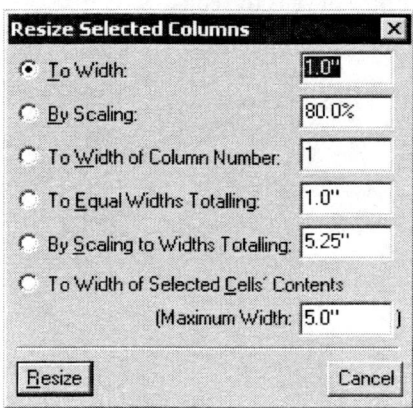

3. Select the resize setting which is to be used to resize the current selection.

   - **Width:** Resizes table column(s) to the exact value specified.
   - **Scaling:** Resizes table column(s) to the percentage of current width specified.
   - **Width of Column Number:** Resizes table column(s) to the width of the column specified.
   - **Equal Widths Totalling:** Sets the width of all selected columns to the same width, based on the total amount specified.
   - **Scaling to Widths Totalling:** Resizes table column(s) to proportional widths.
   - **Width of Selected Cells' Contents:** Resizes table column(s) to the width of longest selected paragraph up to a maximum specified value.

4. Click Resize .

Merging or splitting cell content

This topic explains how to merge or split two or more cells into one.

In FrameMaker, this function is called straddling. Straddling combines a range of cells to act as a single large cell, with content extending across borders.

Merge cell content	1.	Select the range of cells to merge.
		The cells must all be of the same type. That is, Heading, Body or Footing cells may be merged only with the same type of content.
	2.	Select Table > Straddle.

Split cell content	1.	Select the range of cells to split.
		The initial cell range selected must be made up of content already merged.
	2.	Select Table > Unstraddle.

Chapter 15

Images

Overview

This topic teaches you how to work with graphical and multimedia objects.

The following topics are covered:

- *Anchored frames*
- *Supported formats*
- *Inserting images*
- *Manipulating images in frames*

Anchored frames

Whenever images are inserted, FrameMaker creates an anchored frame to contain the image. The anchored frame has the option to contain multiple objects, including more than one image or FrameMaker text boxes and line art, or a combination of these. There are also numerous supported formats that are available to choose from in FrameMaker, but only a limited set of these are supported outside of the application by the DITA Open Toolkit. It is therefore important to plan your images in advance.

Anchored frames

An anchored frame is fixed to a specific location within text and therefore repositions itself (and its content) in relationship to the text. Therefore, moving text that contains an anchored frame also moves the content of the frame as well.

If text is added prior to an anchored frame, the frame moves down in its position relative to the rest of the text. If text is removed prior to an anchored frame, the frame moves up in its position relative to the rest of the text.

Anchored frames may only be inserted within text frames. Upon the insertion of an anchored frame an anchor symbol is inserted at the insertion point within text. This anchor symbol is a non-printing character. It displays as shown below.

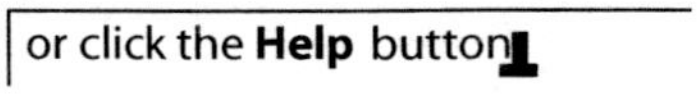

> or click the **Help** button▌

Modify an anchored frame

Once an image is inserted, the frame can be modified to display in a different anchoring location, to resize or to modify the offset from the baseline or margins.

📝 **Note**

Is is possible that not all anchored frame properties export to XML for use with other applications.

1. Select the anchored frame to modify.

    To select an existing anchored frame, click the border of the frame.

2. Select Special > Anchored Frame and edit settings.

3. Click Edit Frame .

Supported formats

When inserting images be aware of restrictions that may be imposed on content outside of FrameMaker.

The DITA Open Toolkit supports the following image formats:

-   GIF
-   JPEG/JPG
-   PNG
-   EPS
-   SVG

Note that while FrameMaker supports all of these image formats (and more), you should test to make sure the formats you want to work with are supported by the tools that are going to be used to view your output. In general, GIF, JPEG and PNG are the most widely supported image formats.

Inserting images

You can insert images into many of the elements found in concept, task, and reference topics. For example, paragraphs, step results, and examples can all contain images.

When you insert an image in FrameMaker, you are actually inserting a link to an existing image stored on your computer, network, or content management system. Plan the names and locations of your image files and FrameMaker documents carefully. Changes to file names and locations could break existing links, making it necessary to re-create them.

Both the Insert menu and the Element Catalog bring up the Insert Image dialog. You can use this dialog to set image properties such as size and alignment. You can go back and modify these properties at anytime.

Insert an inline image   This topic explains how to insert an inline styled image into a document. This type of image is most often inserted in the middle of text content.

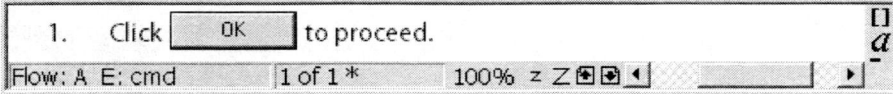

1. Position the insertion point at the location to insert an image.

2. Using the Element Catalog, double click <image>.

    The Import dialog displays.

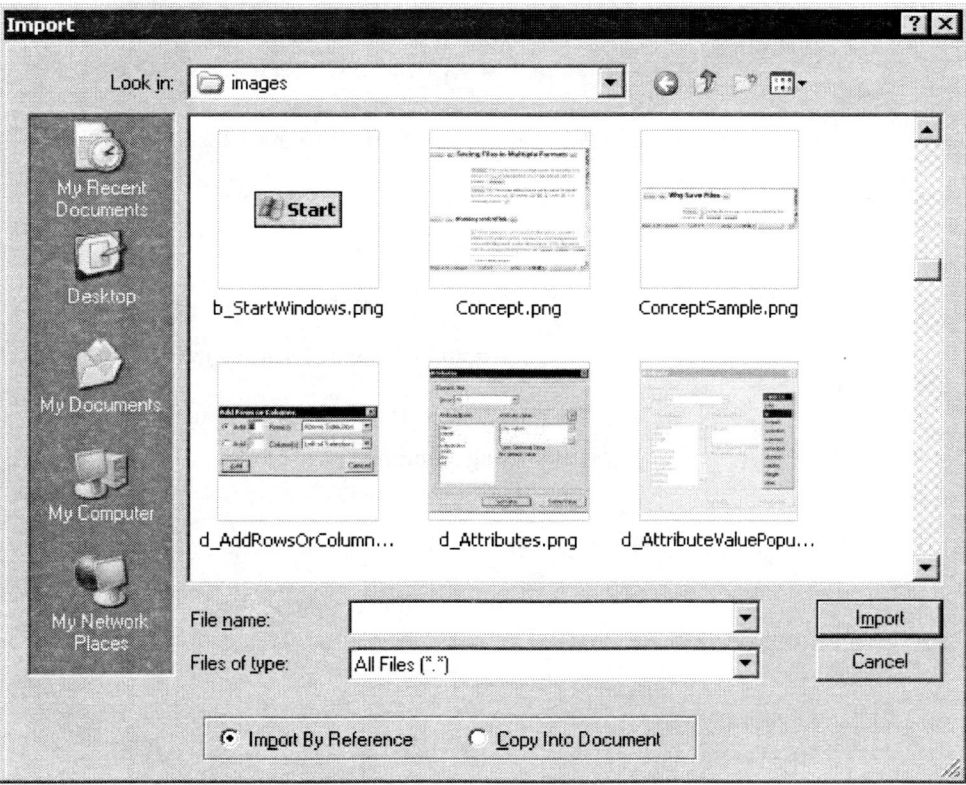

3. Select Import By Reference.

4. Select the graphic from its location and click Import .

5. If required, specify the page or the dots per inch.

   If importing a multiple page pdf file, you need to specify the page to import. If importing a raster image, the dpi (dots per inch) needs to be set.

Insert an image with a title

This topic explains how to insert an image with a title into a document. Images with titles must be wrapped in a figure <fig> element.

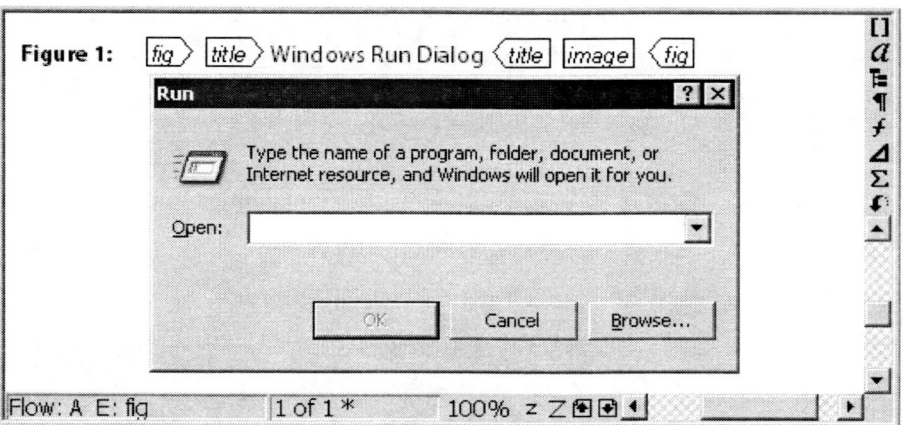

1. Position the insertion point at the location to insert a figure.

2. Using the Element Catalog, double click <fig>.
   The Import dialog displays.

3. Select Import By Reference.

4. Select the graphic from its location and click Import .

5. If required, select the page of a graphic or the dots per inch.

   If importing a multiple page pdf file, you need to specify the page to import. If importing a raster image, the dpi (dots per inch) needs to be set.

6. In the Structure View, display the current <fig> element.

7. Click above the <image> element.

8. Using the Element Catalog, double click <title>.

9. Type a title.

Add a title to an image

To add a title to an existing image, you must first wrap it in a figure <fig> element.

1. Display the Structure View.

2. Select the <image> element tag.

3. From the Element Catalog, wrap the element in a <fig>.

4. Click above the <image> element.

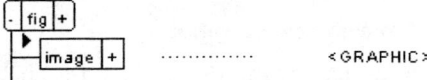

5. Using the Element Catalog, double click <title>.

6. Type a title.

Modify image properties

You can change image properties from the initial insertion settings.

1. Select the image you want to modify.

2. Select Graphic > Object Properties.
   The Object Properties dialog displays.

3. Change properties as required.

4. Click ⬚ Set ⬚.

Delete an image

This topic explains how to remove images or figures.

1. Using the Structure View, select the image or figure to delete.

2. Press *Delete*.

Manipulating images in frames

Rotating objects

1. Select the object to rotate.

2. Select Graphics > Rotate.

3. Specify the number of degrees by which to rotate, under Rotate By.

4. Select Clockwise or Counterclockwise, under Direction.

5. Click Rotate .

Move an image

1. Select the image to be moved.

2. Take the mouse pointer to the border of the image to be moved but not over any of the sizing dots.

3. Click and hold the primary button.

4. Drag the image to a new location.

   It is important that the image remain in the anchored frame or it will no longer be included in the XML export.

5. Release the primary button.

Resize an image

1. Select the image to resize.

2. Take the mouse pointer to one of the sizing dots.

   To change the width and height of the image at the same time drag a corner sizing handle. To change the size of an image and keep the width to height ratio, hold down *Shift* when resizing.

3. Click and drag the mouse pointer to the desired location to resize the image.

4. Release the primary button.

   If changing the size of the image while keeping its width to height ratio, release *Shift*.

Chapter 16

Developing references

Overview

This topic teaches you how to create and develop the <reference> element.

The following topics are covered:

- *Basic reference example*
- *Commonly used elements in a reference*
- *Detailed reference example*
- *Create a new reference*

Basic reference example

The element <reference> is used as a container for facts or information that needs to be looked up for technical information that is not conceptual.

A reference is generally only read by a user when specific technical information is required, usually while doing a specific job. The reference provides the facts without background information or procedural steps. Any reference may be heavily linked to other related reference materials.

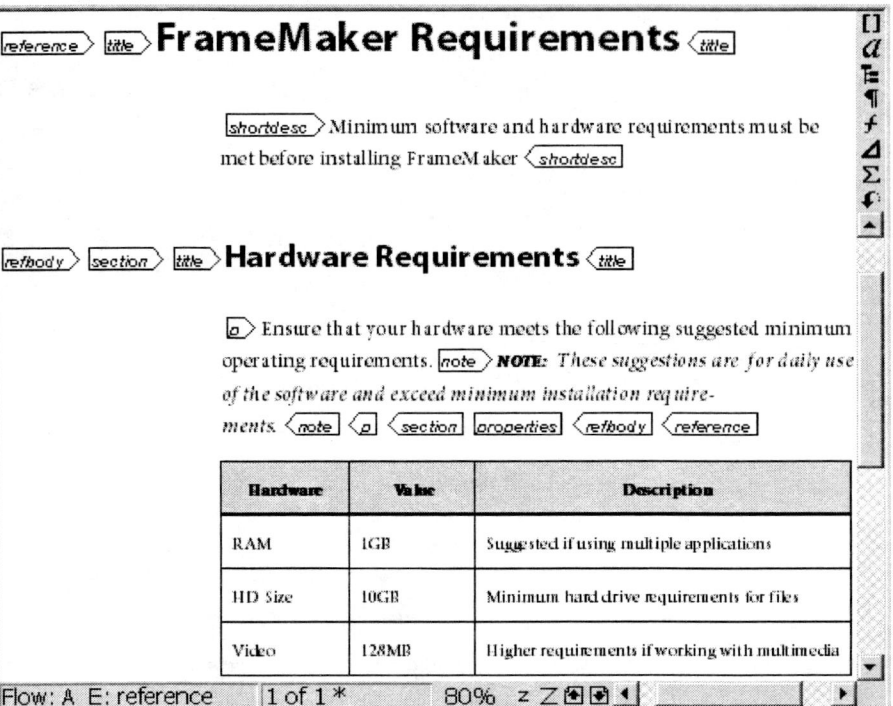

This basic sample contains a title and a section. The section has its own title and a single paragraph of content.

Commonly used elements in a reference

This topic provides a detailed list of commonly used elements in a DITA reference.

References may contain most of the element types that a concept contains. However, the body of the reference has a limited set of element types when compared with a concept. Reference body content must be contained in section, refsyn, example, table, simpletable, or properties elements.

Reference syntax
<refsyn>

The element <refsyn> is used to represent syntax content such as an API's signature. It contains a brief description of the subject's interface or high-level structure. This may then be further defined following the reference syntax.

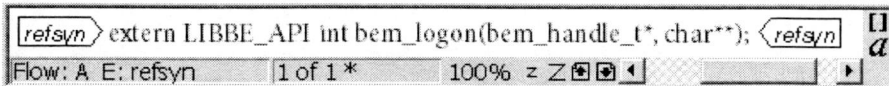

```
refsyn  extern LIBBE_API int bem_logon(bem_handle_t*, char**);  refsyn
Flow: A  E: refsyn        1 of 1 *           100%  z Z ⊞ ⊡ ◄                    ►
```

Properties
<properties>

The element properties is used to represent a list of properties for a topic. This includes the type, value, and description. It is generally represented in a table format.

Type	Value	Description
RGB	0,0,0	Set color using a red, green, blue color model.
CMYK	0,0,0,0	Set color using a cyan, magenta, yellow, black color model.

```
Flow: A  E: propvalue     1 of 1 *           90%  z Z ⊞ ⊡ ◄                    ►
```

Detailed reference example

This topic provides an example of a more involved reference and the elements it may contain.

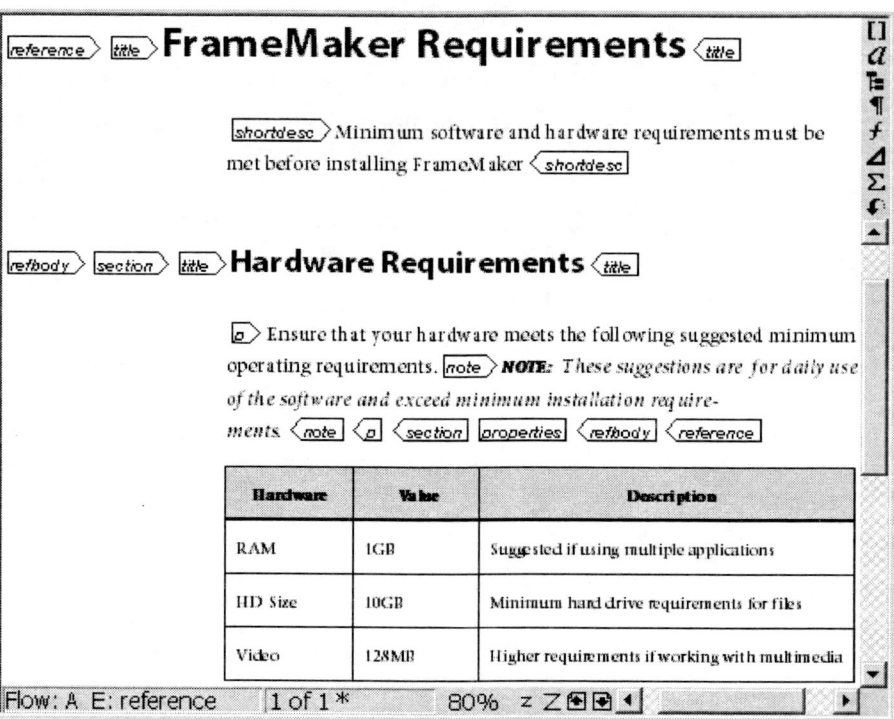

Create a new reference

A new reference can be created as needed.

1. Select DITA > New DITA File.

2. From the DITA topic list, select New <reference>.

3. Specify a file name and location.

4. Click [Select].

5. Modify the document as required.

Chapter 17

Sections and examples

Overview

This topic teaches you how to create and manage sections and examples to organize information.

The following topics are covered:

- *Comparing sections and examples with nested topics*
- *Commonly used elements in a section or example*
- *Working with section and example elements*

Comparing sections and examples with nested topics

While the appearance of content in sections and content in nested topics may be similar, their purposes and capabilities are different.

A section or an example may be fairly generic in its use, but a task, concept, or reference provides a specific usage model. Therefore, the decision to use sections or nested topics may be relatively simple to make.

Purpose of sections

Sections are used to organize information within a topic. Sections are siblings with other sections, not nested within each other. Sections have an optional title; it is a best practice to specify a title for each section.

Purpose of examples

Examples are used to provide support or to demonstrate information in a topic. Examples are siblings with other examples (and sections), not nested within each other. Examples have an optional title; it is a best practice to specify a title for each example.

Purpose of nested topics

Nested topics are used to organize specific information types (such as tasks or concepts) within a topic. Each topic requires a title.

Sample structure of a section

The element <section> is used to represent a collection of organized information. It represents subsets of content that are related to a larger topic. Typically, you use sections when you want to break up a long topic using subheadings. The section title becomes a subheading within the topic.

In this example, neither <section> element is able to be a standalone topic. Instead, each is dependent on the content of the other for clarity. Both are logical supporting information to their parent element.

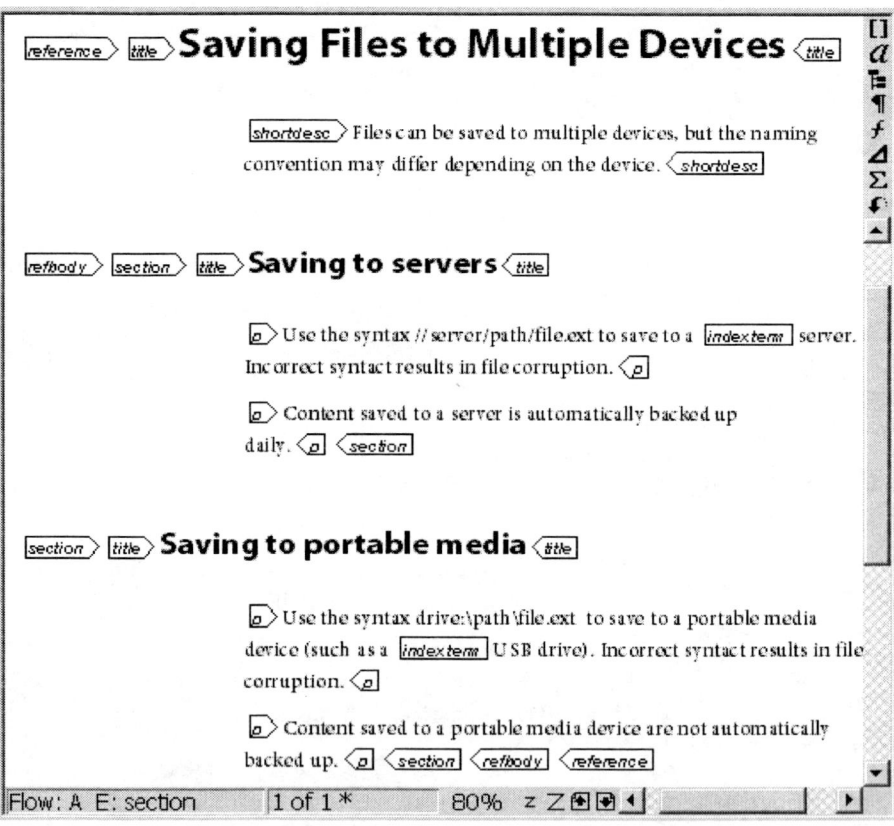

Sample structure of an example

The element <example> is used to represent a sample to further illustrate a topic. An example is otherwise identical to a <section> element.

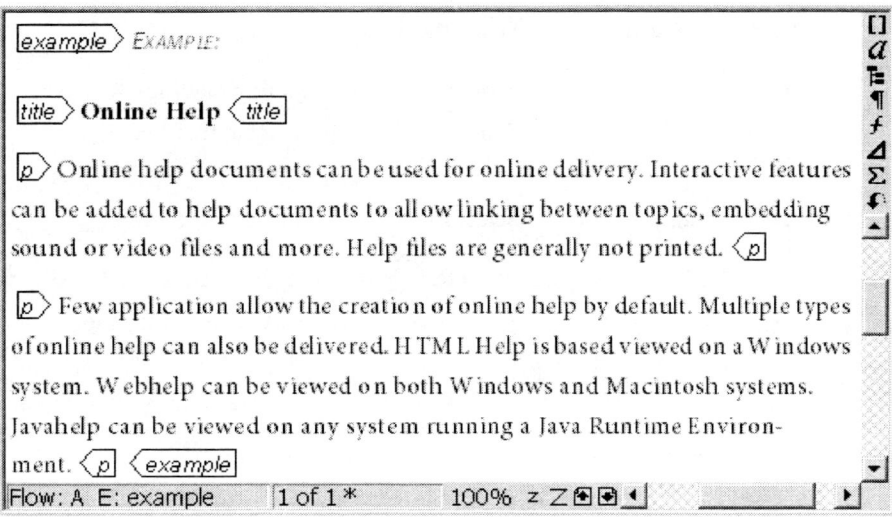

Sample structure of a nested topic

The nested topic elements can each be treated as a standalone topic. Each would make sense on its own and could be reused in other instances of the documentation. In addition, each nested topic may contain additional nested topics as required. Some content management system (CMS) tools do not work well with nested topics and it is suggested that you nest topics in a DITA map instead.

Commonly used elements in a section or example

This topic provides a detailed list of commonly used elements in a DITA section or example.

Common elements

The elements <section> and <example> use many of the same elements that are used in a concept.

Restricted elements

However, <section> and <example> cannot contain other <section> or <example> elements. They also cannot contain topics, references, concepts, or tasks.

Working with section and example elements

Insert a section

1. Select the location to insert a section.

2. From the Element Catalog, double-click <section>.
   A new section is inserted at that location.

Insert an example

1. Select the location to insert an example.

2. From the Element Catalog, double-click <example>.
   A new example is inserted at that location.

Chapter 18

Developing tasks

Overview

This topic teaches you how to create and develop the <task> element.

The following topics are covered:

- *Basic task example*
- *Commonly used elements in a task*
- *Detailed task example*
- *Create a new task*

Basic task example

The element <task> is used as a container for a procedure. This element provides instructions related to addressing how to do a specific thing and the order of steps to follow.

The purpose of a task is to tell the user how to accomplish a set of steps to achieve a goal. It is often read while a user is performing a specific task and should provide enough information to guide the user through the steps to a clear end point, the completion of the task.

Tasks provide detailed, step-by-step instructions and provide context and examples as required. They may have explicit prerequisites or postrequisites that must be performed by the user. Within the task, there are usually multiple single-step procedures to follow.

Each step may be made up of a variety of information including an explicit command (a call to action) and related supporting information.

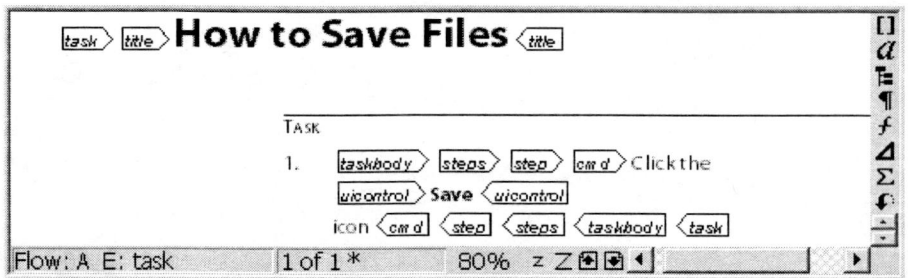

This basic sample contains a title and a task. The task has a single step and the step has a command in it.

Commonly used elements in a task

This topic provides a detailed list of commonly used elements in a DITA task.

The task contains a variety of elements including a single title, an optional short description, one or more paragraphs, index entries, lists, tables, figures or images, examples, and more. However, most importantly, tasks have a set of specific elements that can only be used within the <taskbody> element.

The <taskbody> may contain a variety of elements including a task prerequisite, the context in which the task is performed, a variety of steps (which may be numbered or unordered), a result, an example, and a postrequisite. Each of these elements may have additional specific set of descendents. For example, the steps element must contain one or more step elements. The step elements contain a command and an optional set of elements that may include additional information, substeps, choices, and so on.

Task prerequisite <prereq>
The element prereq is used to inform the user of specific things that must be done before the task is started.

Task context <context>
The element context is used to provide background information related to a task. It provides information to help the user be successful at the task and understand the reason for it.

Task steps <steps>
The element steps is used to contain the main set of procedural information related to a task.

Task step \<step>	The element \<step> is used to contain a specific action that the user must perform to accomplish a task. It contains one command.
Step command \<cmd>	The element \<cmd> is an active voice instruction to the user that is usually a single sentence.
Step result \<stepresult>	The element \<stepresult> is used to provide feedback to the user on the expected result of a command.
Substeps \<substeps>	The element \<substeps> is used to provide additional steps that must be taken within a major step. The output is usually the same as a nested list in appearance. A substep contains all the same element options as a step, except it cannot contain further substeps.
Step choices \<choices>	The element \<choices> is used to provide a selection that has more than one option.
Step choice tables \<choicetable>	The element \<choicetable> is used to present table-based choices, which usually include an option and a related description.
Step example \<stepxmp>	The element \<stepxmp> is used to provide a sample of what the step involves.
Information \<info>	The element \<info> is used to contain additional content related to the command.
Result \<result>	The element \<result> is used to provide feedback to the user on the expected result of a overall task upon completion of all steps.
Post requisite \<postreq>	The element \<postreq> is used to contain additional content related to the command.

Detailed task example

This topic provides an example of a more involved task and elements it may contain.

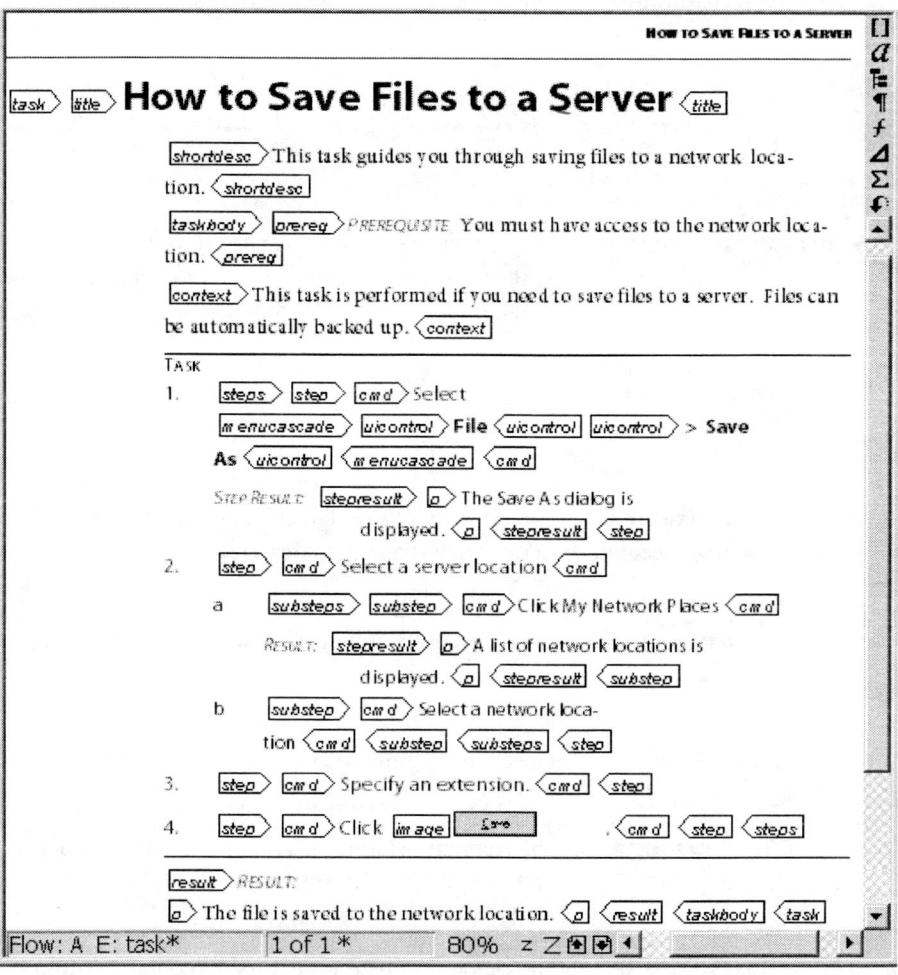

The same task may display as seen below in Normal View.

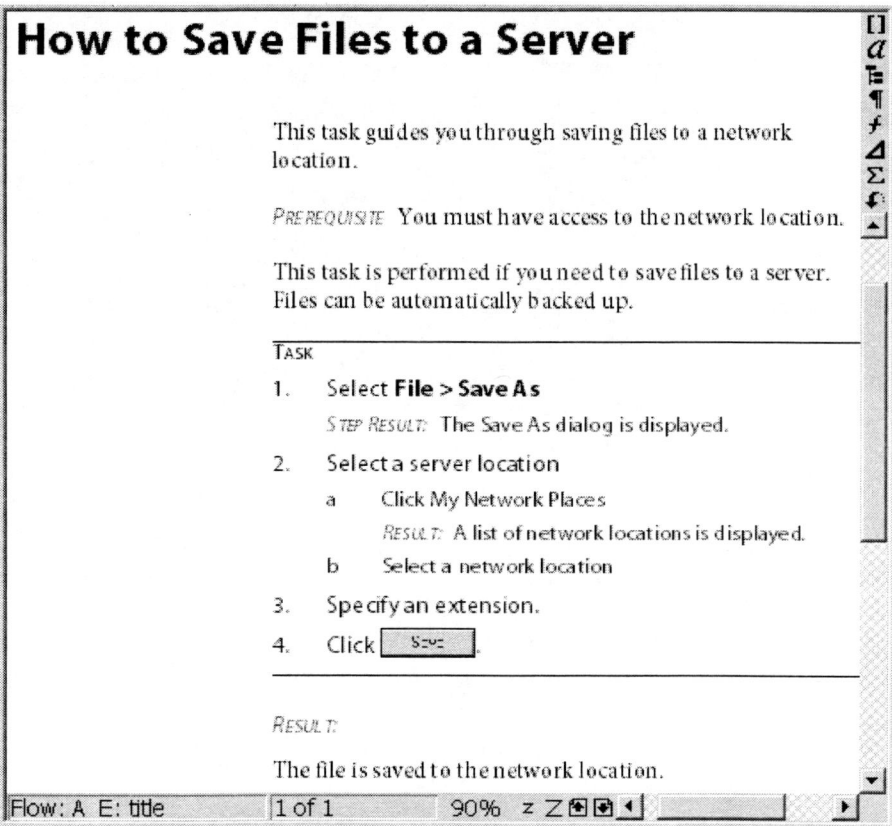

Create a new task

A new task can be created as needed.

1. Select DITA > New DITA File.

2. From the list, select New <task>.

3. Specify a file name and location.

4. Click [OK].

5. Modify the document as required.

Chapter 19

Track text edits

Overview

This topic teaches you how to note modifications when content is added, deleted or modified in a file.

The following topics are covered:

- *Tracking text edits*
- *Track text edits display*
- *Working with track text edits*

Tracking text edits

You can set FrameMaker to track all text edits made to documents.

Tracking text edits records edits made to text or the elements in the Structure view, but does not record all of the changes you make within your file.

⚠ **Caution**

Changes that are tracked are marked up in the XML output using processing instructions that only FrameMaker understands.

Text edits tracked

A variety of modifications to documents can be automatically tracked. These include:

- Text inserted or pasted
- Text deleted or cut

- Text moved by dragging and dropping in the Structure or normal view
- New elements added

Changes not tracked   Several modifications to documents are not tracked. These include:

- Changes to markup, including elements that are split or joined
- Changes to attribute values
- Changes to marker text
- Addition or deletion of rows and columns in tables

Track text edits display

Once the tracking of text edits is enabled, text that you add or delete appears formatted according to system defaults. You cannot change the default color and format of revision indicators.

You can navigate through all the text edits and accept or reject them. You can also view the document before the track text edits were turned on and view it as it would be with all text edits accepted.

Appearance of tracked text edits

Text removed displays with a strike through and is red in color. Text added is underlined and is green in color.

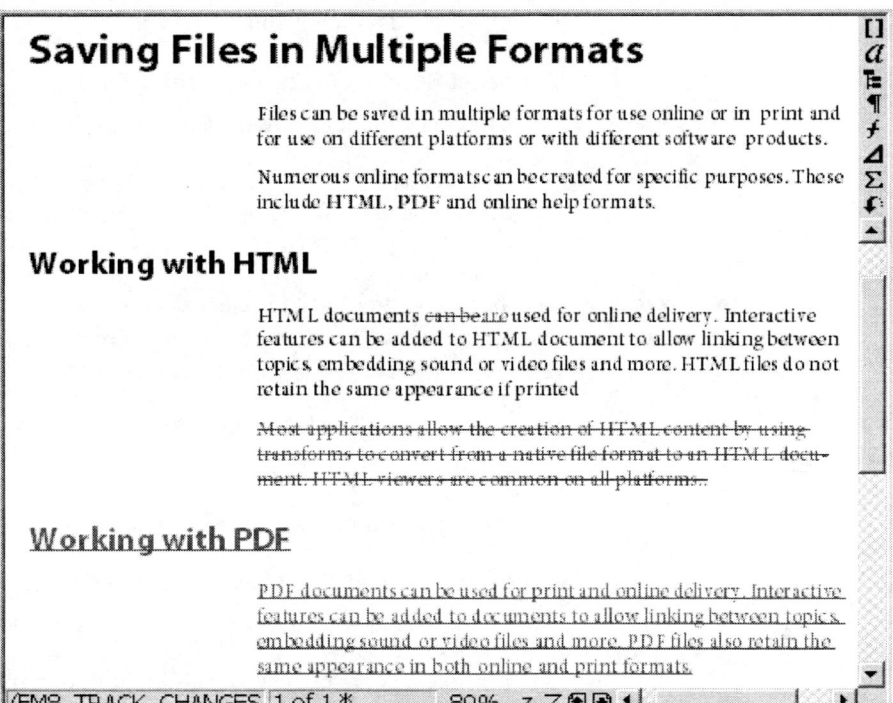

Working with track text edits

Track Text Edit toolbar

The Track Text Edit toolbar can be used to work with change tracking.

1. Select View > Track Text Edit Bar.

    The Track Text Edit toolbar displays.

Turn track text edits on or off

Turning track text edits off prevents further changes from being tracked. It does not accept, reject, or hide any changes made while track text edits was on.

1. Open the document you want to edit.

2. Select Special > Track Text Edits > Enable.

   The check mark next to the Enable option indicates whether track text edits is on or off.

3. Select Special > Track Text Edits > Enable again to turn track text edits off.

Accept or reject tracked text edits

Use the toolbar to accept or reject all text edits in a document, or to accept or reject each change individually. Accepted text edits are incorporated into the document and the revision marks are removed from the relevant text. Rejected text edits are undone.

1. Select View > Track Text Edit Bar.

   The Track Text Edit toolbar displays.

2. Use the toolbar to do one of the following:

   • Move to the next or previous change using ▶ or ◀ .

   • Accept or reject text edits one at a time by clicking ✔ or ✗ .

   • Accept or reject all text edits in the document at once by clicking ✔ or ✗ .

Chapter 20

Validation

Overview

This topic teaches you how to validate documents.

The following topics are covered:

- *Understanding valid versus invalid documents*
- *Checking validity*
- *Allowing or ignoring errors*
- *Fixing invalid documents*

Understanding valid versus invalid documents

Validation in XML

All DITA documents have a set of rules they need to adhere to. These rules are called a content model. For example, one of the rules is that all concepts must contain a <title> element before the <shortdesc> or <conbody> element. The Document Type Definition (DTD) or the schema contains the structural rules for DITA documents. The DITA Architectural Specification document describes these rules in detail. It is available at www.oasis-open.org.

A valid document is one that adheres to these DITA rules; an invalid document is one that does not. Validation errors are the errors in the document that make it invalid. Note that if the DTD you are working with has been specialized, it may help to understand how it differs from the standard DITA DTD.

Understanding how validation works in FrameMaker

In Structure View, FrameMaker displays visual cues to indicate validation errors. This is called rules checking, so named because FrameMaker checks that the action you perform is valid according to the rules in the DTD.

As you write, FrameMaker does not ensure that you insert all of the required elements, attributes, and values. A missing required element, attribute, or value is one of the most common causes of a validation error. At any time, however, you can perform a check to find possible validation errors in your document.

The first step in fixing the errors is finding them. Run FrameMaker validation to help you find all validation errors in your document.

Checking validity

You can validate your document at any time. If you have many validation errors, you may find it useful to validate a selection at a time.

Check if a document is valid

1. Select Element > Validate.

   If your document is valid, a message displays indicating validation success.

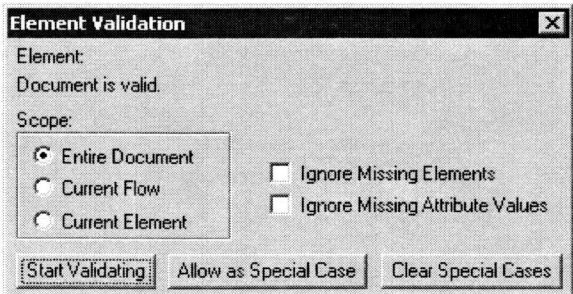

   If your document is invalid, you are taken to the first validation error.

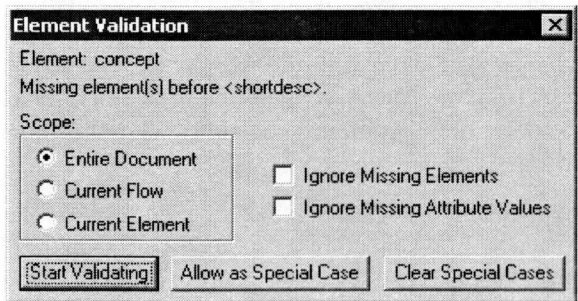

Check if a selection is valid

1. Select Element > Validate.

2. Place your cursor in the text you want to validate.

3. Select Scope: Current Flow.

4.   Click `Start Validating` .

If your document is valid, a successful validation message displays in the Element Validation dialog.

If your document is invalid, you are taken to the first error in your document.

Allowing or ignoring errors

This topic explain how to allow specific errors or types of errors in documents. This is done most often in a document that is not yet complete, where errors are expected and a fully valid document is not required. In addition, if you are unsure of how to fix an error at the current time, you may want to allow it as a special case.

Ignore missing elements

All missing elements can be ignored when validating.

1.   Launch the Element Validation dialog.

2.   Select or deselect Ignore Missing Elements.

3.   Begin validating.

Ignore missing attribute values

All missing attributes can be ignored when validating.

1.   Launch the Element Validation dialog.

2.   Select or deselect Ignore Missing Attribute Values.

3.   Begin validating.

Allow errors as special cases

Specific errors can be ignored when validating.

1.   Launch the Element Validation dialog.

2.   When an error is found, click `Allow as Special Case` .

Special cases are only remembered as long as the document is open. They are not stored as part of the file.

3.   Continue validating.

Reset special cases   If you have allowed specific errors in validation to exist you can reset them at any time.

1.   Launch the Element Validation dialog.

2.   Click `Clear Special Cases`

Any special cases are cleared.

3.   Continue validating.

Fixing invalid documents

If you have errors when you check the validity of your document, you must fix the errors before your document can be valid. To help you resolve errors, you are taken to the next error in the document when you run the validation.

When fixing validation errors, it helps to understand the types of errors that can occur. A very common type of validation error is the "missing" error. This error indicates that a required element, attribute, or value is missing. It may be missing from the document altogether or it may be missing from the required position.

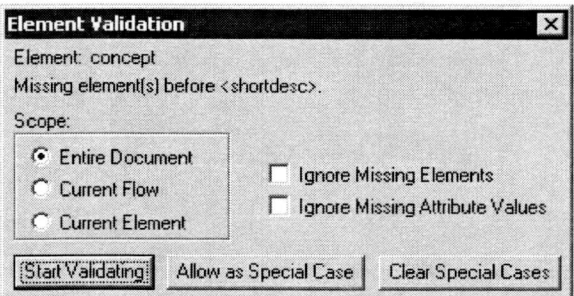

To fix this type of error, you must insert the required element, attribute, or value in the required position. You may need to check the DITA specifications to figure out which required elements, attributes, or values are missing from your document.

Another common type of validation error is the "invalid" error. This error indicates that either an element or attribute is invalid in its current location or that an attribute value is invalid. In the case of an element or attribute, it may be in the wrong place or it may be that a required element is missing before it, making it seem as though it is in the wrong place.

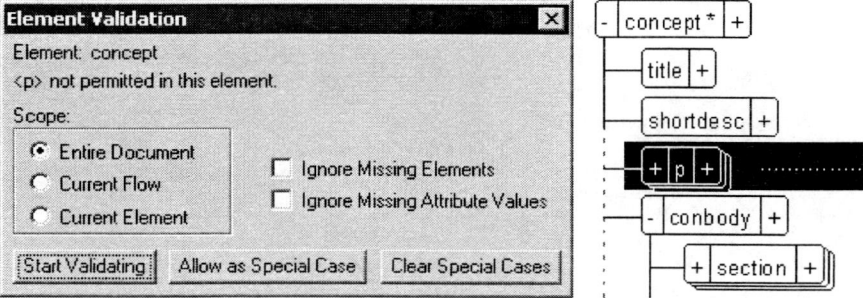

To fix an invalid element or attribute, try resolving all missing required element and attribute errors first. If the "invalid" errors still exist after rechecking validation, try moving the invalid element by cutting and pasting it. Another option is to change the element to a different element that is valid in that location.

In the case of an invalid attribute value, the problem may be that the same value is being used in multiple places. For example, IDs must have unique values. Another possible problem may be that the value restrictions are not being met. For example, letters may be being used when only numbers are allowed.

FrameMaker prevents you from defining a unique value twice in a file. However, it is possible that a document is modified outside of FrameMaker and invalidated externally by specifying an ID that is already used.

If you have further problems resolving "invalid" errors, you may need to check the DITA specifications to figure out how to best meet its requirements.

Example of fixing an invalid document

In this example, the title element is removed from a concept topic, resulting in an invalid document:

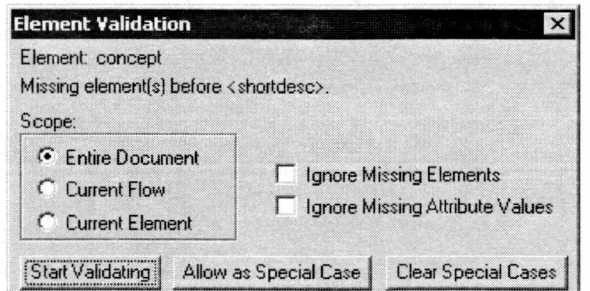 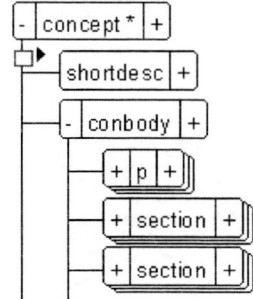

The Structure View displays a red box to indicate a missing required element. In this case, the missing element is <title>. After adding a <title> before <shortdesc> and rerunning validation, the following message indicates that all of the errors have been fixed:

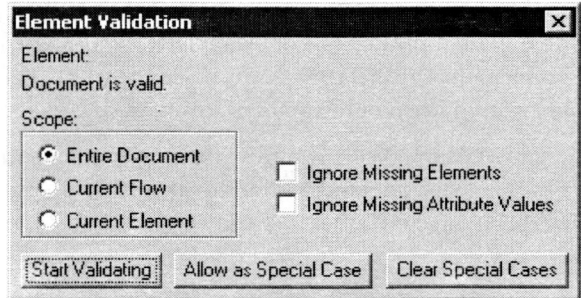

Chapter 21

Linking in topics

Overview

This topic teaches you how to work with links and related elements.

The following topics are covered:

- *Types of links*
- *Working with links*

Types of links

The DITA specification allows links to be created inline, within a collection of related links, or in a relationship table. If links are created inline or as a set of related links within a file, dependencies are built. Should the link destination file change in name or path, the hard coded links need to be updated. Instead, the relationship table and a map provide more control and greater flexibility in content reuse and linking.

Inline links

An inline link is usually inserted within the body of the document. It directs the reader to a location either internal to the document or to an external location. Common inline links may include, for example, cross-references between steps in a task, references to an external document such as a PDF file, or URL links to websites or email addresses.

Cross-reference

A cross-reference is a link to a destination in either the current topic or another topic. The cross-reference is the best type of link for inline references. This type of a link can generally be inserted anywhere and link to a variety of elements. A cross-reference to other external topics will build dependency on that external topic and reduce the overall reuse of a topic. Generally this type of cross-reference should be avoided for the most compliancy with the best practices of DITA.

Web link

A Web link is a link to an internet location or an email address. This type of a link is relatively easy to manage and does not require the link destination to be included in the delivered topic.

Related links

Related links to topics, Web pages, or files are handled in a unique fashion when processing topics in DITA. The link information is not an internal component of your content but is instead included at the end of the topic.

 **Note**

The default related link mechanism that is provided does not offer a great deal of support on the insertion and management of related links.

This allows the related links to be processed in a specific way and may include the reorganization of content, the automatic placement of the links in the output that is generated, or even the removal of the links if the target does not exist. Related links display at the end of their respective topics. However, the related links do build dependency on other topics and therefore are not the most ideal way to create links.

Rather than using related links, the <reltable> element used with a map document may provide far more benefit.

Working with links

The initial steps associated with inserting a link are the same for all link types. However, specific options related to any given link vary.

Developing inline links

Inline links display within the content of an element (such as paragraph).

Support for the FrameMaker cross-reference link is provided, but generally the DITA xref element provides greater support for the types of elements that can be referenced and the way that the links are managed in external DITA enabled software tools.

Insert a FrameMaker cross-reference link

This type of link is based on the traditional FrameMaker cross-reference. It allows links to be inserted between FrameMaker objects that support the unique ID.

1. Position the insertion point where you want a cross-reference.

2. Using the Element Catalog, double click <fm-xref>.

   The Cross Reference dialog displays.

3. Under Source Type, click 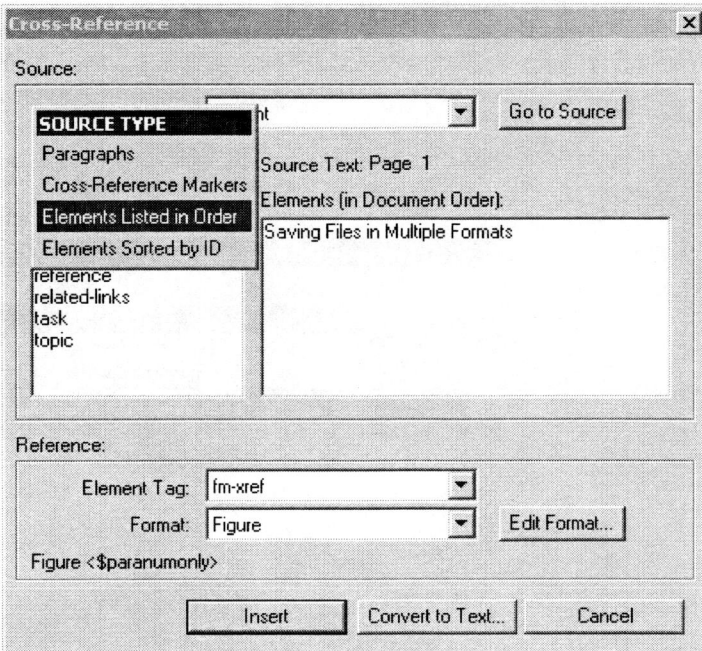.

4. From the Source Type drop-down list, select the type of content to reference to.

    For use with DITA, this should be either Elements Listed in Order or Elements Sorted by ID.

    - **Elements Listed in Order** displays elements in the order of their appearance in the document

    - **Elements Sorted by ID** displays elements in the alpha-numeric order, base on their unique identification value

5. Select the specific content to reference.

6. From the Format drop-down list, select the format to display the reference as.

7. Click Insert.

    The cross-reference is inserted and, if it does not yet exist, a unique ID is assigned to the element the reference is linked to.

Insert a DITA cross-reference link to topic content

This type of link is based on the DITA styles of a cross-reference. It allows links to be inserted between elements that support the unique ID.

1. Position the insertion point where you want a cross-reference.

2. Using the Element Catalog, double click <xref>.

   The DITA Reference Manager dialog displays.

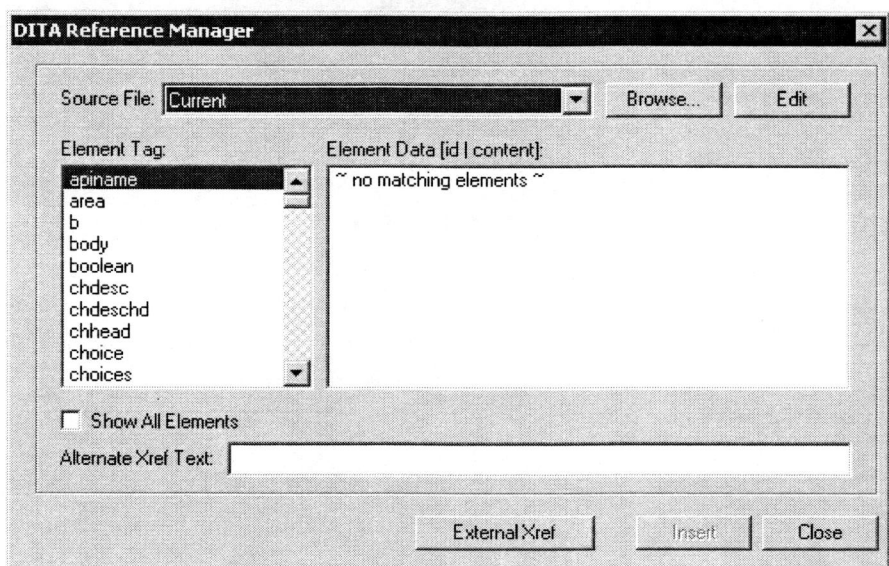

3. Under Source File, select a file to reference to.

4. If the file is not currently open click  and specify the server, drive, or folder to open the topic from, then select the topic to reference.

5. Under Element Tag, select the type of element to reference to.

📝 **Note**

Only a limited number of file types are supported since FrameMaker attempts to open the file to link to.

6. The dialog updates to display any matching element types that have an ID assigned to them. If the Element Data [id | content] is blank, select Show All Elements.

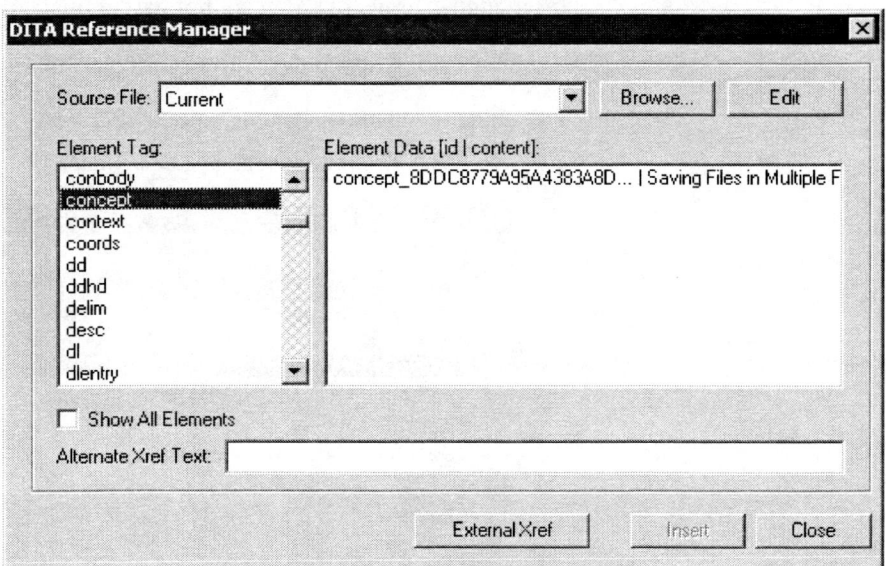

7. Under Alternative Xref Text, type the text to display with the link.

8. Click Insert .

The cross-reference is inserted and, if it does not yet exist, a unique ID is assigned to the element the reference is linked to.

Insert a DITA cross-reference link to an external file

This type of link is based on the DITA styles of a cross-reference. It allows links to be inserted to external files that are not part of the DITA specification.

1. Position the insertion point where you want a cross-reference.

2. Using the Element Catalog, double click <xref>.

   The DITA Reference Manager dialog displays.

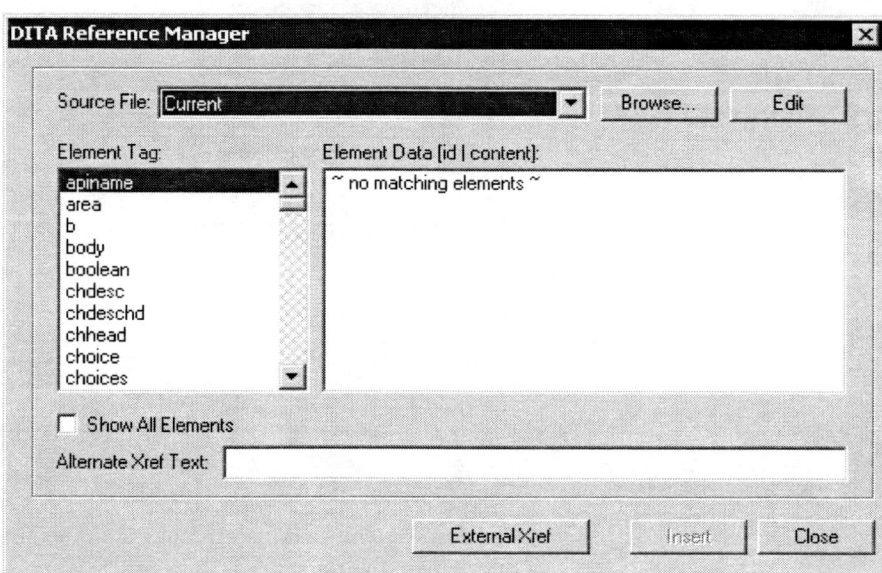

3. Click [External Xref].

   The DITA External Xref dialog displays.

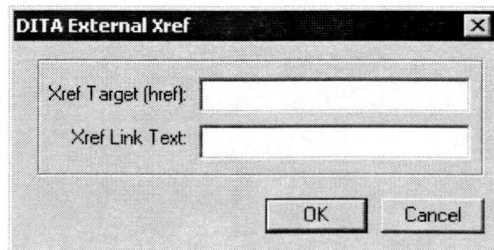

> **Note**
>
> This type of link depends on effective file and folder management and is not generally due to the work involved in creating and managing the link and the target.

4. Under Xref Target (href), type the relative path and file name to link to.

5. Under Xref Link Text, type the on-screen message to be displayed.

6. Click [OK].

   The cross-reference is inserted.

Insert a DITA cross-reference link to web links

This type of link is based on the DITA styles of a cross-reference. It allows links to be inserted to websites.

1. Position the insertion point where you want a cross-reference.

2. Using the Element Catalog, double click <xref>.

    The DITA Reference Manager dialog displays.

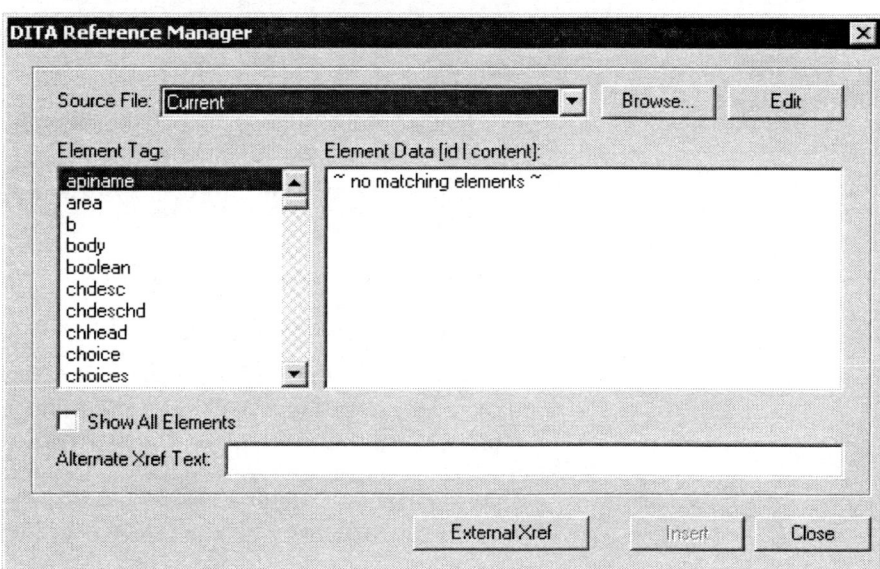

3. Click [External Xref].

    The DITA External Xref dialog displays.

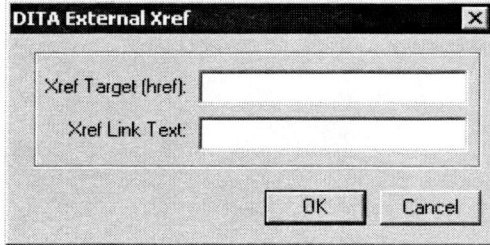

4. Under Xref Target (href), type the full URL to link to.

5. Under Xref Link Text, type the on-screen message to be displayed.

6. Click [OK].

    The cross-reference is inserted.

Developing related links

Related links display at the end of the content of a higher level element (such as a Topic, Task, Reference, or Concept).

Note

This type of link depends on manual development of links and related information and is not recommended due to the work involved in creating and managing the link and the target.

Insert a related links to a topic

1. Using the Structure view, place your cursor at the end of a <topic>, <concept>, <task> or <reference> element.

2. From the Element Catalog, double-click **Related Links**.

3. From the Element Catalog, select what type of related links you want.

   - Link: A simple link.
   - Linklist: A list of links output in the author preferred order based on processing instructions in the DITA Open Toolkit.
   - Linkpool: A group of links output based on processing instructions in the DITA Open Toolkit.

4. Add the required and optional elements for your link and link description.

5. Expand the attributes for the element <link>.

   If you add text to the <link> element, that text becomes what the user clicks on to navigate the related link. Without text, the link automatically takes the title or the topic or file, or the web address you specified.

6. Double-click the attribute `href` and specify the file name that has the topic you want to link to followed by # and the ID of the element you want to link to.

   For example, the href attribute when linking to a topic within a file could look like this: introduction.xml#overview.

Chapter 22

Reusing content

Overview

This topic teaches you how to work with reuseable content and strategies to effectively create, insert, modify, and update shared content.

The following topics are covered:

- *About reuse*
- *Conditional content*
- *Filter by attribute*
- *Working with content references*
- *Working with variables*

About reuse

FrameMaker allows you to create content once and reuse that same content in multiple places. Note that reusing content is different from copying content. With copies, any updates you need to make to the original also have to be made manually to every copy. This is not only inefficient, but makes it more difficult to ensure the accuracy and consistency of your content. With reused content, you only need to update the content once, and every place that reuses that content also gets updated.

Reuse examples

Consider the following examples where the same content can be reused in multiple places:

- A copyright and trademark page that displays at the front of every manual.
- A company logo that displays numerous times in different documents.
- Standardized notes and warnings that display multiple times throughout a document set.

- An online help system that is customized for basic users or administrators.
- Three products that share 50% of the same topics.
- An online help system and a printed manual that share 80% of the same topics.

Plan reuse

To plan for reuse, we suggest the following steps:

1. Read through the topics in this manual describing DITA maps, conditional content, and content references so that you understand how these tools will help you to reuse information.

2. Analyze your document sets to find content that is repeated. Create a representative list of the content you find.

3. For each example in your list, figure out which method or combination of methods will allow you to reuse information in the way you need. Here is a simple guide to get you started:
   - Reusing entire topics—DITA maps
   - Reusing topics with customizations—Conditional content
   - Reusing parts of topics—Content references

Conditional content

Conditional content allows you to reuse a topic and customize it based on audience, platform, product, or the specifications of your choosing. When you generate output for a topic, you can specify which conditional content is included and which is excluded.

 **Note**

Using the default conditional content options may result in undesired effects if the XML content is used by other applications. Avoid selecting **Special** > **Conditional Text** if using structured content.

FrameMaker inserts processing instructions into the XML to manage conditions. A better approach is to use the Filter by Attribute options.

You can conditionalize almost any element that is optional in the DITA specification. Some element types that can be conditionalized include paragraphs, steps, examples, tables, table rows, and images. You can also conditionalize text within an element, which is especially useful if you are restricted from conditionalizing the whole element. For example, while a Task requires a Title, and so cannot be conditionalized, you can conditionalize a phrase <ph> element within the Title. Similarly, while you cannot conditionalize a table column, you can conditionalize phrase <ph> elements within a table column.

Since best practice in DITA is to avoid using tool specific processing instructions, this chapter does not document procedures related to working with the Conditional Content options

Filter by attribute

While FrameMaker inserts processing instructions into XML to manage conditional content it makes sense to use the Filter by Attribute option. This applies conditions based on elements, attributes and values. This is a much better approach to working with DITA.

Default conditions   No default options are defined.

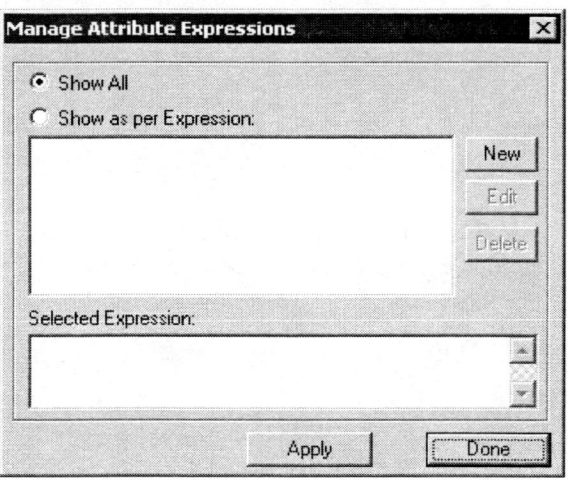

Sample of conditional user information

For example, the following topic has conditional content for two audiences: user and administrator. The administrator conditional content is indicated by the attribute audience set to admin. The user conditional content is indicated by the attribute audience set to user.

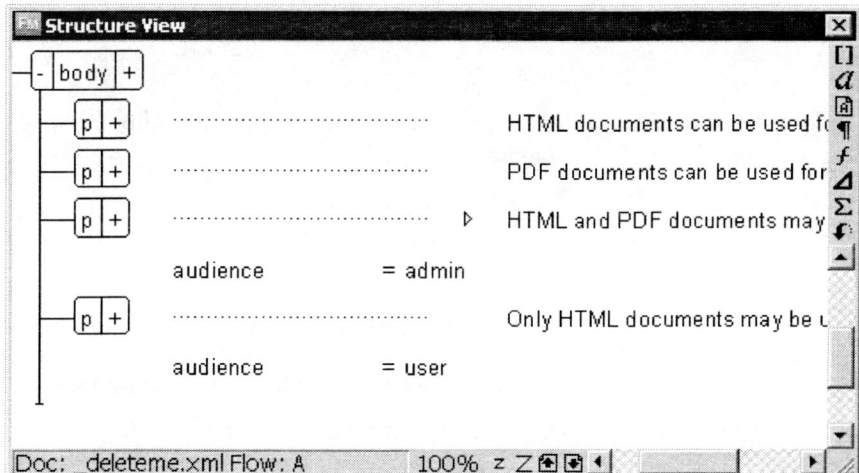

When this topic is generated with the administrator condition included and the user condition excluded, the topic reads as follows:

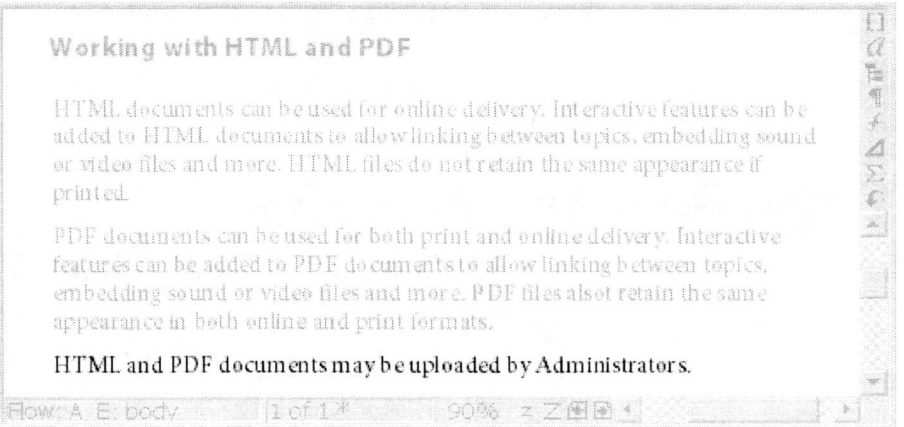

When this topic is generated with the user condition included and the administrator condition excluded, the topic reads as follows:

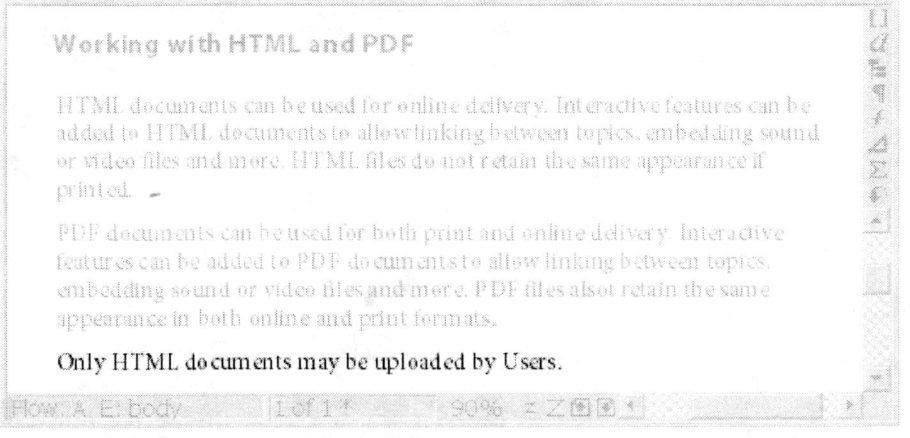

Apply a condition

This topic explains how to apply a condition to content including text, tables, and graphics.

1. Select the element to conditionalize.

2. Display the Attribute Editor.

3. Select the attribute to modify.

4. Select the attribute value you want to apply.

5. Click OK .

Remove a condition

This topic explains how to remove a condition once it has been applied.

1. Select the element to remove the condition from.

2. Click a plus sign to expand the currently applied attribute.

3. Display the Attribute Editor.

4. Clear the attribute value.

5. Click OK .

Display the Filter by Attribute dialog

This topic explains how display the Filter by Attribute dialog as needed.

1. Select Special > Filter by Attribute.

   The Manage Attribute Expressions displays.

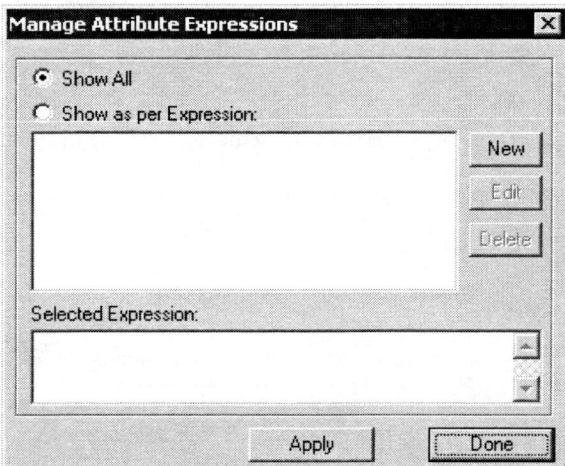

2. If expressions exist the Selected Expression displays the code of the Expression when a specific Expression Tag is selected.

Purpose of expressions

The expressions drive conditional content. Depending on the phrasing of the expression specific content does or does not display in the document.

Any element that does not have an attribute with a specified value is considered to be unconditional and therefore displays by default. However, elements with specific attributes set to defined values can be shown or hidden as required.

Samples

The following code, when applied, only displays elements where the attribute for *audience* is set to a value of *admin* or where the *audience* is not defined at all:

```
(audience="admin")
```

The following code, when applied, only displays elements where the attribute for *audience* is set to a value of *user* or where the *audience* is not defined at all:

```
(audience="user")
```

The following code, when applied, only displays elements where the attribute for *audience* is set to a value of *user* or where the *audience* is not defined at all AND the *platform* is set to *unix* or where the *platform* is not defined at all.

```
(audience="user") AND (platform="unix")
```

The following code, when applied, only displays elements where the attribute for *audience* is set to a value of *user* or *support* or where the *audience* is not defined at all AND the *platform* is *xp* or where the *platform* is not defined at all:

```
(audience="admin" OR audience="support") AND (platform="xp")
```

Create filter by attribute settings

This topic explains how to create a new filter by attribute setting.

1. Display the Manage Attribute Expressions dialog.

2. Click [New].

   The Build Expression dialog displays.

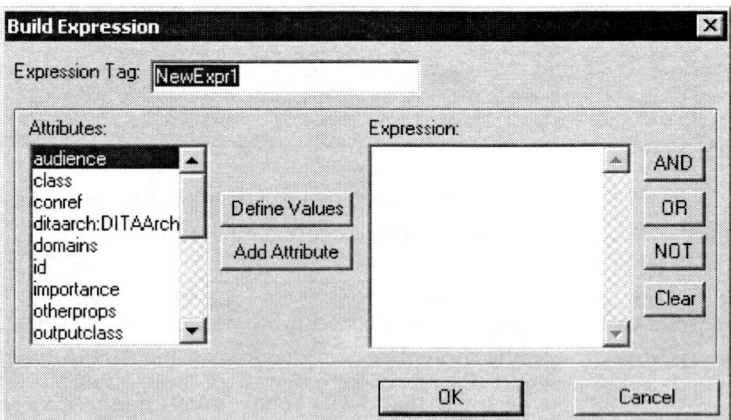

3. Under Expression Tag, type the name to display in the Manage Attribute Expressions dialog.

   Use a descriptive name that helps the user such as *Administrator Guide*.

4. Define the Expression.

    This can be done by typing the entire expression or by using the Attributes to start. For example to automatically add *audience* or *platform* or *product*:

    a. Under Attributes, select an attribute to drive the filter.

    b. Click [Add Attribute] to place the attribute in the Expression.

5. Complete the Expression.

6. Click [OK].

Publish conditional content   You publish topics with conditional content in the same way that you publish regular topics, except that you additionally indicate which conditions should be output.

1. Display the Manage Attribute Expressions dialog.

2. Select Show as Per Expression.

3. Select an expression to apply.

4. Click [Apply].

5. Click [Done].

6. Publish the content.

Working with content references

Content references allow you to reuse individual elements or groups of elements within your topics. For example, you may have certain paragraphs, phrases, keywords, notes, or tables that can be used in many contexts. Phrases and keywords make especially good content references because they can be reused inside so many other elements.

When you insert a content reference, you are actually inserting a link to the file containing the original content. It is this link that allows the update of all content references when the original content is updated.

A content reference can be inserted as part of an existing topic. For example, if you have topic containing a note, you could take the note and reuse it within the topic at an other location as reuseable information. If the source is updated the subsequent instance is also modified.

Your second choice is to take advantage of FrameMaker's reusable component tools for content references. In this case, every reusable component is stored as a separate file. Each note, then, would be stored as a separate file, and then the separate files would each be inserted as content references into a collection of content. To reuse a single note in a concept topic, you would insert a reusable component content reference to the individual note file.

Plan how to store your reusable content so that it is easy to find when you need it. You must also be careful when you update a piece of content that is reused elsewhere so that the changes you make are applicable in all the places that reference it.

Insert a content reference

1. Place your cursor where your want to insert the content reference.

    Ensure that the type of content reference you want to insert is valid at this location.

2. Select DITA > Insert Conref.

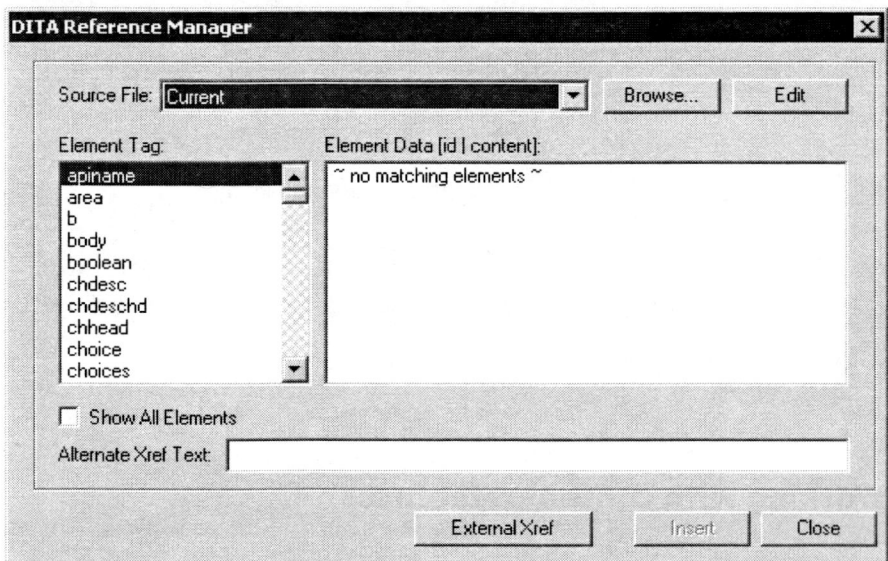

3. If the source content you want to insert is located in a different file, browse to the source file and click [**Open**].

4. From Element Tag, select the element type to insert.

5. From Element Data (id | content), select the ID of the element you want to insert.

6. Click [Insert].

    FrameMaker inserts the content reference.

Modify a content reference

Before you modify a content reference, ensure that the changes you want to make are applicable in all the places where you are reusing that content reference.

1. Select File > Open.

2. Select the file containing the content reference to be modified and click ⬚Open .

3. Edit the content as needed.

4. Select File > Save.

5. Select File > Close.

Update a content reference

Once you have modified content references and reusable component content references, you can update your current file to reflect the changes. Any file that is opened after modifying a content reference automatically reflects the changes.

1. Select DITA > Update References.

Working with variables

Variables allow you to reuse short strings of text throughout your topic. Phrases and keywords make especially good variables because they can be reused inside so many other elements.

Insert a user defined variable

To insert a user defined variable, there must be existing user defined variables. These are usually managed on a template level and already defined for use in the template.

1. Place your cursor where your want to insert the user defined variable.

2. Select Special > Variables.
   The Variables dialog displays.

3. Select the Variable you want to insert and click ⬚Insert .

Delete a variable instance

You can delete a variable that is in use in a specific topic.

1. Select the variable you want to delete.

2. Press *Delete*.

Chapter 23

Maps

Overview

This topic teaches you how to create, manage, and publish maps.

The following topics are covered:

- *Introduction to maps*
- *Attributes and maps*
- *Attributes and topicrefs*
- *Working with maps*
- *Publish a map*
- *Adding content to a map*
- *Organizing maps*
- *Modifying relationships between map or topicref elements*

Introduction to maps

Maps are organizational objects in DITA. They bring together a variety of topics to help create a finished product. The map is often used to assemble the topics into various deliverables based on product lines or releases or other criteria related to publishing. A map is also used to manage multiple maps and topics and combine references between them. Content is organized in a hierarchy that forms the basic structure of the map and organizes topics into relationships based on this hierarchy.

Relationships between topics

The element <map> provides information about the relationships between topics. The map may contain additional maps, assorted topics, nested topics, links between topics, and other information to organize content. It could be compared in general terms to a book or a master document that links to other documents and defines relationships between them.

Navigational support   The relationship in the map can be represented as navigational for tables of contents or for the purpose of developing related links. This relationship can be used to generate a table of contents, to combine topics into a help or PDF deliverable, and to manage content in regards to links between topics. The map can then be published as required.

Multiple outputs   Since topics are written as standalone units of information, they need a way to be added to a larger deliverable for true functionality of content. A discrete unit of information (the topic) may still be a small part of a final file set. The map would combine topics in a specific order for publishing and this may differ for print (or PDF) output when compared to online (or Help) content. Therefore, multiple maps may be created for multiple types of output.

Visually representing maps   The map has both a document view and a Structure view. Within the map are a wide range of elements used to link to topics. The document view displays subordinate topics indented under primary topics.

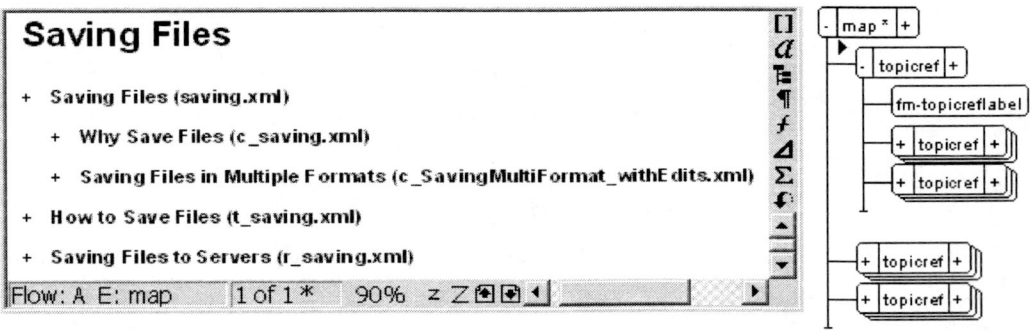

Topic reference <topicref>   The element <topicref> is used to identify a topic so that a map can identify the location of a required resource.

Attributes and maps

Attributes of maps can be used to configure a wide range of settings that impact the way that output is created from a map.

Attributes in maps   Attributes allow changes to the map title as well as control over content in regards to the output appearance in a variety of display configurations. Other attributes allow control over how the map is managed in revisions or translations.

The map attributes can be configured using the Attributes editor.

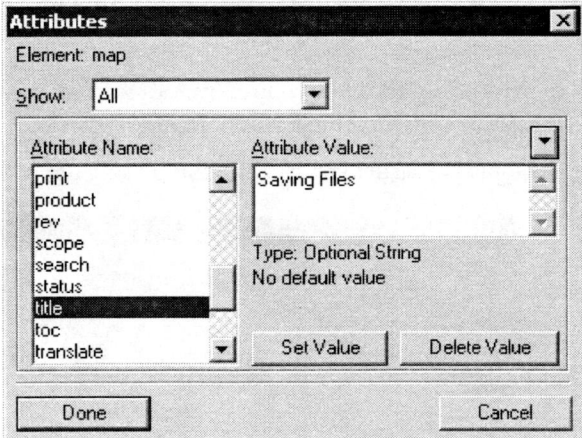

- Collection Type provides a description of how links relate to each other.

- Format sets the format of a target being cross-referenced.

- Importance indicates the degree to which the content is important.

- Include in TOC provides a way to exclude or include content from the table of contents.

- Language indicates the language of the content.

- Linking sets the linking relationship between elements.

- Lock title provides a way to use the navtitle of a topic rather than the title.

- Other properties lets you add your own properties. You can customize an output generator to process these properties as needed.

- Print provides a way to exclude or include content from the print output.

- Revision indicates the revision number of the content.

- Scope sets the relationship between the current elements and the output.

- Status indicates whether the content is new, changed, deleted, or unchanged.

- Title specifies the book title.

- Translate indicates whether or not the content needs to be translated.

- Type sets the target of cross-references.

Attributes and topicrefs

Attributes of topicrefs in maps can be used to configure a wide range of settings that impact the way that output is created from a map. These are organized into two primary categories. Special attributes and Other Attributes.

Attributes of topicrefs in maps

Topicref attributes allow control over topicrefs in regards to the output appearance of the topicref in a variety of display configurations.

The topic properties can be configured using the Attributes Editor.

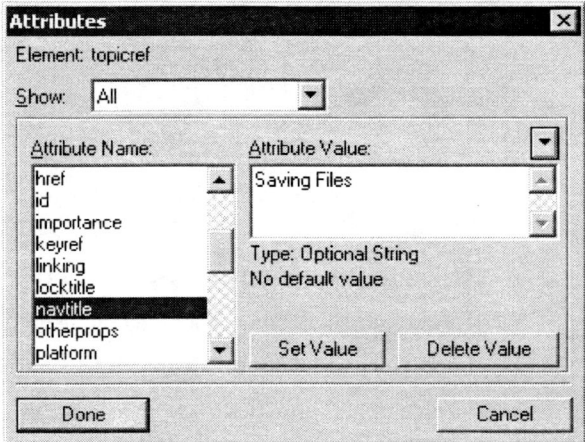

- Collection Type provides a description of how links relate to each other.

- Format sets the format of a target being cross-referenced.

- Importance indicates the degree to which the content is important.

- Include in TOC provides a way to exclude or include content from the table of contents.

- Language indicates the language of the content.

- Linking sets the linking relationship between elements.

- Navigation title provides the default title of the element.

- Other properties lets you add your own properties. You can customize an output generator to process these properties as needed.

- Print provides a way to exclude or include content from the print output.

- Revision indicates the revision number of the content.

- Scope sets the relationship between the current elements and the output.

- Specify provides an alternate title that can be used if the Navigation Title is changed.

- Status indicates whether the content is new, changed, deleted, or unchanged.
- Translate indicates whether or not the content needs to be translated.
- Type sets the target of cross-references.

Working with maps

A variety of tasks can be performed when working with maps.

Open a map   This topic explains how to open an existing map.

1. Select File > Open.

2. Specify the server, drive, or folder to open the map from.

3. Select the map to open.

4. Click [Open].

5. If required, select the Structured Application to use.

    By default this is usually named DITA-Map-FM or DITA-Book-FM.

Create a map   This topic explains how to create a map.

1. Select DITA > New DITA File > New <map>.

2. Type a file name and browse to a location.

3. Click [Select].

4. Replace the default text with a title for the map.

5. Modify the map as required.

Saving maps   You have two menu options to choose from when saving maps: Save As, and Save. When a new map is created, or an existing map is to be saved with a new name, use the Save As menu option. Once a file has been created and saved, the Save command replaces the original map with any changes you make to the material, effectively deleting the older versions of the map. Therefore, if you want to keep the original version of a map, use the Save As command to save new maps under a different name.

Save a map with a new name or path

The Save As option allows you to specify a path and name for a map.

1. Select File > Save As.

   The Save As dialog box displays.

2. Specify the server, drive, or folder to save the map to.

3. Name the map.

4. Click [Save].

Save an existing map

The Save option saves your current map.

1. Select File > Save.

Save an existing map under a new name

The Save As option allows you to specify a path and name for a map.

1. Select File > Save As.

   The Save As dialog box displays.

2. Specify the server, drive, or folder to save the map to.

3. Name the map.

4. Click [Save].

Open files from within maps

Files that are referenced by a map may be opened for editing, printing, and so on.

1. Double click the title of the file to open.

Publish a map

By default, you cannot publish a map from FrameMaker. However, you can convert a ditamap to a FrameMaker file or to a book and publish that. You can also use the DITA Open Toolkit (if installed and configured) to publish.

Publish to a FrameMaker document

The following steps outline how to convert a map to a FrameMaker document.

1. Open a map to publish.

2. Select DITA > Build FM Document from DITA Map.

3. If required, browse to specify the server, drive, or folder to save to.

4. Name the file.

   If the name is the same as an existing file the file must first be deleted before you can continue.

5. Click [Select].

   FrameMaker converts the map and its topicrefs into a FrameMaker document. Once the output is generated, you can create a book, add a TOC and Index if required, generate book content to update numbering, page layout, generated files and so on and save as PDF.

Publish to a book

The following steps outline how to convert a map to a FrameMaker book.

1. Select DITA > Build FM DITABook from DITA Map file.

2. If required, browse to specify the server, drive, or folder containing the map to publish to a book.

3. Select the map to publish.

4. Click [Select].

   The Save Book dialog displays.

5. If required, browse to specify the server, drive, or folder to save the book to and enter the name of the book.

6. Click [Save].

   FrameMaker converts the map and its topicrefs into a FrameMaker book and files. Once the output is generated, you can add a TOC and Index if required, configure the book, generate the book content to update numbering, page layout, generated files and so on and save as PDF.

Adding content to a map

Topics that have been created can be added to a map. This includes topic, concept, task, and reference files. Files that are not XML based or DITA compliant can also be added to maps.

Add a topic

1. In the Structure View, select a valid location for a topicref.

2. In the DITA map, display the Element Catalog.

3. Double-click topicref.
   The Select a Topic dialog displays.

4. Browse to the path and topic to link to and double-click the topic file.
   The topic title and file name display in the map file.

5. Using the Attributes Editor, configure attributes as required.

Add non-DITA files to a map

1. In the Structure View, select a valid location for a topicref.

2. In the DITA map, display the Element Catalog.

3. Double-click topicref.
   The Select a Topic dialog displays.

4. Browse to the path and file to link to and double-click the file.
   The file name and placeholder text NO TITLE display in the map file.

5. Using the Attributes Editor, configure attributes as required.

6. Enter a navigation title.
   This is the text that displays in generated output as the link to the file.

7. Click [Set Value] .

8. Click [Done] .

Organizing maps

Content that is in a map may be reorganized in a variety of ways to modify the hierarchy and relationship of topics.

Rearrange topics in a map

Topics that are in a map may be rearranged to organize siblings using drag and drop editing.

1. In the Structure view, select the topic to move.

2. Click and drag the topic to a new location.
   A check mark indicates where the topicref is valid.

3.   Release the mouse button to drop the topic.

Nest topics in a map

Topics that are in a map may be nested to create a parent and child relationship using drag and drop editing.

1.   In the Structure view, select the topic to move.

2.   Click and drag the topic to a new location.
A check mark indicates where the topicref is valid.

3.   Release the mouse button to drop the topic.

Group topics with topic headings

Within a map, topics can be grouped with a common heading.

1.   In the Structure view, select the object to act as the parent of the new content.

2.   In the Element Catalog, double-click topichead.
The topicref is wrapped in a topic heading.

3.   Specify a navtitle for the topic heading.

4.   Drag and drop any other topicrefs into the topic heading.

Work with submaps

Maps can be added to maps. This allows content to be organized into maps and be reused as required in other maps.

1.   In the Structure View, select a valid location for a topicref.

2.   In the DITA map, display the Element Catalog.

3.   Double-click topicref.
The Select a Topic dialog displays.

4.   Browse to the path and map to link to and double-click the topic file.
The navtitle (if set) and file name display in the map file.

5.   Using the Attributes Editor, configure attributes as required.

Remove topics from a map

Topics that are in a map may be removed from the map. The topic still exists, it is simply no longer a part of the map.

1.   In the Structure view, select the topicref to remove.

2.   Press *Delete* to remove the topic reference.

Modifying relationships between map or topicref elements

Attributes related to topicrefs allow relationships and function to be further defined.

Many of the relationships between map elements can also be configured for entire maps. This allows the reuse of entire maps with different configurations across volumes of content.

> ✍️ **Note**
>
> Many modifications to DITA content are not reflected in FrameMaker and only apply when processed using the DITA Open Toolkit.

Display topicref attributes

The topicref attributes display in two different ways depending on the view of the map.

1. In the map, click the topicref to modify.

2. Display the attributes of the topicref by opening the Attributes Editor.

Exclude a topic from the generated table of contents

Topics can be excluded from the generated table of contents as required in a map.

1. Display the topicref attributes.

2. Change the attribute toc to **no**.

Exclude a topic from the print output

Topics can be excluded from the print output (the PDF) as required in a map.

1. Display the topicref attributes.

2. Change the attribute print to **no**.

Change the display title of a topicref

If alternate titles are configured in a topicref they can be used when building the navigation system contents.

1. Display the topicref attributes.

2. Change the attribute navtitle to **Specify other title** and type a new title under Specify.

Use alternate titles from within a topic

If a topic is configured with alternate titles and has a navtitle the map can reference it automatically when building the navigation system contents.

1. Display the map attributes.

2. Change the attribute locktitle to **yes**.

Link topic references as source or target only

Topics may be configured to act as only a source or only a target in a map. That is, they can be set up to only allow references into the topic from other topics (target only) or out of the topic to other destination (source only) using attributes.

1. In the map, click in the topicref to modify.

2. Display the topicref attributes

3. Change the attribute linking (in the XML view) to one of the following values:

    *   *none* defines that no links to or from the <topicref> are created
    *   *normal* defines that links to or from the <topicref> are created using DITA defaults
    *   *sourceonly* defines that no links to the <topicref> are created, but links to other <topicref> elements may be created
    *   *targetonly* defines that no links from the <topicref> are created, but links from other <topicref> elements may be created

Link topicrefs as a collection-type

A collection type allows links between nested topicrefs to be customized for output purposes.

1. In the map, select either a parent or a collection of sibling topicrefs.

2. Using the Attributes Editor, modify the collection-type attribute value.

    *   *choice* defines that the links can be treated as a selection where two or more are specifically ordered choices and may display as a numbered list. Parent elements link to child elements. Child elements link up to parent elements only.
    *   *unordered* defines a relationship with no specific order. Links display in a default format, one after the other. Parent elements link to child elements. Child elements link up to parent elements only.
    *   *sequence* defines a relationship with a specific order. Links display in a numbered format. Parent elements link to child elements. Child elements link up to parent elements and link to the previous or the next sibling.
    *   *family* defines that the entire collection should also link to each other option. All parents and children link up and down the hierarchy.

Chapter 24

Relationship tables

Overview

This topic teaches you how to work with relationship tables.

The following topics are covered:

- *Introduction to relationship tables*
- *Working with relationship tables*
- *Add a topicref to a relationship table*
- *Organizing relationship tables*
- *Working with topicref attributes and reltables*

Introduction to relationship tables

The DITA specification allows links to be created inline, within a collection of related links, or in a relationship table. If links are created inline or as a set of related links within a file, dependencies are built. Should the link destination file change in name or path the hard-coded, links need to be updated. Instead, the relationship table and a map provide more control and greater flexibility in content reuse and linking.

Purpose of relationship tables

The element <reltable> is used in a map document to provide information about the relationships between topics. The map may contain numerous topics, nested topics, links between topics, and other information to organize content.

The relationship table is used to define links between topics within a map. This is done by arranging topic references and specifying attributes within a semantic table used for the express purpose of linking files. The columns of the table define the various information types, the rows define the relationships between topics, and the cells contain references to topics.

Topic Reference **<topicref>**	The element <topicref> is used to identify a topic so that a map can identify the location of a required resource.

Relationship table **<reltable>**	The element <reltable> is used to build a set of relationships between topics based on the table model of rows, columns, and cells. Each cell contains one or more <topicref> elements, which are related to other topics in the same row.

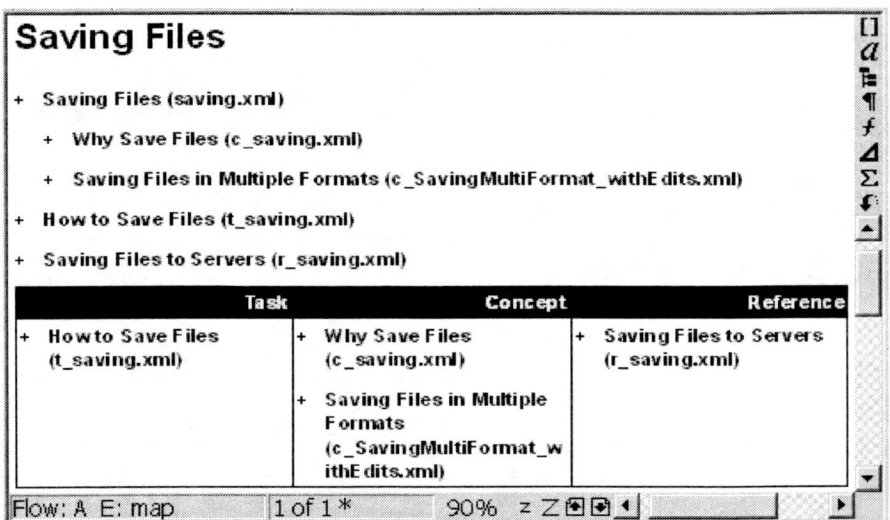

Relationship table **header <relheader>**	The element <relheader> is used to contain a common heading under which one or more DITA topics are grouped logically.

Relationship table **row <relrow>**	The element <relrow> is used to build a single row in a relationship table. This row creates a relationship between the elements for linking purposes.

Relationship table cell **<relcell>**	The element <relcell> is used to contain one or more DITA topics that are grouped logically under a common heading. By default, the content within a cell does not link to other content in the same cell. Rather it links to content in related cells.

Working with relationship tables

Before working with a relationship table, a map document must exist and be open.

Create a relationship table

This topic explains how to create a relationship table.

1. In the Structure view, place your cursor to insert the last of the map elements.

1. Using the Element Catalog, double-click reltable.

   The Insert Table dialog displays.

2. Select the relationship table you want.

   A standard relationship table usually has three or four columns and one header row.

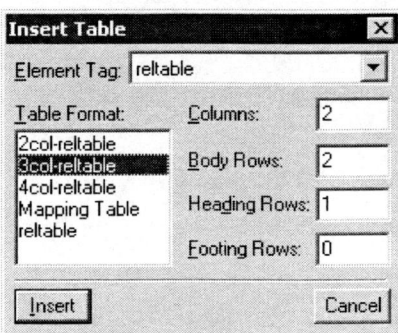

3. Click Insert.

   The relationship table displays.

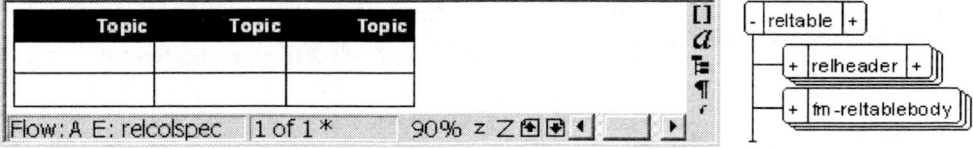

4. Set the type attribute in the relcolspec elements to task, concept, and reference.

   If you have a fourth column, set type="topic".

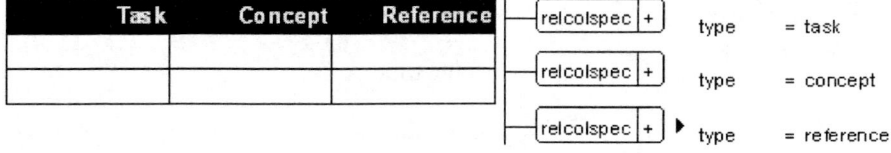

5. Modify the relationship table as required.

Add a topicref to a relationship table

Topics that are referenced by a map can be added to a relationship table.

1. In the Relationship Table, select the cell to add a <topicref> in.

2. With the Element Catalog, double-click <topicref>.

3. Specify the server, drive, or folder to open the topic from.

4. Click [Select].

5. Configure Attributes as required.

Organizing relationship tables

Content in a relationship table needs to be organized to develop relationships between topics. The types of relationships that are developed determine the order, links, and even the appearance of the finished deliverable files.

Rearrange topicrefs in a relationship table

Topics that are in a relationship table may be rearranged using drag and drop editing.

1. In the Structure view, select the topicref to move.

2. Click and drag the topic to a new relcell.

3. Release the mouse button to drop the topic.

Create hierarchies between topicrefs in a relationship table

Hierarchies in relationship tables determine the relationship (siblings or parent and child) between the topics.

1. Select the topic to nest.

2. Click and drag the topic to a location within another topic.

3. Release the mouse button to drop the topic.

| Fine tune relationship tables | You may have a relationship table where the output has too many or badly organized links on output. Refine the relationship table until you have cleaner (and possibly fewer) links. |

1. Open a relationship table to modify.

2. Duplicate rows that have too many links.

    By creating the duplicate rows, all the original topic references exist and modifications can be made without having to re-create topic references.

3. Modify the duplicated rows to contain appropriate content.

| Remove topicrefs from a relationship table | Topics that are in a relationship may be removed from the table. The topic still exists—it may even still be in the map—however, it is no longer a part of the relationship table. |

1. In the Structure view of the relationship table, select the topic to remove.

2. Press *Delete*.

Working with topicref attributes and reltables

Attributes related to rows, columns, cells or topicrefs allow relationships to be further defined.

| Link topic references as source or target only | Topics may be configured to act as only a source or only a target in a relationship table. That is, they can be set up to only allow references into the topic from other topics (target only) or out of the topic to other destination (source only) using attributes. |

1. In the relationship table, click in the topicref or cell or column or row to modify.

2. Using the Attributes Editor, modify the linking attribute value.
    *   *none* defines that no links to or from the <topicref> are created
    *   *normal* defines that links to or from the <topicref> are created using DITA defaults
    *   *sourceonly* defines that no links to the <topicref> are created, but links to other <topicref> elements may be created
    *   *targetonly* defines that no links from the <topicref> are created, but links from other <topicref> elements may be created

Link columns as source or target only

Entire columns (all concepts, references, or tasks) may be configured to act as only a source or only a target in a relationship table.

1. In the relationship table, click in the column header to modify.

2. Using the Attributes Editor, modify the linking attribute value.

    - *none* defines that no links to or from the <topicref> are created
    - *normal* defines that links to or from the <topicref> are created using DITA defaults
    - *sourceonly* defines that no links to the <topicref> are created, but links to other <topicref> elements may be created
    - *targetonly* defines that no links from the <topicref> are created, but links from other <topicref> elements may be created

Link cell content as a collection-type

Entire cells of content may be configured to act as related information to create links between topicrefs in a cell.

1. In the relationship table, select all the content in a cell.

2. Using the Attributes Editor, modify the collection-type attribute value.

    - *family* defines that content in the cell should be treated as siblings with links between them
    - all other attributes have no impact on cell content

Appendix A

DITA Primer

Overview

These topics introduce a variety of DITA elements and provide basic examples of them in context.

While not a definitive document with regards to DITA, this is a companion piece to the book you are working with and provides background information that may be of use to you. We are providing a primer on the DITA specification. We presume you to have a very basic familiarity with XML syntax.

While DITA provides numerous elements, these topics addresses only some of the common elements that a new user should initially be aware of. For more detailed information about any element, or about the full set of available elements, review the documentation included with the DITA Open Toolkit.

DITA defined

DITA is an emerging specification that provides a cost-effective way to create, publish, reuse, and exchange structured information.

DITA refers to the Darwin Information Typing Architecture (DITA). It is based on the idea of building information types for specific representation of structured content from a common initial topic.

Like any structured architecture, it is based on a set of rules referenced in a DTD or a schema. The key information types include topic, concept, reference, and task. However, additional specialized information types can be created including, for example, outlines, FAQ documents, and so on.

The DITA specification is also an approach to organizing information types into logical groups that can be either standalone, or can be published as part of a volume or set of materials using a map to reference and link these information types together.

Origin of DITA

The Darwin Information Typing Architecture was first developed in March 2001 by IBM. After three years of work, IBM donated the DITA technology to the OASIS Consortium in March of 2004. The formal standard was published in May 2005 as an open source standard. Version 1.1 of DITA DTDs and Schemas are now available.

Benefits of working with DITA

There are a variety of benefits to be gained by working with DITA.

The key to DITA is that it separates form and format from the content. In other words, the appearance of content is removed from the structure when the file is saved. Format is applied by a software tool in a programmatic way without the author having to manually decide on formatting options as he writes. The raw XML code associated with the DITA specification is formatted based on a standard set of rules that are defined once and reused as needed.

DITA contains a predefined set of information types that are already developed and can be worked with immediately. The information types are often predefined in how they work with software applications, including FrameMaker, so less initial work is required when starting with DITA.

Examples of DITA-specific content can be found online, though it may take some careful searching to find appropriate material for your company. Some companies can provide you with samples of DITA-specific content. They can then create a customized DITA-compliant solution for your needs and help you implement it.

Third-party development of tools that work with content adhering to the DITA specification is ongoing. Therefore, it is becoming easier to work with software that is already configured to manage content. Without the need for large investments in tools, it becomes easier to do more with default software configurations. This includes tools to author content, to manage content, and to deliver content.

Difficulties in working with DITA

The DITA specification does have some specific elements that may only be used in a given context and therefore do not apply to all users. Due to this, it may be difficult at first to learn the elements.

The elements adhere to a set of predefined rules that must be learned. It may be frustrating early on to work with elements and not see the 'right' element at any given time. However, with exposure to the elements and proper training, the DITA specification can be learned quickly.

Content that has previously been published may not match the requirements of the DITA specification. This may require an analysis of legacy content to understand how it can be modified to meet the specifications needs. It may also be required that a set of specializations be created to manage exceptions that exist in a specific information architecture.

Not all content is supported by DITA. There are numerous types of materials that are not a good fit with DITA and many may require either a great deal of additional work to adhere to the specification or may simply not be a good candidate for DITA.

Key information types

There are several elements that must be identified as 'highest level' elements when working with the DITA specification. Without using these elements, any content created would not be compliant with DITA. They represent the core group of information types and also include the <dita> element for topic nesting.

One of the key benefits of breaking out information into these information types is in the creation of content. By having experts in specific areas work with content and then combine the content into a deliverable, the relative strengths of different resources can be best used. In one writing environment, engineers may provide technical reference content, marketing may provide conceptual content, and courseware developers may create task-specific content. An information development team may then review the materials for consistency and accuracy before publishing finished topics into a deliverable format such as help materials, PDF files, and so on.

Authors benefit from this model by being able to design new information quicker and with greater consistency. By identifying task, concept, or reference information, specific authors can be assigned to specific work.

A reader benefits from this model by being able to quickly find the information he needs because it is presented in a consistent format. Task, concept, and reference information can be quickly identified and reviewed, skimmed, or skipped as the reader's needs change. Information is also more concise and a reader can quickly find a detailed set of task information without the need to read additional conceptual or reference materials in mid step.

DITA <dita>   The element <dita> is used to provide a top level for nesting topics. It supports any combination of topic, concept, task, and reference topics.

Element representation:

```
<dita>
```

Markup example:

```
<dita>
<concept id="intro">...</concept>
<reference id="requirements">...</reference>
<task id="installation">...</task>
<task id="configuration">...</task>
</dita>
```

Display example:

Not applicable. The output may be an entire publication, help system, or other deliverable that can not be represented here.

Topic <topic>

The element <topic> is used as a container for a single-subject topic or article. It should be short enough to give users answers to a question without breaking away from the problem they are trying to solve. It should be long enough to make sense as a standalone unit of information. Other more content-specific top-level elements include concept, task, and reference.

Topics are written as standalone units of information. For use in a larger project, topics need a way to be added to a larger deliverable. DITA uses the map file to combine topics in a specific order for publishing to print (or PDF) output or to online (or Help) content.

Element representation:

```
<topic>
```

Markup example:

```
<topic id="saving">
<title>Saving Files</title>
<body>
<p>This topic addresses saving files.</p>
</body>
</topic>
```

Display example:

Concept <concept>

The element <concept> is used as a container for an answer to a "what is" question. It provides background information that a user must know to successfully work with a product.

A concept explains and teaches ideas to help users build on experience and knowledge they may already have before using a product or performing a task. In this capacity, they are one of the first information types a user is exposed to.

The concept introduces the system, solution, process, or characteristics and provides background information the user should know before starting a task or exploring a reference. Features and benefits of the product would be described in the concept and more detailed information is usually found here.

A concept is focused on providing information on the technology, user concerns, information concerning decisions that may need to be made, background information, product overview, or relationships between products.

The concept contains a variety of elements including a single title, an optional short description, one or more paragraphs, index entries, lists, tables, figures or images, sections and examples, and more.

Element representation:

```
<concept>
```

Markup example:

```
<concept id="c_saving">
<title>Why Save Files</title>
<conbody>
<p>Saving files is an easy way to store content for later retrieval.</p></conbody></concept>
```

Display example:

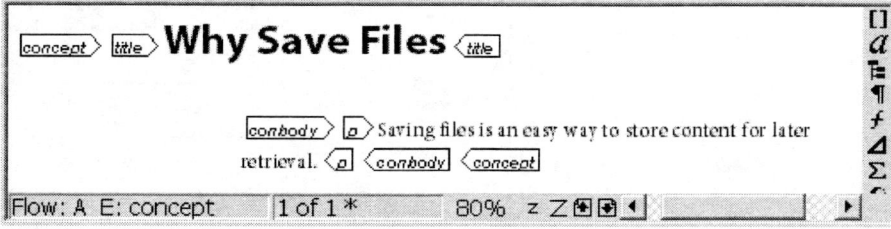

Reference <reference>

The element <reference> is used as a container for facts or information that needs to be looked up for technical information that is not conceptual. This is usually done by creating specific sections and populating them with concise information.

A reference is generally only read by a user when specific technical information is required, usually while doing a specific job. The reference provides the facts without background information or procedural steps. Any reference may be heavily linked to other related reference materials.

Element representation:

`<reference>`

Markup example:

```
<reference id="r_saving">
<title>Saving Files to Servers</title>
<refbody>
<section>
<p>Use the syntax //server/path/file.ext to save to a server. Incorrect syntax results in file corruption.</p></section></refbody></reference>
```

Display example:

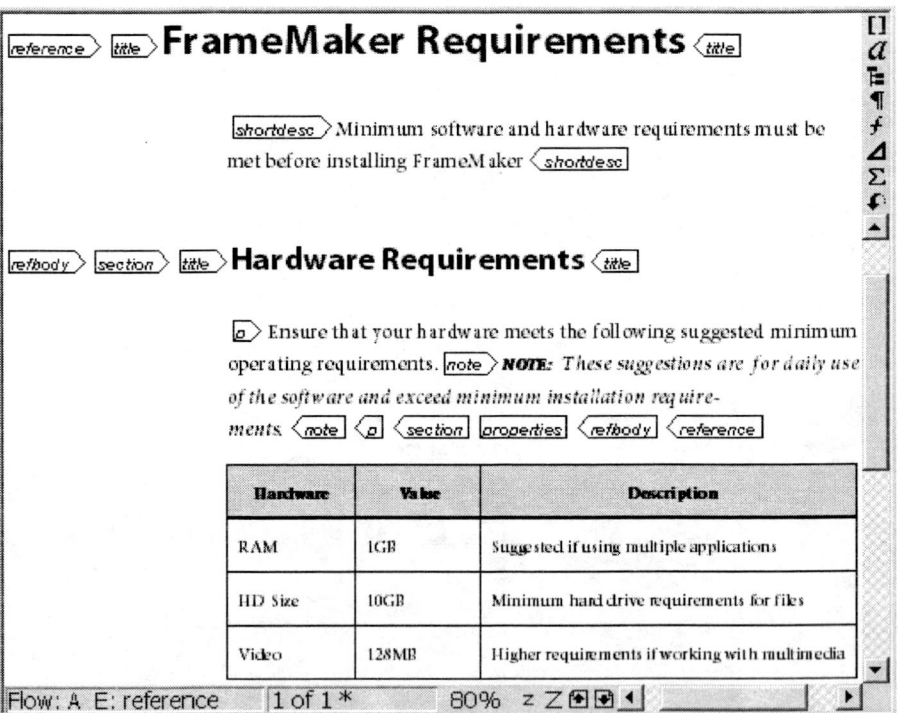

Task `<task>`   The element `<task>` is used as a container for a procedure. This element provides instructions related to addressing how to do a specific thing and the order of steps to follow.

The purpose of a task is to tell the user how to accomplish a specific set of procedures to achieve a goal. It is often read while a user is performing a specific task and should provide enough information to guide the user to a logical conclusion.

Tasks provide detailed, step-by-step instructions and provide context and examples as required. They may have explicit prerequisites or postrequisites that must be performed by the user. Within the task, there are usually multiple single-step procedures to follow. Each step may be made up of a variety of information including an explicit command (a call to action) and related supporting information.

Element representation:

```
<task>
```

Markup example:

```
<task id="t_saving">
<title>How to Save Files</title>
<taskbody>
<steps>
<step>
<cmd>Click the <uicontrol>Save</uicontrol> icon</cmd>
</step>
</steps>
</taskbody>
</task>
```

Display example:

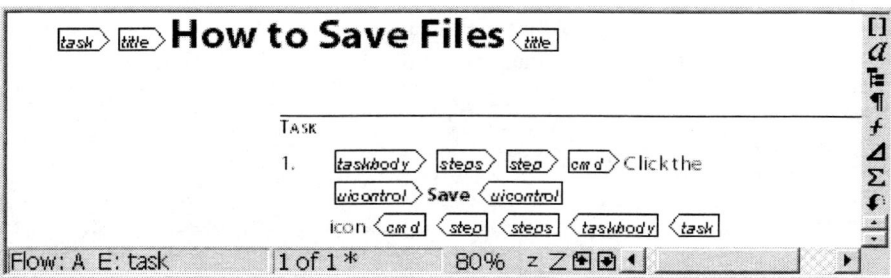

Commonly used elements

While DITA provides numerous elements, these topics address only some of the common elements that a new user should initially be aware of. For more detailed information, review the documentation included with the DITA Open Toolkit.

Title \<title\>

The element \<title\> is used as a heading or label for a variety of elements including topic, concept, reference, task, section, example, table, and so on.

Element representation:

`<title>`

Markup example:

`<title>Why save files</title>`

Display example:

Short description \<shortdesc\>

The element \<shortdesc\> is used to represent the purpose of the content that follows. A \<shortdesc\> may also be used as a link preview and in when returning search results. The short description should be a concise statement that provides a summary of the topic.

Within a concept, the short description answers "what is this?" This may simply be a key term or idea, and a related basic definition.

Within a task, the short description answers "what is the purpose of this task?" or "when should this task be performed?" with a brief overview of the task.

Within a reference, the short description addresses "technically this is" type of information with a brief statement about the technical content to follow.

As a generalization, the short description is likely no more than 1 to 3 sentences and usually no more than 40 or 50 words. It is not a lead-in paragraph.

Element representation:

`<shortdesc>`

Markup example:

`<shortdesc>Used to provide a brief introduction to the topic and often used in links, summary documents and search results.</shortdesc>`

Display example:

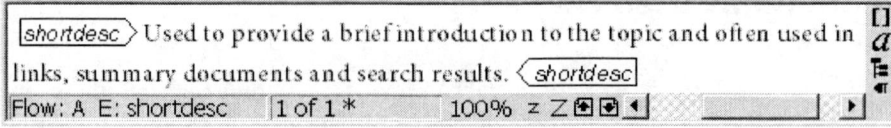

Paragraph <p>

The element <p> is used to identify a string of text that has a single main idea. Element representation:

<p>

Markup example:

> <p>Saving files is an easy way to store content for later retrieval.</p>

Display example:

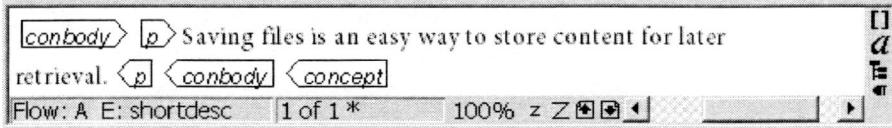

Note <note>

The element <note> is used to identify content that displays in a different format from the default of a document and draws attention to a point.

Element representation:

<note>

Markup example:

> <note>Failure to shut down the device before opening the containment compartment can result in radiation leakage.</note>

Display example:

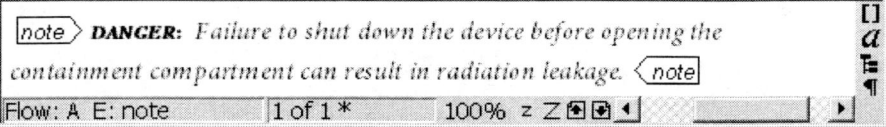

Short quotation <q>

The element <q> is used to identify a short string of text that is a quotation from another source and is usually treated as an inline element, similar to a character range.

Element representation:

<q>

Markup example:

> <p>Yogi Berra said <q>It ain't over till it's over</q> close to the end.</p>

Display example:

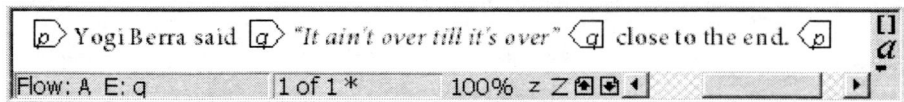

Long quotation <lq>

The element <lq> is used to identify a longer string of text that is a quotation from another source and is usually treated as a standalone element, similar to a paragraph.

Element representation:

`<lq>`

Markup example:

> <p>Napoleon Bonaparte has said: <lq>If I always appear prepared, it is because before entering an undertaking, I have meditated long and have foreseen what might occur. It is not genius where reveals to me suddenly and secretly what I should do in circumstances unexpected by others; it is thought and preparation.</lq></p>

Display example:

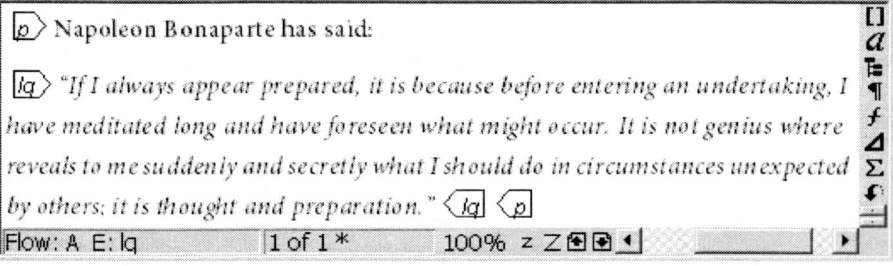

Index entries <indexterm>

The element <indexterm> is used to represent content that is not displayed in the <indexterm> specific topic, but rather in a generated, sorted document.

Element representation:

`<indexterm>`

Markup example:

> <p>To open files you must have access to either a <indexterm>server </indexterm> server or a local drive on a <indexterm>workstation</indexterm> workstation where files have been saved.</p>

Display example:

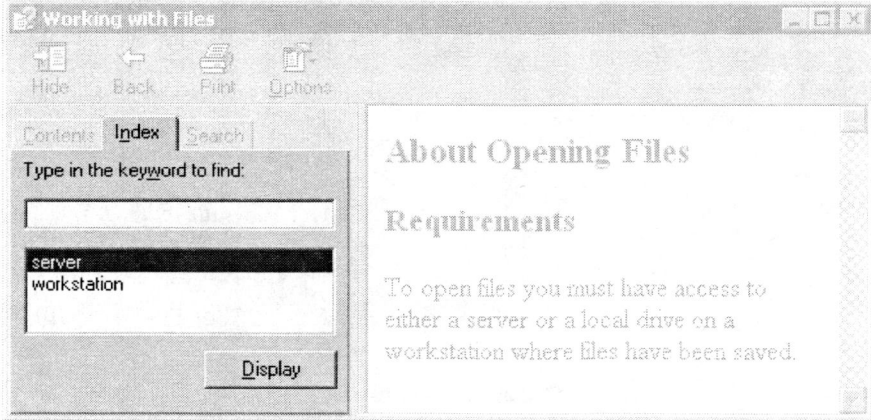

Lists <ul> and <ol>

While DITA provides numerous list-related elements, this topic addresses only some of the common elements that a new user should initially be aware of. For more detailed information, review the documentation included with the DITA Open Toolkit.

Unordered List <ul>

The element <ul> is used to identify a collection of items in which the order is not relevant.

Element representation:

```
<ul>
```

Markup example:

```
<p>Assorted breakfast items are available including:
<ul>
<li>Waffles, pancakes or french toast</li>
<li>Assorted meats and cheeses</li>
<li>Fresh fruit (pineapple, grapes, oranges, apples and more)</li>
<li>Coffee, tea</li>
</ul>
</p>
```

Display example:

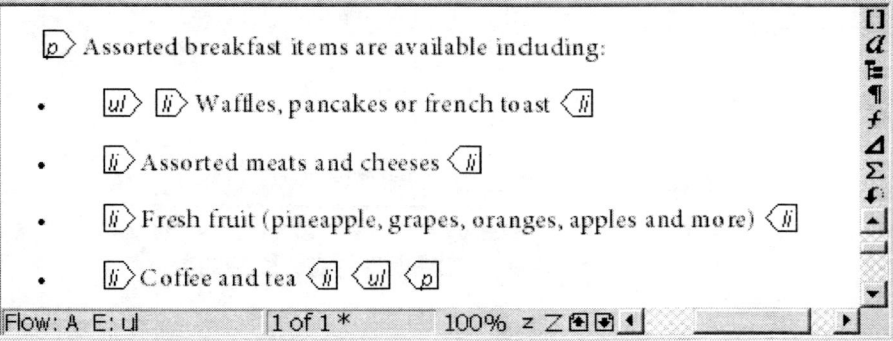

Ordered List <ol>

The element <ol> is used to identify a collection of items in which the order is relevant.

Element representation:

```
<ol>
```

Markup example:

```
<p>After accessing our ftp server:
<ol>
<li>Agree to the licensing terms</li>
<li>Download the software</li>
</ol>
</p>
```

Display example:

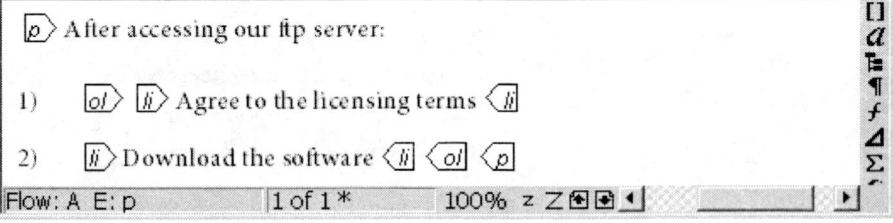

List Item <li>

The element <li> is used to contain content that has a single main idea within a list. If <li> is contained in an <ol> element, the <li> element is usually displayed as a numbered list (using traditional numbering, roman numerals, or alphabetical characters in order). If <li> is contained in a <ul> element, the <li> is usually displayed as a bullet or dash.

Element representation:

```
<li>
```

Markup example:

```
<p>After accessing our ftp server:
<ol>
<li>Agree to the licensing terms</li>
<li>Download the software</li>
</ol>
</p>
```

Display example:

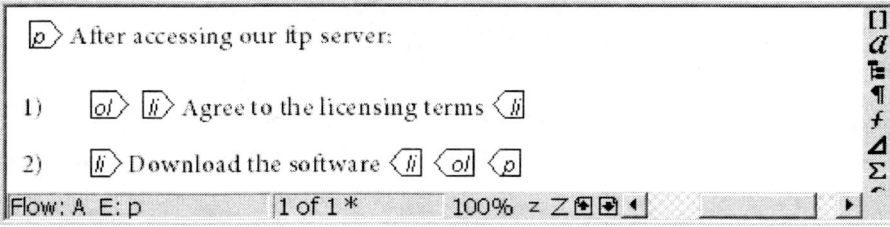

Definition lists <dl>

While DITA provides numerous definition list-related elements, this topic addresses only some of the common elements that a new user should initially be aware of. For more detailed information, review the documentation included with the DITA Open Toolkit.

Definition list <dl>

The element <dl> is used to build a list of terms and definitions.

Element representation:

```
<dl>
```

Markup example:

```
<dl>
<dlentry>
<dt>XML</dt><dd>eXtensible Markup Language</dd>
</dlentry>
<dlentry>
<dt>CSS</dt><dd>Cascading Style Sheet</dd>
</dlentry>
<dlentry>
<dt>HTML</dt><dd>HyperText Markup Language</dd>
```

```
</dlentry>
</dl>
```

Display example:

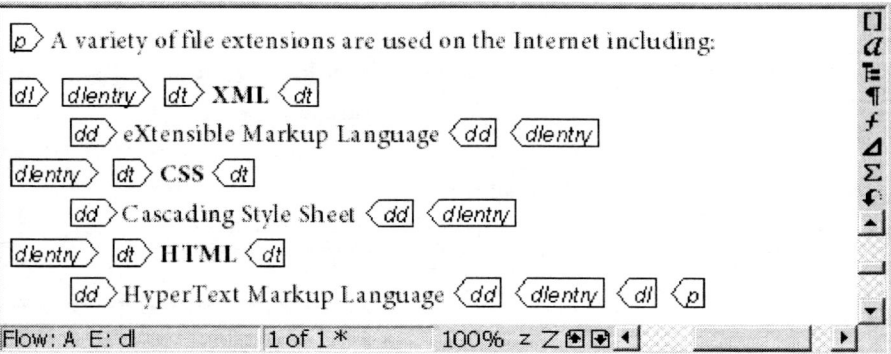

Definition list entry <dlentry>

The element <dlentry> is used to create a single item within a definition list.

Element representation:

```
<dlentry>
```

Markup example:

```
<dl>
<dlentry>
<dt>...</dt><dd>...</dd>
</dlentry>
<dlentry>
...
</dlentry>
</dl>
```

Definition term <dt>

The element <dt> is used to identify the content that the entry relates to.

Element representation:

```
<dt>
```

Markup example:

```
<dl>
<dlentry>
<dt>XML</dt><dd>...</dd>
```

```
...
</dl>
```

Definition description <dd>

The element <dd> is used to expand on the meaning of the term. Element representation:

```
<dd>
```

Markup example:

```
<dl>
<dlentry>
<dt>...</dt><dd>eXtensible Markup Language</dd>
</dlentry>
...
</dl>
```

Table <table>

While DITA provides numerous table-related elements, this topic addresses only some of the common elements that a new user should initially be aware of. For more detailed information, review the documentation included with the DITA Open Toolkit.

The element <table> is used to organize a set of information into tabular constructs. This allows the representation to be displayed in a grid-like fashion with content spanning rows or columns. An optional title can be included to further identify the table.

Element representation:

```
<table>
```

Markup example:

```
<table>
<title>File formats</title>
<tgroup cols="2">
<colspec colnum="1" colname="col1" colwidth="1.00*"/>
<colspec colnum="2" colname="col2" colwidth="3.00*"/>
<thead>
<row>
<entry colname="col1">Extension</entry>
<entry colname="col2">Definition</entry>
</row>
</thead>
<tbody>
<row>
```

```
<entry colname="col1">.xml</entry>
<entry colname="col2">eXtensible Markup Language</entry>
</row>
<row>
<entry colname="col1">.html</entry>
<entry colname="col2">Hyper Text Markup Language</entry>
</row>
…
</tbody>
</tgroup>
</table>
```

Display example:

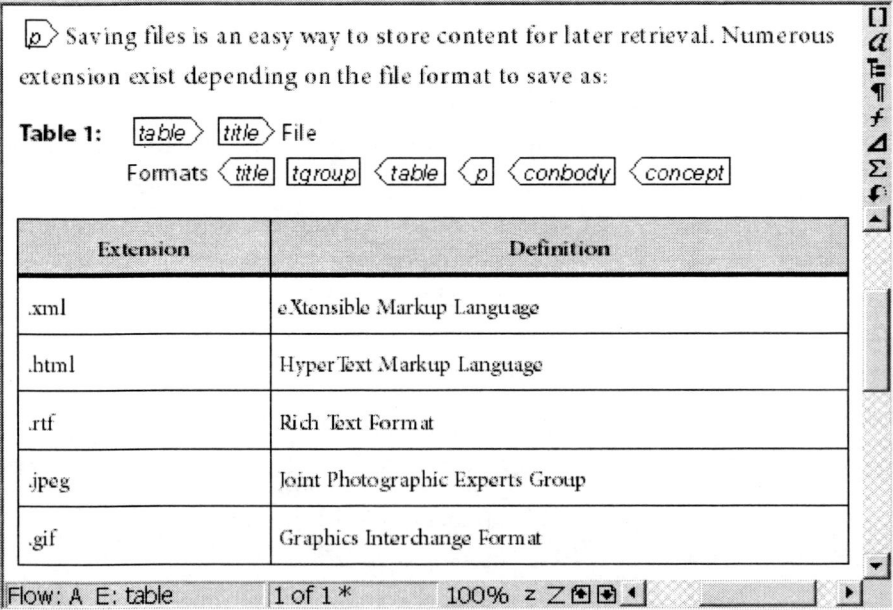

Column specifications <colspec>

The element <colspec> is used to organize the columns of a table including the name of the column and information associated with the column and cells within it. This element does not have to be modified by the user.

Element representation:

```
<colspec>
```

Markup example:

```
<table>
<title>File formats</title>
<tgroup cols="2">
<colspec colnum="1" colname="col1" colwidth="1.00*"/>
<colspec colnum="2" colname="col2" colwidth="3.00*"/>
...
</tgroup>
</table>
```

Table group <tgroup>

The element <tgroup> is used to organize the elements within a table including the columns, rows, headers, and the body of the table.

Element representation:

`<tgroup>`

Markup example:

```
<table>
<title>File formats</title>
<tgroup cols="2">
...
</tgroup>
</table>
```

Table header <thead>

The element <thead> is used to organize the elements within the header of the table.
Element representation:

`<thead>`

Markup example:

```
<thead>
<row>
<entry colname="col1">Extension</entry>
<entry colname="col2">Definition</entry>
</row>
</thead>
```

Table body <tbody>

The element <tbody> is used to organize the elements within the body of the table. Element representation:

<tbody>

Markup example:

```
<tbody> … </tbody>
```

Table row <trow>

The element <trow> is used to organize the elements within the rows of the table. Element representation:

<row>

Markup example:

```
<row>
<entry colname="col1">.xml</entry>
<entry colname="col2">eXtensible Markup Language</entry>
</row>
```

Table entry or table cell <entry>

The element <entry> is used to organize the elements within one cell of the table. Element representation:

<entry>

Markup example:

```
<row>
<entry colname="col1">.xml</entry>
<entry colname="col2">eXtensible Markup Language</entry>
</row>
```

Figure <fig>

The element <fig> is used as a container for an image and an optional title that acts as a figure caption.

Element representation:

<fig>

Markup example:

```
<fig>
<title>Windows Run dialog</title>
<image href="run.png" />
</fig>
```

Display example:

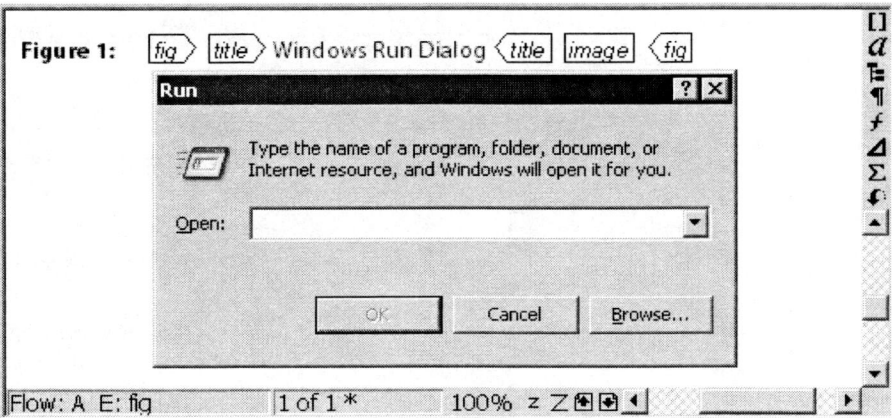

Image <image> The element <image> is used to display an image and may be displayed on its own line (often the default for large images) or inline (often the default for an icon or button).

Element representation:

`<image>`

Markup example:

> `<p>Click <image placement="inline" href="ok.jpg" /> to proceed.</p>`

Display example:

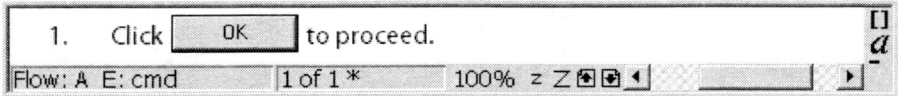

Section <section> The element <section> is used to represent a collection of organized information. It represents subsets of content that are related to a larger topic and are treated as siblings to each other. An optional title may be used.

Element representation:

`<section>`

Markup example:

> `<section>`
> `<title>Saving to servers</title>`
> `<p>Use the syntax //server/path/file.ext to save to a server. Incorrect syntax results in file corruption.</p>`…`</section><section>` … `</section>`

Display example:

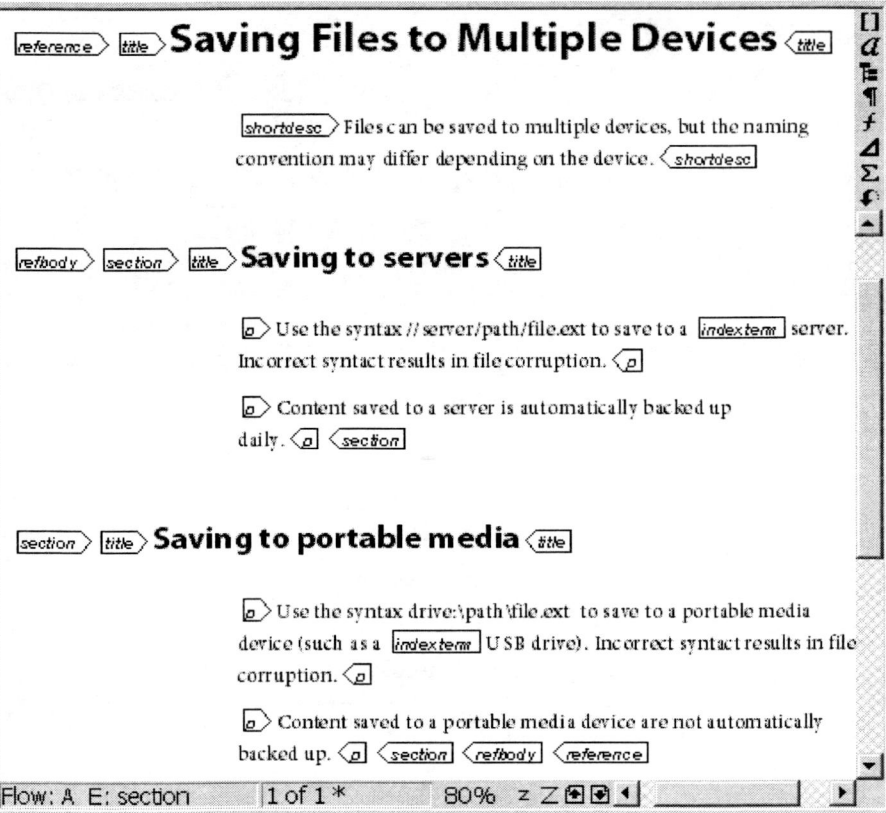

Example <example>

The element <example> is used to represent a sample to further illustrate a topic. An example is otherwise identical to a <section> element.

Element representation:

<example>

Markup example:

```
<example>
<title>Online help</title>
…
</example>
```

Display example:

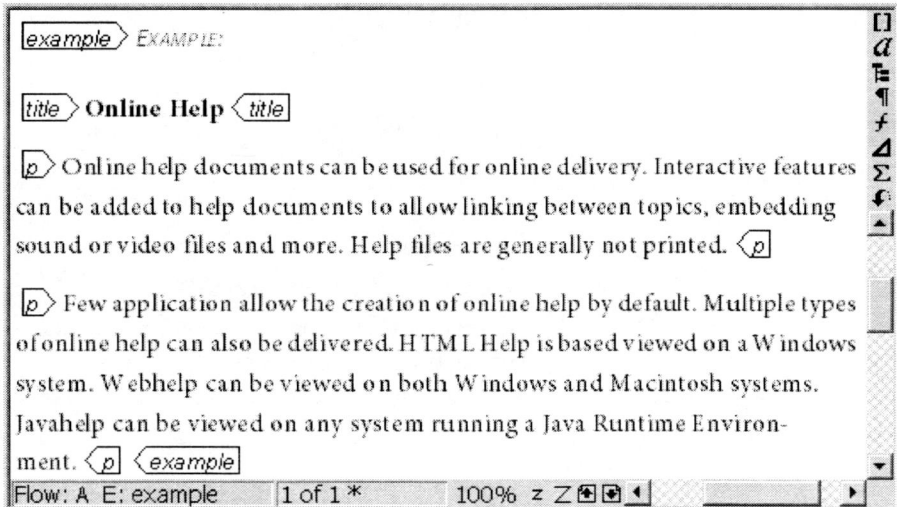

Reference syntax
<refsyn>

The element <refsyn> is used to represent syntax content such as an API's signature. It contains a brief description of the subject's interface or high-level structure. This may then be further defined following the reference syntax.

Element representation:

```
<refsyn>
```

Markup example:

```
<refbody><refsyn>extern LIBBEM_API int bem_logon(bem_handle_t *, char *,
char *, char **);</refsyn></refbody>
```

Display example:

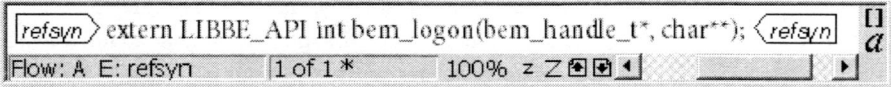

Properties
<properties>

The element <properties> is used to represent a list of properties for a topic. This includes the type, value, and description. It is generally represented in a table-like format.

Element representation:

```
<properties>
```

Markup example:

```
<refbody>
```

```
<properties>
<prophead>
<proptypehd>Type</proptypehd>
<propvaluehd>Value</propvaluehd>
<propdeschd>Description</propdeschd>
</prophead>
<property>
<proptype>RGB</proptype>
<propvalue>0,0,0</propvalue>
<propdesc>Set color using a red, green, blue color model.</propdesc></
property> … </properties>
 </refbody>
```

Display example:

Type	Value	Description
RGB	0,0,0	Set color using a red, green, blue color model.
CMYK	0,0,0,0	Set color using a cyan, magenta, yellow, black color model.

Flow: A E: propvalue   1 of 1 *   90% z Z

Task body elements
<taskbody>

While DITA provides numerous task body-related elements, this topic addresses only some of the common elements that a new user should initially be aware of. For more detailed information, review the documentation included with the DITA Open Toolkit.

The element <taskbody> is used to organize a set of information into task-specific constructs. This allows the <taskbody> to have a specific flow of information to guide the user through a set of procedural steps.

Element representation:

```
<taskbody>
```

Markup example:

```
<taskbody>
<steps>
<step>
<cmd>Click the <uicontrol>Save</uicontrol> icon</cmd>
</step>
```

```
</steps>
</taskbody>
```

Display example:

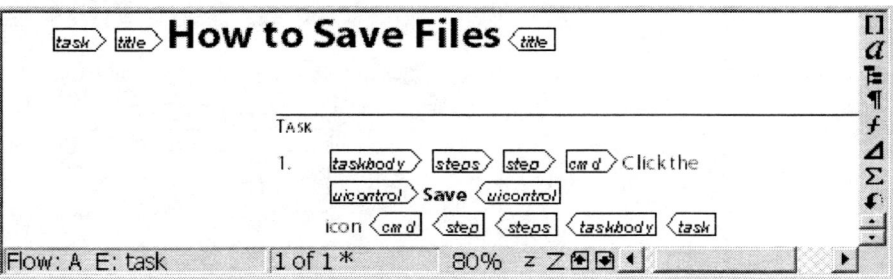

However, far more complex tasks can be created which incorporate a wide range of elements.

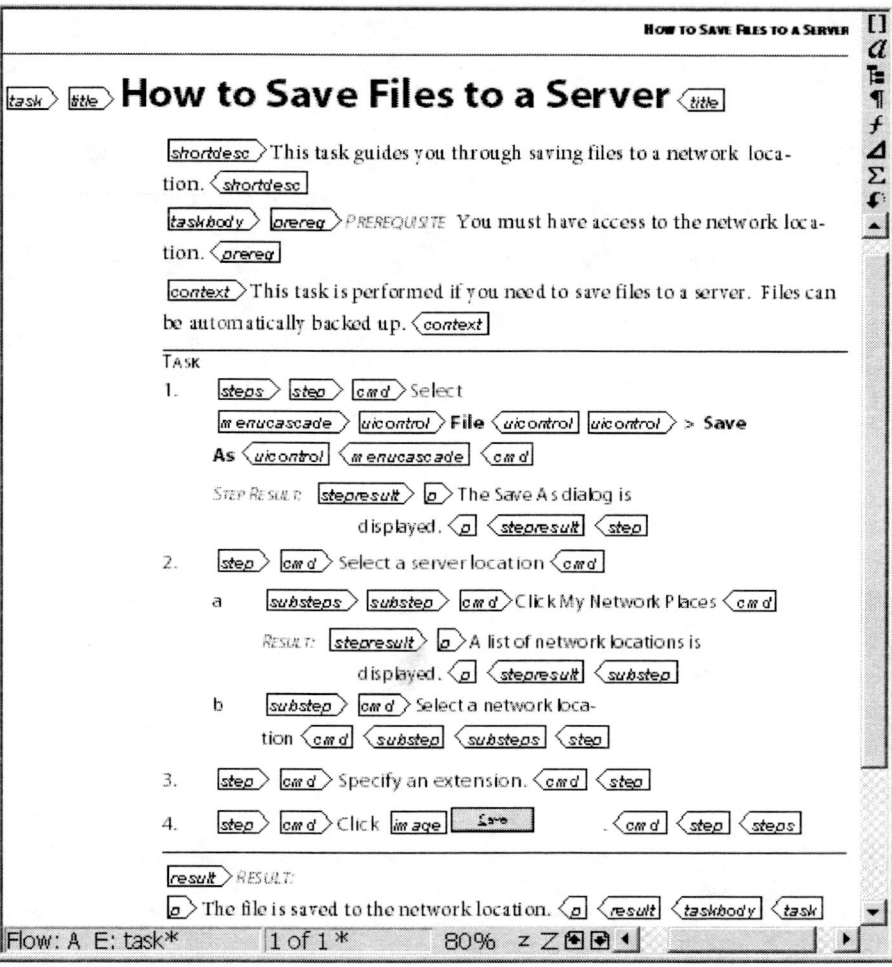

Task prerequisite <prereq>

The element <prereq> is used to inform the user of specific things they must do before starting the task.

Element representation:

<prereq>

Markup example:

<taskbody>

<prereq>You must have an XML editor installed.</prereq> ... </taskbody>

Task context <context>

The element <context> is used to provide background information related to a task. It provides information to help the user be successful at the task and understand the reason for it.

Element representation:

<context>

Markup example:

```
<taskbody>
<context>This task must be done on a PC or a Mac.</context>
…
</taskbody>
```

Task steps <steps>

The element <steps> is used to contain the main set of procedural information related to a task.

Element representation:

<steps>

Markup example:

```
<steps>
<step>…</step>
<step>…</step>
…
</steps>
```

Task step <step>

The element <step> is used to contain a specific action that the user must perform to accomplish a task. It contains a minimum of one command.

Element representation:

<step>

Markup example:

```
<steps>
<step>
<cmd>Open an XML file in your editing software.</cmd>
</step>
</steps>
```

Step command <cmd>

The element <cmd> is an active voice instruction to the user that is usually a single sentence.

Element representation:

```
<cmd>
```

Markup example:

```
<step>
<cmd>Open an XML file in your editing software.</cmd>
</step>
```

Information <info>

The element <info> provides information about the command.

Element representation:

```
<info>
```

Markup example:

```
<step>
<cmd>…</cmd>
<info>The filename can be any combination of upper or lowercase letters as well as numbers and underscores. No other characters are supported.</info>
</step>
```

Step result <stepresult>

The element <stepresult> is used to provide feedback to the user on the expected result of a specific command.

Element representation:

```
<stepresult>
```

Markup example:

```
<step>
<cmd>…</cmd>
<stepresult>The XML file is displayed.</stepresult></step>
```

Substeps <substeps>

The element <substeps> is used to provide additional steps that must be taken within a major step. The output is usually the same as a nested list in appearance. A subset contains all the same element options as a step, except for further substeps.

Element representation:

`<substeps>`

Markup example:

```
<step>
<cmd>Save the file.</cmd>
<substeps>
<substep><cmd>Select File.</cmd></substep>
<substep><cmd>Select Save.</cmd></substep>
</substeps>
</step>
```

Step choices <choices>

The element <choices> is used to provide a selection that has more than one option.
Element representation:

`<choices>`

Markup example:

```
<step>
<cmd>Save the file.</cmd>
<choices>
<choice>Click the Save icon.</choice>
<choice>Press Ctrl+s.</choice>
</choices>
</step>
```

Step choice tables <choicetable>

The element <choicetable> is used to present table-based choices, which usually include an option and a related description.

Element representation:

`<choices>`

Markup example:

```
<step>
<cmd>Choose an extension.</cmd>
<choicetable>
<chhead>
<choptionhd>Option</choptionhd>
<chdeschd>Description</chdeschd>
```

```
</chhead>
<chrow>
<choption>XML</choption>
<chdesc>eXtensible Markup Language</chdesc>
</chrow>
<chrow><choption>HTML</choption>
<chdesc>HyperText Markup Language</chdesc>
</chrow>
</choicetable>
</step>
```

Step example <stepxmp>

The element <stepxmp> is used to provide a sample of what the step involves. Element representation:

```
<stepxmp>
```

Markup example:

```
<step>
<cmd>Name the file.</cmd>
<stepxmp>For example, name the file WorkingWithCode.xml.</stepxmp>
</step>
```

Result <result>

The element <result> is used to provide feedback to the user on the expected result of a overall task upon completion of all steps.

Element representation:

```
<result>
```

Markup example:

```
<taskbody>
<steps>
…
</steps>
<result>The file is stored on the server.</result>
</taskbody>
```

Postrequisite <postreq>

The element <postreq> is used to provide information after a step is completed.

Element representation:

`<taskbody>`

Markup example:

> </steps>
>
> <postreq>Once you have updated the file ensure that it is checked back into the CMS server and update your job list.</postreq>
>
> </taskbody>

Linking in DITA

While DITA provides numerous linking elements, this topic addresses only some of the common elements that a new user should initially be aware of. For more detailed information, review the documentation included with the DITA Open Toolkit.

Cross reference
<xref>

The element <xref> is used in the body of a topic to link to virtually any other element. <xref> This includes related locations within the current file, external files, or external links (such as a URL or an email address). The href attribute provides the location to link to.

Whenever possible, the cross reference should remain internal to allow the greatest amount of reuse.

Element representation:

`<xref>`

Markup example:

> <p>Read info on opening: <xref href="c_Opening.xml">Opening Files</xref></p>
>
> <p>Look up info on opening: <xref href="http://www.google.com">Google</xref>.</p>
>
> <p>Print a copy of our quick reference card <xref href="quickref.pdf" format="pdf">Opening Files</xref>.</p>

Display example:

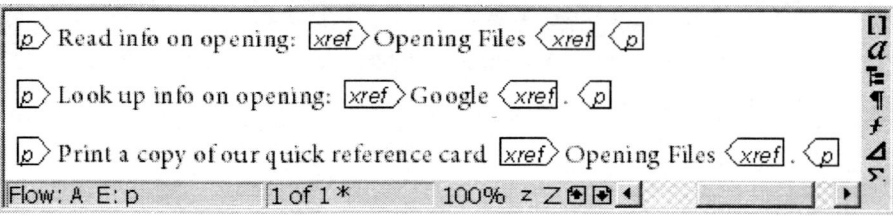

Related links

Related links are different from cross-references. Unlike cross-references, the related links cannot occur within the body of a topic and cannot target any element. Instead, related links only target other topics or non-topic objects.

Special processing instructions can be applied when related links are output. These may group links together, sort them, or place them in a specific frame of a help system.

Related links can also be used with DITA maps as a way to avoid embedding links within topics.

While DITA provides numerous related links-related elements, this topic addresses only some of the common elements that a new user should initially be aware of. For more detailed information, review the documentation included with the DITA Open Toolkit.

Related links <related-links>

The element related-links is used to support navigation between topics as well as link to external files, or to external links (such as a URL or an email address).

Element representation:

```
<related-links>
```

Markup example:

<related-links> ... </related-links>

Display example:

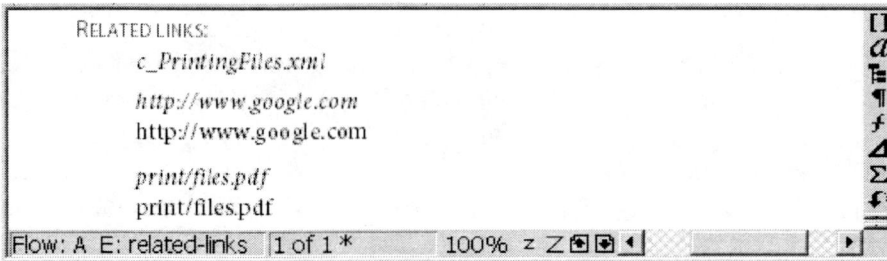

Link <link>

The element <link> is used to define a target for navigation to connect to. It contains an href attribute that is used to identify the target.

Element representation:

`<link>`

Markup example:

```
<link href="c_PrintingFiles.xml"></link>
<link href="http://www.google.com" scope="external" format="html">
<linktext>http://www.google.com</linktext>
</link>
<link href="print/files.pdf"><linktext>print/files.pdf</linktext>
</link>
```

Display example:

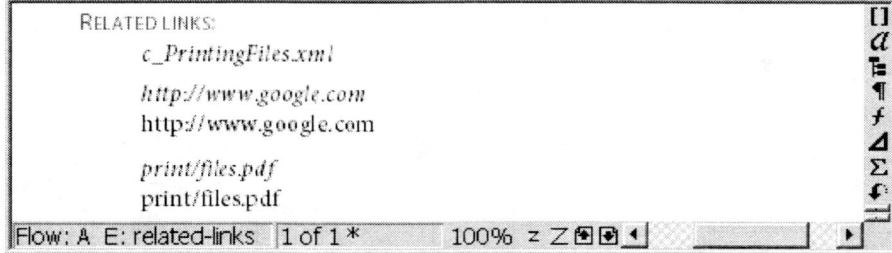

Link text <linktext>

The element <linktext> is used to provide a string of text to be used when representing a link visually. Normally, though, the destination that a <link> element references contains content that is automatically used.

Element representation:

<linktext>

Markup example:

```
<link href="http://www.google.com" scope="external" format="html">
<linktext>http://www.google.com</linktext>
</link>
```

Domain elements

Domain elements support a variety of terms that relate to programing, software, and user interface-specific writing. They also include conventions related to common typographical conventions. A generalization can be made that domain elements relate to the idea of creating specific ranges of structure that are transformed into the equivalent of character range formats.

While DITA provides numerous domain-related elements, this topic addresses only some of the common elements that a new user should initially be aware of. For more detailed information, review the documentation included with the DITA Open Toolkit.

Typographical

Typographical elements are generally used to apply styles such as bold or italic to a range of characters. It is a generally accepted best practice that they are avoided if a semantically specific element could be used instead.

Bold <b>

The element <b> is used to apply bold to a text range. Element representation:

<b>

Markup example:

<p>If possible, <b>avoid</b> typographical elements.</p>

Display example:

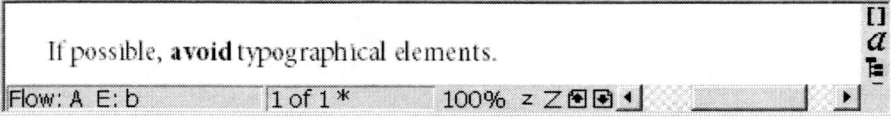

Italic <i>

The element <i> is used to apply italic to a text range. Element representation:

<i>

Markup example:

<p>If possible, <i>avoid</i> typographical elements.</p>

Display example:

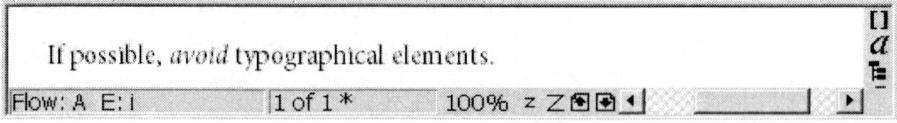

Underline <u>

The element <u> is used to apply underline to a text range. Element representation:

<u>

Markup example:

<p>If possible, <u>avoid</u> typographical elements.</p>

Display example:

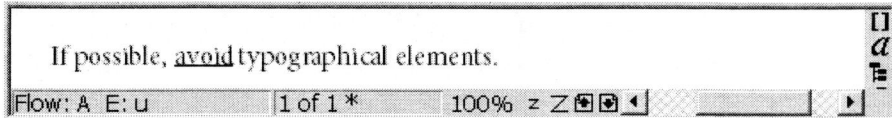

Type text <tt>

The element <tt> is used to apply typetext (usually a monospace font, such as Courier) to a text range.

Element representation:

```
<tt>
```

Markup example:

<p>If possible, <tt>avoid</tt> typographical elements.</p>

Display example:

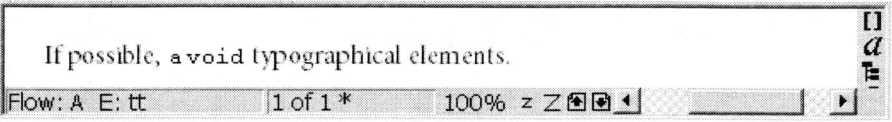

Superscript <sup>

The element <sup> is used to apply superscript to a text range. Element representation:

```
<sup>
```

Markup example:

<p>Albert Einstein stated, in 1905, that E=mc² where E is the speed of light, m is the mass, and c is thespeed of light in a vacuum.</p>

Display example:

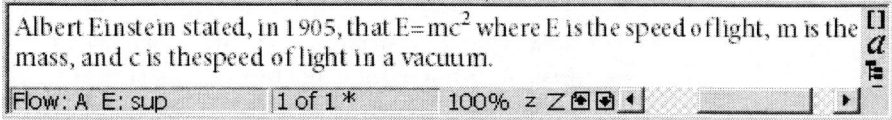

Subscript <sub>

The element <sub> is used to apply subscript to a text range. Element representation:

```
<sub>
```

Markup example:

<p>The chemical formula for water is H₂O where H is hydrogen and O is oxygen.</p>

Display example:

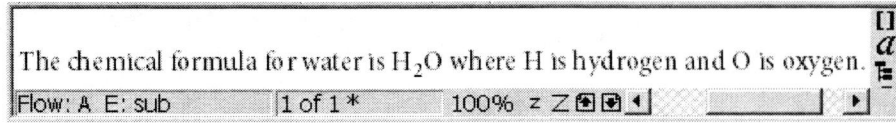

Programing elements

The elements related to programing are used to define syntax and samples related to programing languages (HTML, XML, XSL, FO, Java, Python, PHP, C#, ASP, JavaScript, Perl and so on) and code.

While DITA provides numerous programing-related elements, this topic addresses only some of the common elements that a new user should initially be aware of. For more detailed information, review the documentation included with the DITA Open Toolkit.

Code phrase <codeph>

The element <codeph> is used to document a specific phrase of code (usually displayed as a monospace font, such as Courier) as an inline text component.

Element representation:

```
<codeph>
```

Markup example:

```
<p>Type <codeph>dir</codeph> to list the directory.</p>
```

Display example:

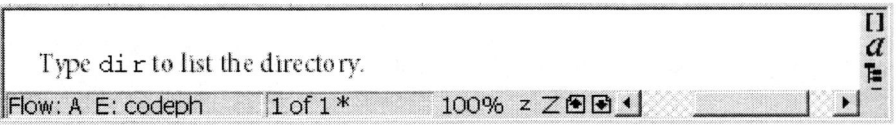

Codeblock <codeblock>

The element <codeblock> is used to document a collection of multiple lines of code (usually displayed as a monospace font, such as Courier) as a collection of lines with line endings.

Element representation:

```
<codeblock>
```

Markup example:

```
<p>A variety of commands exist to list directory information:
<codeblock>
dir /s
dir /p
```

```
dir /w
dir /s /w /p
</codeblock>
</p>
```

Display example:

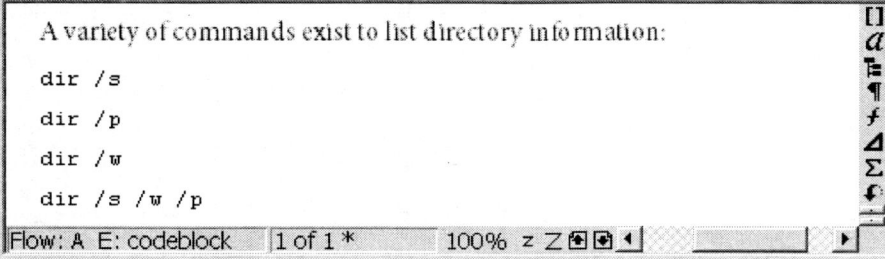

Additional programing elements

A variety of additional elements exist, to support parameters, syntax, operators, delimiters, separators, options, keywords, variables, and API names. However, they are not addressed here. For more detailed information, review the documentation included with the DITA Open Toolkit.

Software elements

The elements related to software are used to document the way that a software tool is operated.

While DITA provides numerous software-related elements, this topic addresses only some of the common elements that a new user should initially be aware of. For more detailed information, review the documentation included with the DITA Open Toolkit.

Message phrase <msgph>

The element <msgph> is used to document the text of a message that is created by an application.

Element representation:

<msgph>

Markup example:

```
<p>The phrase <msgph>copy complete</msgph> displays.</p>
```

Display example:

File path <filepath>

The element <filepath> is used to document the name and location, including the directory path, of an object on a computer.

Element representation:

```
<filepath>
```

Markup example:

<p>The file is in <filepath>c:\</filepath> by default.</p>

Display example:

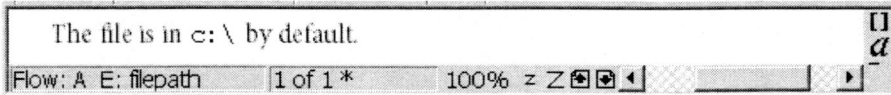

User input <userinput>

The element <userinput> is used to document the text a user should input when prompted by an application.

Element representation:

```
<userinput>
```

Markup example:

<p>Type <userinput>confirm</userinput> to close the file.</p>

Display example:

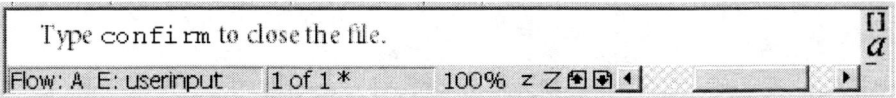

Additional software elements

A variety of additional elements exist, to support messages, commands, system outputs, and variables. However, they are not addressed here. For more detailed information, review the documentation included with the DITA Open Toolkit.

User interface

The elements related to user interface are used to document the components that make up a software application's visual appearance.

While DITA provides numerous user interface elements, this topic addresses only some of the common elements that a new user should initially be aware of. For more detailed information, review the documentation included with the DITA Open Toolkit.

User interface control <uicontrol>

The element <uicontrol> is used to document the names of objects in an application. This may include a button or dialog name.

If a menu item is referenced, and only one level of entry is referenced, the element <uicontrol> can be used. However, for nested entries, use the element <menucascade> (for example, File > Close should use the element menucascade, which contains two or more <uicontrol> elements).

Element representation:

`<uicontrol>`

Markup example:

```
<p>Click the <uicontrol>Close</uicontrol> icon.</p>
```

Display example:

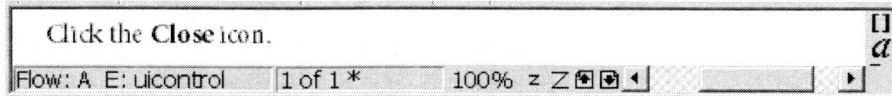

Menu cascade <menucascade>

The element <menucascade> is used to document a set of menu choices that branch off each other.

For nested entries, use the element <menucascade> with the element <uicontrol> (for example, File > Print should use the element <menucascade>, which contains two or more <uicontrol> elements). However, if a menu item is referenced, and only one level of entry is referenced, the element <uicontrol> can be used.

Element representation:

`<menucascade>`

Markup example:

```
<p>Select <menucascade><uicontrol>File</uicontrol><uicontrol> Close</uicontrol></menucascade> to close the file.</p>
```

Display example:

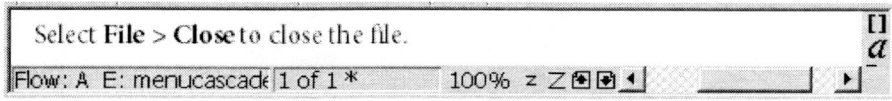

Window title <wintitle>

The element <wintitle> is used to document the names of windows or dialogs. Element representation:

```
<wintitle>
```

Markup example:

```
<p>The <wintitle>Print</wintitle> dialog is displayed.</p>
```

Display example:

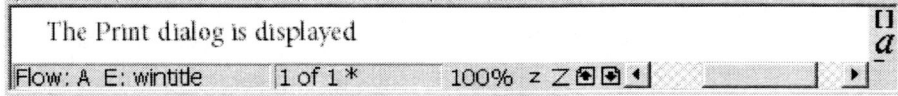

Additional user interface elements

A variety of additional elements exist to support shortcuts and screens. However, they are not addressed here. For more detailed information, review the documentation included with the DITA Open Toolkit.

Prolog elements

The elements related to prolog are used to add information to the document being created. This information is generally not displayed in generated output. The metadata may also be used for publishing purposes to identify content that may or may not be published. It may also be used to build a navigation system, customize the index entries, or even to automatically include or exclude specific topics in the published version depending on the permissions granted.

While DITA provides numerous prolog-related elements, this topic addresses only some of the common elements that a new user should initially be aware of. For more detailed information, review the documentation included with the DITA Open Toolkit.

Prolog <prolog>

The element <prolog> is used to provide information about the topic.

Element representation:

```
<prolog>
```

Markup example:

```
<prolog>
<author>Vicky Lee</author>
<author>Noah Macleander</author>
```

```
<publisher>BPS Incorporated</publisher>
<copyright>
<copyryear year="2007"/>
<copyrholder>BPS Incorporated</copyrholder>
</copyright>
<critdates>
<created date="1999-02-07"/>
<revised modified="2006-05-16"/>
<revised modified="2006-10-11"/>
<revised modified="2006-11-02" golive="2007-01-23"/>
</critdates>
<permissions view="entitled"/>
</prolog>
```

Author <author>

The element <author> is used to provide information about the person or persons who wrote the topic.

Element representation:

`<author>`

Markup example:

```
<author>Vicky Lee</author><author>Noah Macleander</author>
```

Publisher <publisher>

The element <publisher> is used to provide information about the company or person who is responsible for publishing the topic.

Element representation:

`<publisher>`

Markup example:

```
<publisher>BPS Incorporated</publisher>
```

Copyright <copyright>

The element <copyright> is used to provide information about a single copyright entry including copyright years and copyright holder.

Element representation:

`<copyright>`

Markup example:

```
<copyright> ... </copyright>
```

Copyright year <copyryear>

The element <copyryear> is used to provide the year that the copyright is specific to. Element representation:

```
<copyryear>
```

Markup example:

```
<copyryear year="2007"/>
```

Copyright holder <copyrholder>

The element <copyrightholder> is used to provide information about the company or person who holds the legal rights of a topic and its content.

Element representation:

```
<copyright>
```

Markup example:

```
<copyrholder>BPS Incorporated</copyrholder>
```

Critical dates <critdates>

The element <critdates> is used to provide information such as creation date and revision dates.

Element representation:

```
<critdates>
```

Markup example:

```
<critdates> ... </critdates>
```

Creation date <created>

The element <created> is used to provide information about the date a document was first created. This is done through the use of the date, golive, and expiry attributes.

Element representation:

```
<created>
```

Markup example:

```
<created date="1999-02-07"/>
```

Revision date <revised>

The element <revised> is used to provide information about the date a document was modified. This is done through the use of the modified, golive, and expiry attributes.

Element representation:

```
<revised>
```

Markup example:

```
<revised modified="2006-10-11">
<revised modified="2006-11-02" golive="2007-01-23" expiry="2008-05-16"/>
```

Permissions
<permissions>

The element <permissions> is used to provide information about how a topic is allowed <permissions> to be accessed by setting the view attribute. Values include: internal, classified, all, and entitled.

Element representation:

`<permissions>`

Markup example:

```
<permissions view="entitled"/>
```

Additional prolog
elements

A variety of additional elements exist, to support source, metadata (including audience, category, keywords, prodinfo [including prodname, vrmlist (including vrm), brand, series, platform, prognum, featnum and component], and othermeta), and resourceid. However, they are not addressed here. For more detailed information review the documentation included with the DITA Open Toolkit.

Common attributes and values

The attributes are used to add information to the document being created. The metadata may be used for a variety of purposes including the appearance and placement of content, the creation and management of navigational links, the flagging of information for specific publishing or distribution purposes, the building of maps, translation, and more.

While DITA provides numerous attributes and values related to elements, this topic addresses only some of the common attributes that a new user should initially be aware of. For more detailed information review, the documentation included with the DITA Open Toolkit.

Display attributes
<display-atts>

Display related attributes are used primarily for formatting the appearance of content.

Scale <scale>

An optional attribute used to increase or decrease the font size by using a fixed and predefined value.

Attribute options:

```
(50 | 60 | 70 | 80 | 90 | 100 | 110 | 120 | 140 | 160 | 180 |
   200)
```

Markup example:

```
<codeblock scale="90">
```

Frame or border <frame>

An optional attribute used to create a border around an element by using a fixed and predefined value.

Attribute options:

```
(top | bottom | topbot | all | sides | none)
```

Markup example:

```
<codeblock frame="all">
```

Expanse or placement <expanse>

An optional attribute used to horizontally place an element by using a fixed and predefined value.

Attribute options:

```
(page | column | textline)
```

Markup example:

```
<codeblock expanse="column">
```

Identification attributes <id-atts>

ID-related attributes are used primarily for naming and referencing elements.

Unique identifier <id>

An optional attribute used to uniquely identify an element. While optional, the best practice is to define a value for at least topic, concept, reference, and task elements.

Attribute options:

```
unique value
```

Markup example:

```
<concept id="saving">
```

conref

An optional attribute used to reference to a uniquely identified element. While optional, the best practice is generally to define a value for topic, concept, reference, and task elements.

Attribute options:

```
unique value
```

Markup example:

```
<concept id="saving">
```

**Selection attributes
<select-atts>**

Selection-related attributes are used to flag and filter elements based on a variety of criteria.

Platform <platform>

Indicates operating system and hardware that is applicable to the element. Attribute options:

```
text string
```

Markup example:

```
<concept platform="windows">
```

Product <product>

Indicates the product name that is applicable to the element.

Attribute options:

```
text string
```

Markup example:

```
<concept product="Widget-O-Matic2K">
```

Audience <audience>

Indicates the audience that is applicable to the element. Attribute options:

```
text string
```

Markup example:

```
<concept audience="developers">
```

Importance <importance>

Indicates the priority that is applicable to the element. Attribute options:

```
obsolete | deprecated | optional | default | low | normal |
    high | recommended | required | urgent
```

Markup example:

```
<concept importance="low">
```

Revision <rev>

Indicates the revision or version level that is applicable to the element.

Attribute options:

```
text string
```

Markup example:

```
<concept rev="2.0">
```

Status <status>

Indicates the state or modification that is applicable to the element.

Attribute options:

```
new | changed | deleted | unchanged
```

Markup example:

```
<concept status="new">
```

Additional attributes

A variety of additional attributes exist including univ-atts, rel-atts, topicref-atts, and topicref-atts-no-toc. However, they are not addressed here. For more detailed information, review the documentation included with the DITA Open Toolkit.

Map elements

While DITA provides numerous map-related elements, this topic addresses only some of the common elements that a new user should initially be aware of. For more detailed information, review the documentation included with the DITA Open Toolkit.

Map <map>

The element <map> is used to provide information about the relationships between topics. The map may contain numerous topics, nested topics, links between topics, and other information to organize content. It could be compared in general terms to a book or a master document that links to other documents and defines relationships between them.

A map is generally used to manage multiple topics and combine references between them. Content is organized in a hierarchy that forms the basic structure of the map and organizes topics into relationships based on this hierarchy.

The relationship in the map can be represented as navigational for tables of contents or for the purpose of developing related links. This relationship can be used to generate a table of contents, to combine topics into a help or PDF deliverable, and to manage content in regards to links between topics. The DITA map can then be published as required.

Maps are organizational objects in DITA. They bring together a variety of topics to help create a finished product. The map is then used to assemble the topics into various deliverables based on product lines or releases or other criteria related to publishing.

Since topics are written as standalone units of information they need a way to be added to a larger deliverable for true functionality of content. A discrete unit of information (the topic) may still be a small part of a final file set. The map would combine topics in a specific order for publishing and this may differ for print (or PDF) output when compared with online (or Help) content. Therefore, multiple maps may be created for multiple types of output.

The representation of the map is a simple XML file. This XML file contains references to specific topics and instructions that are used when processing the map for output.

Element representation:

`<map>`

Markup example:

```
<map title="Managing Files">
<topicref href="c_OpeningFiles.xml"/>
…
</map>
```

Display example:

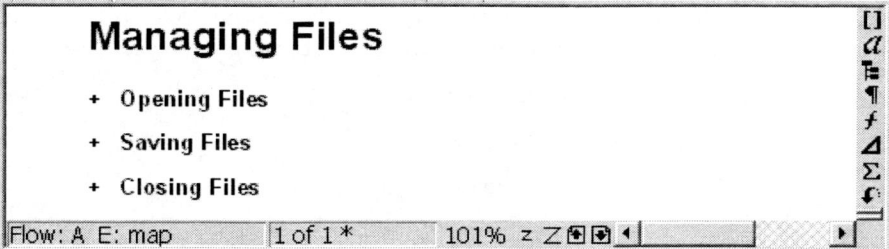

Topic reference
<topicref>

The element <topicref> is used to identify a topic so that a map can identify the location of a required resource.

Element representation:

`<topicref>`

Markup example:

```
<map title="Managing Files">
<topicref href="c_Opening.xml" navtitle="Opening Files"/>
```

```
<topicref href="c_Saving.xml" navtitle="Saving Files"/>
<topicref href="c_Closing.xml" navtitle="Closing Files"/>
</map>
```

Display example:

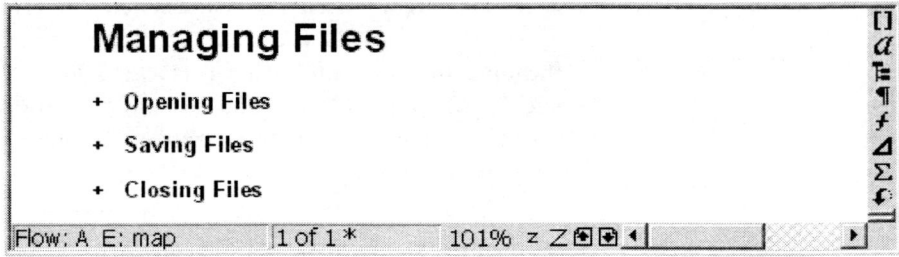

Relationship table

While DITA provides numerous relationship table-related elements, this topic addresses only some of the common elements that a new user should initially be aware of. For more detailed information, review the documentation included with the DITA Open Toolkit.

**Relationship table
\<reltable\>**

The element \<reltable\> is used to build a set of relationships between topics based on the table model of rows, columns, and cells. Each cell contains one or more \<topicref\> elements, which are related to other topics in the same row.

Element representation:

```
<reltable>
```

Markup example:

```
<reltable title="Saving Files">
<relheader>
<relcolspec type="task"/>
<relcolspec type="concept"/>
<relcolspec type="reference"/>
</relheader>
<relrow>
<relcell>
<topicref format="dita" href="t_HowToSave.xml"/>
</relcell>
```

```
<relcell>
<topicref href="c_Save.xml" navtitle="When Saving Files"/>
</relcell>
<relcell>
<topicref href="r_MultipleDevices.xml"/>
<topicref href="r_PathNames.xml"/>
</relcell>
</relrow>
</reltable>
```

Display example:

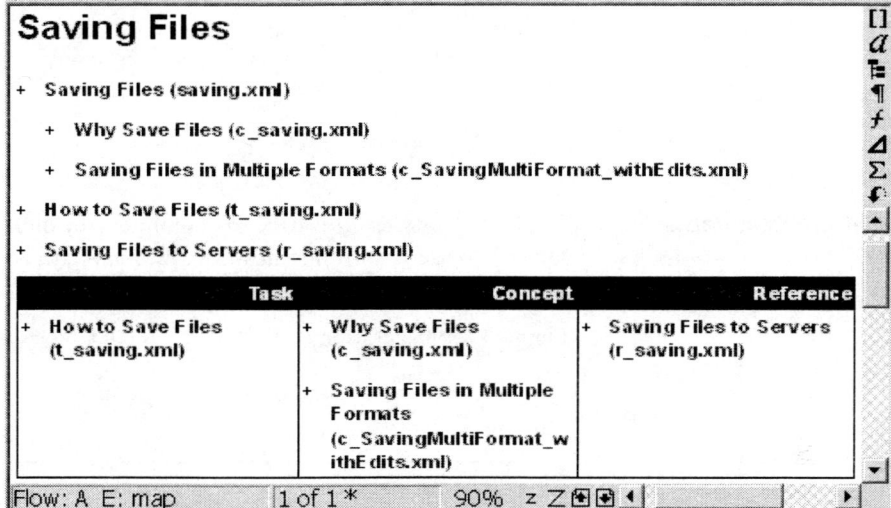

Relationship table header <relheader>

The element <relheader> is used to contain one a common heading under which one or more DITA topics are grouped logically.

Element representation:

```
<relheader>
```

Markup example:

```
<relheader>
<relheader>
<relcolspec type="reference"/>
<relcolspec type="concept"/>
<relcolspec type="task"/>
</relheader>
```

```
</relheader>
```

Relationship table row <relrow>

The element <relrow> is used to build a single row in a relationship table. This row creates a relationship between the elements for linking purposes.

Element representation:

```
<relrow>
```

Markup example:

```
<relrow>
<relcell>
<topicref href="t_Saving.xml" navtitle="Saving Files"/>
</relcell>
<relcell>
…
</relrow>
```

Relationship table cell <relcell>

The element <relcell> is used to contain one or more DITA topics that are grouped logically under a common heading. By default, the content within a cell does not link to other content in the same cell. Rather it links to content in related cells.

Element representation:

```
<relcell>
```

Markup example:

```
<relcell>
<topicref href="t_Saving.xml" navtitle="Saving Files/">
</relcell>
```

Publishing from DITA

To publish content from the DITA specification, at least one standalone topic or as much as a full collection of topics in a map using <reltable> content must exist. Depending on the complexity of the content, the finished published file may be as simple as a single PDF file or a standalone Web page. However, a complete set of help documentation, a publication ready for print, or any combination of these can be created.

Publishing a single topic

A single topic can be published to a variety of formats including PDF and HTML Web pages.

Markup example:

```
<?xml version="1.0"?>
<!DOCTYPE concept PUBLIC "-//OASIS//DTD DITA Concept//EN"
"concept.dtd">
<concept id="c_closing_files">
<title>When Closing Files</title>
<shortdesc>Files which have been opened may be closed and changes saved or
discarded.</shortdesc>
<conbody><p>When files are opened and printing or modifications are complete,
they need to be closed. This frees up system resources and makes the file available
to others who may need to use it.</p></conbody>
</concept>
```

Display example:

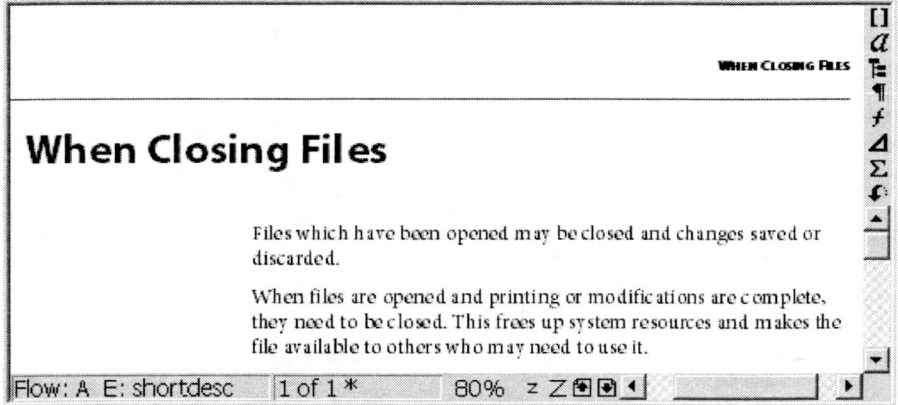

Publishing a map   A map can be published to a variety of formats including PDF, HTML Web pages, and a compiled help system.

Markup example:

```
<?xml version="1.0"?>
<!DOCTYPE map PUBLIC "-//OASIS//DTD DITA Map//EN" "map.dtd">
<map id="saving" title="Saving Files">
<topichead navtitle="Concepts">
<topicref href="c_SavingFiles.xml"/>
</topichead>
<topichead navtitle="Tasks">
<topicref href="t_SavingFiles.xml"/>
<topicref href="t_SavingToNewLocations.xml"/>
```

```
</topichead>
<topichead navtitle="References">
<topicref href="r_SavingToMultipleDevices.xml"/>
<topicref href="r_SavingFiles.xml"/>
</topichead>
<reltable title="Saving Files">
<relheader>
<relcolspec type="task" />
<relcolspec type="concept" />
<relcolspec type="reference" />
</relheader>
<relrow>
<relcell><topicref href="t_SavingFiles.xml"/></relcell>
<relcell><topicref href="c_SavingFiles.xml"/></relcell>
<relcell><topicref href="r_SavingToMultipleDevices.xml"/></relcell>
</relrow>
<relrow>
<relcell><topicref href="t_SavingFiles.xml"/></relcell>
<relcell></relcell>
<relcell><topicref href="r_SavingFiles.xml"/></relcell>
</relrow>
<relrow><relcell></relcell><relcell></relcell>
<relcell collection-type="family">
<topicref href="r_SavingToMultipleDevices.xml"/>
<topicref href="r_SavingFiles.xml"/>
</relcell></relrow></reltable>
</map>
```

Display example:

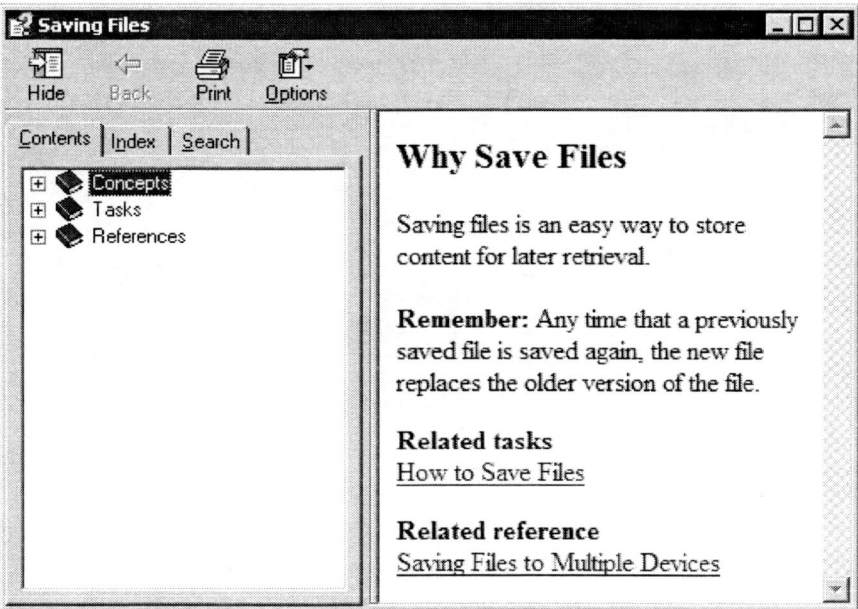

Tutorials

If you need source files for the tutorials, email fmk@brightpathsolutions.com. Note that many of the early tutorials are standalone or built based on earlier tutorials. Sample files are small and will be emailed to you when requested.

When working with the tutorials it is suggested that you work from the first to the last. Read the entire procedure from start to end to ensure that you know what the goal of each one is. Use the screenshots to help orient yourself.

If you expect to jump into a later tutorial, read the content of the earlier ones first as many assumptions are made in later tutorials and these are detailed in the earlier ones.

Adobe FrameMaker 8.0 does not support the DITA Toolkit by default. Therefore it is required that you download and install an additional utility from Adobe.

 Tip

If the online link is invalid, search for the keywords: FrameMaker 8, DITA, plug-in

At the time of publishing this book, the link to the utility is found here: http://www.adobe.com/devnet/framemaker/fm8_opentoolkit.html

Once downloaded and installed the utility and the DITA Open Toolkit provide additional support for publishing content using the toolkit. It also provides sample files, documentation on DITA, assorted transforms and more.

Tutorial 1

Get started with FrameMaker

Overview

This tutorial teaches you the basics of working with the software by creating and populating a DITA concept.

This section contains the following topics:

- *Tutorial overview*
- *Create a new concept*
- *Display and configure the Structure View*
- *Display and configure the Element Catalog*
- *Work with document views*
- *Setting user and compatibility preferences*
- *Close the file*
- *Exit the application*

Tutorial overview

This tutorial guides you through the initial creation of a basic DITA concept.

The tutorial assumes a default installation of Adobe FrameMaker 8.0. If your product has been customized, some of the default options may not be available. If you have previously launched the software and opened files, the default workspace may differ from that shown here.

As the first tutorial, this is a very simple set of procedural information but heavily detailed. Subsequent tutorials build on ideas in this tutorial and may be less detailed.

For example, the first task in this tutorial guides you through the creation of a new concept and provides step–by–step instructions. However, subsequent tutorials may simply instruct you to create a new concept without the step–by–step instructions.

Create a new concept

In this section, you learn how to create a new DITA concept in a specific location.

In this tutorial, the name of the document is based on an arbitrary sample naming convention. The file being worked with is a concept related to printing files. It is an XML-based document. Therefore, the name uses the letter *c* to identify the fact that it is a concept, an *underscore* as a separator, the phrase *PrintingFiles* to identify the content of the document, and the extension *.xml* to identify the file type.

The name of the document is therefore c_PrintingFiles.xml.

1. Launch FrameMaker.

2. Select DITA > New DITA File > New <concept>.
   The Enter a new DITA topic file name dialog box displays.

3. Navigate to your hard drive root directory.
   In the tutorials, the location is assumed to be c:\.

4. Create a new folder named *tutorials*.

5. Within the *tutorials* folder create a new folder named **fm8dita**.
   This folder will contain all the FrameMaker tutorials.

6. If required, within the *fm8dita* folder, create a new folder named **tutorial_01**.
   The path you have created is *c:\tutorials\fm8dita\tutorial_01*.

7. Open the *tutorial_01* folder.
   This is the location the file is to be saved to.

8. Under File name, type **c_PrintingFiles.xml**.

Note

In subsequent tutorials, you may see this procedural information simplified to something similar to: *Create a new concept titled* **Introduction to Printing**.

9. Click ⬚ Select ⬚ .

A new concept is created and automatically populated with placeholder content for the title element.

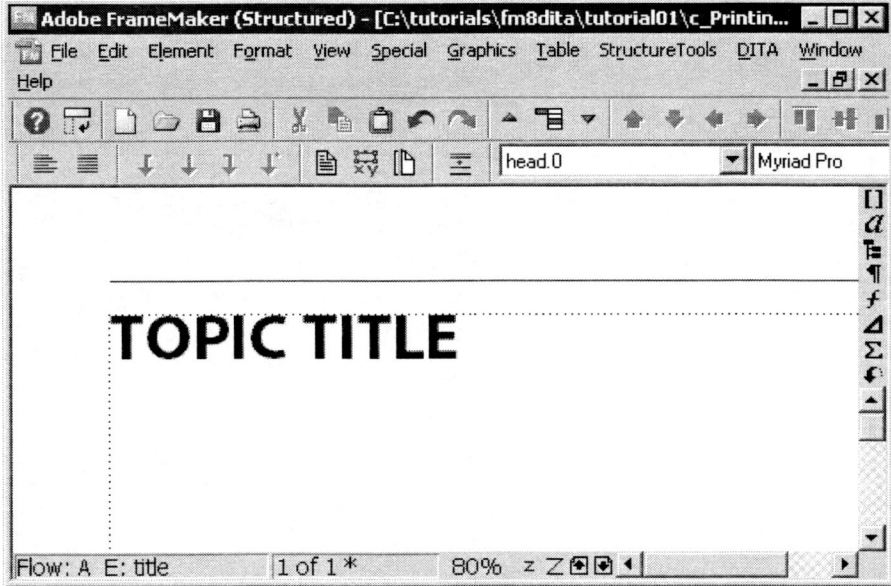

10. Replace the placeholder content *Topic Title* with **Introduction to Printing**.

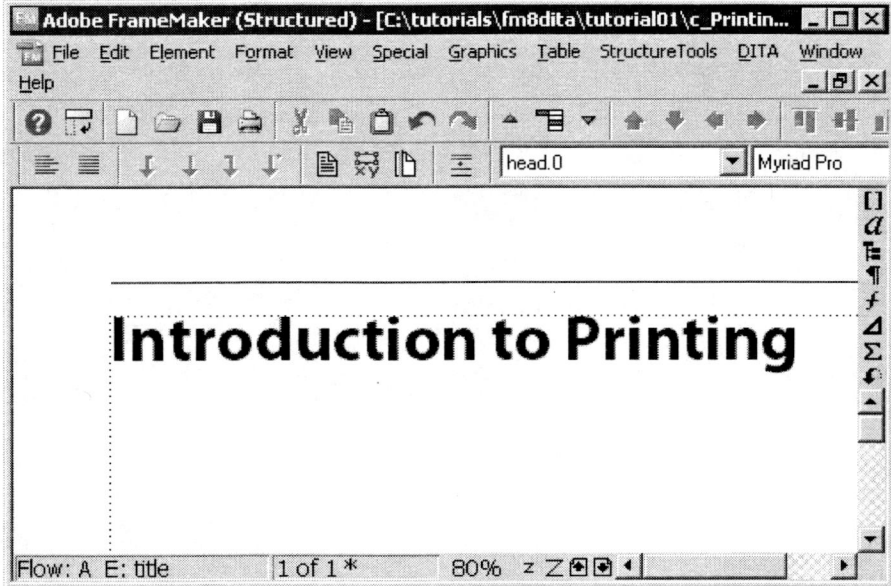

Display and configure the Structure View

In this section you open the Structure View and set it up its placement on screen.

1. Select ⊫ from the sidebar.

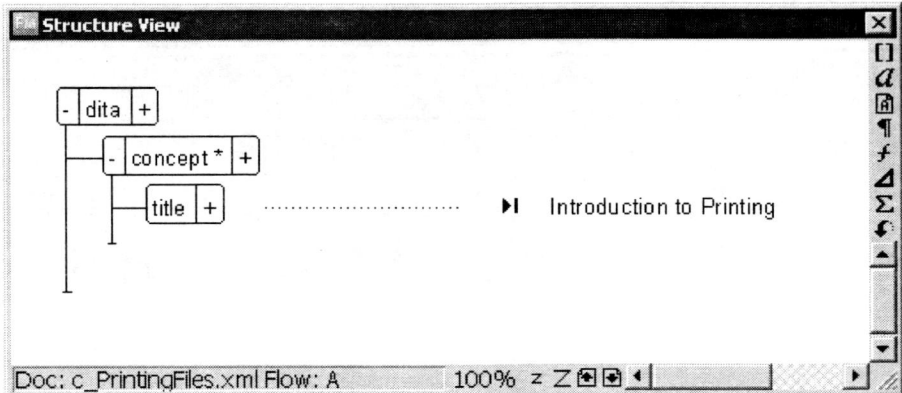

2. Move and resize the Structure View until it is roughly positioned as seen below.

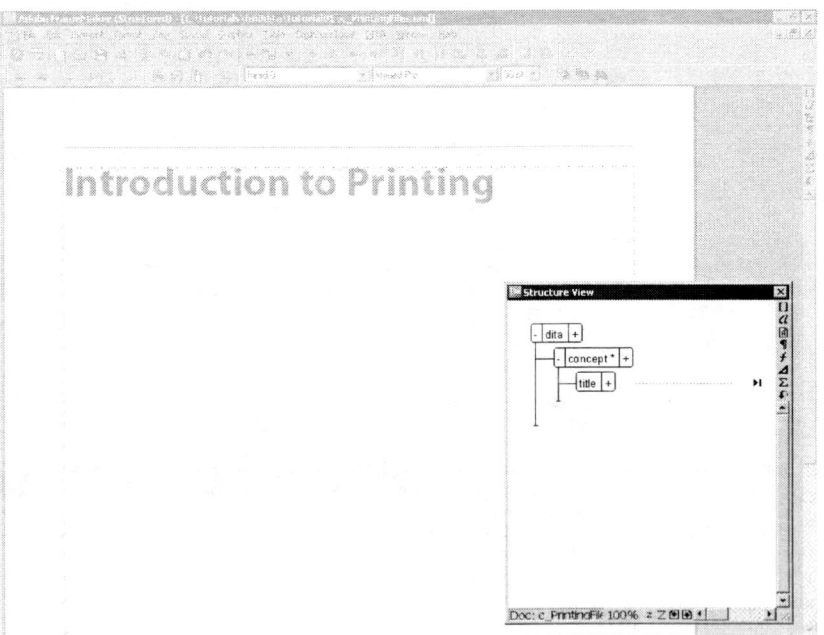

Display and configure the Element Catalog

In this section you open the Element Catalog and set it up its placement on screen.

1. Click [] in the sidebar.

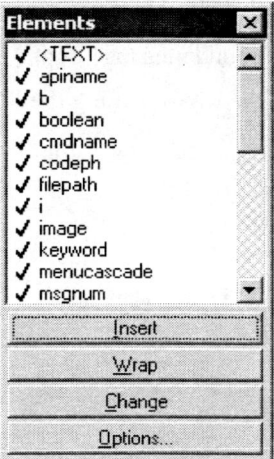

2. Move and resize the Element Catalog until it is roughly positioned as seen below.

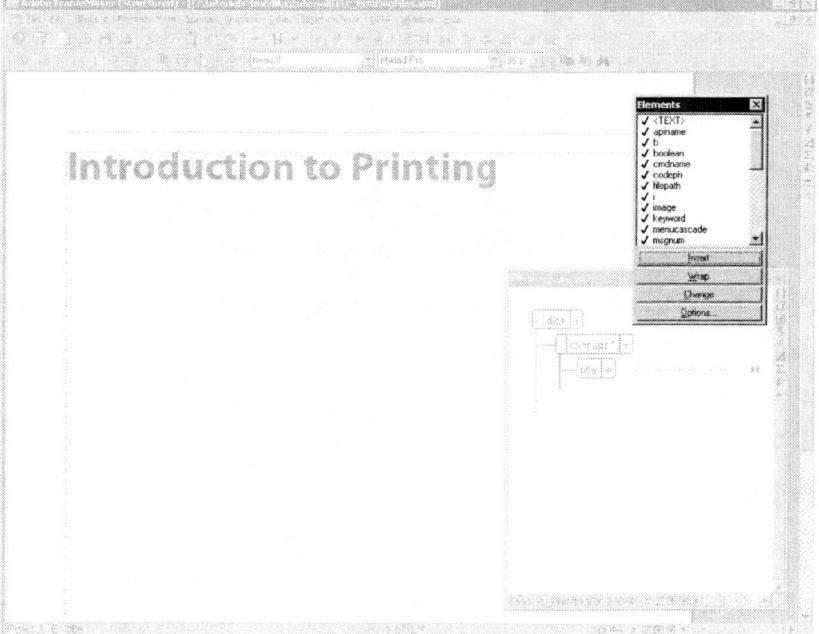

Work with document views

In this section, you learn how to use the various views to display content.

1. Select View > Element Boundaries.

    The structural tags are displayed as brackets.

1. Select View > Element Boundaries (as Tags).

    The structural tags are displayed naming the elements.

2. Select View > Element Boundaries (as Tags).

    The default view is reset.

3. Click Zoom Out z twice.

4. Click Zoom In z three times.

5. Click the Zoom button.

    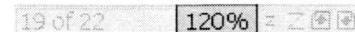

6. Select 100%.

Setting user and compatibility preferences

In this section you cancel the Automatic Backup on Save setting.

1. Select File > Preferences > General.

    The Preferences dialog displays.

2. Deselect Automatic Backup on Save.

3. Click Set .

Close the file

In this section, you learn to close an open file.

1. Select File > Save.

2. Select File > Close.

Exit the application

In this section, you learn how to exit the application.

1.   Select File > Exit.

The application is closed.

Tutorial 2

Work with basic content

Overview

This tutorial teaches you the basics of editing content by creating and populating lists. This tutorial further develops the content created in an earlier tutorial.

This section contains the following topics:

- *Tutorial overview*
- *Opening a previously created DITA concept*
- *Save files to a new location*
- *Add a new paragraph*
- *Add an unordered list*

Tutorial overview

This tutorial guides you through simple addition of content to a basic DITA concept.

As the second tutorial, this is a very simple set of procedural information but heavily detailed. Some procedures from the previous tutorial are simplified. Subsequent tutorials build on ideas in this tutorial and may be less detailed.

Opening a previously created DITA concept

In this section, you open an existing DITA concept. It is stored in a default location. If you are not placing your tutorial files on the root of your local hard drive, some of the following steps may differ.

Information on "Open samples from the previous tutorial" can be found on page 224. Information on "Open a standalone sample" can be found on page 224.

Open samples from the previous tutorial

If you have not completed the previous tutorial, proceed to *Open a standalone sample.*
If you have completed the previous tutorial proceed with the following steps.

 **Note**

In subsequent tutorials, you may see this procedural information simplified to something similar to: Open c_PrintingFiles.xml or Tutorial_02_Start.xml.

1. If required, launch FrameMaker.

2. Select **File** > **Open**.

3. Navigate to your hard drive root directory.
    In this tutorial, the location is assumed to be C:\.

4. Open the folder *tutorials\fm8dita\tutorial_01*.

5. Select the file *c_PrintingFiles.xml,* which was created in the previous tutorial.

6. Click [Open].

7. If required, under Use Structured Application, select DITA-Topic-FM.

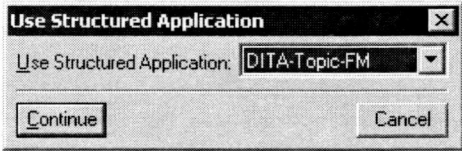

8. Click [Continue].

Open a standalone sample

If you have completed the previous tutorial do not perform the following steps.

1. If required, launch FrameMaker.

2. Select **File** > **Open**.

3. Navigate to your hard drive root directory.
    In this tutorial, the location is assumed to be C:\.

4. Open the folder *tutorials\fm8dita\tutorial_02*.

5. Select the file *Tutorial_02_Start.xml.*

6. Click [Open].

7.   If required, under Use Structured Application, select DITA-Topic-FM.

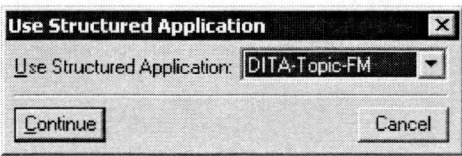

8.   Click .

Save files to a new location

In this section, you create a new folder (if required) in the tutorials folder and save the current file to this folder.

1.   Select File > Save As.

The Save As dialog box displays.

2.   Navigate to your hard drive root directory.

In this tutorial, the location is assumed to be C:\.

3.   Open the folder named *tutorials*.

4.   Within the *tutorials* folder open the folder named *xmad*.

5.   If required, within the *fm8dita* folder create a new folder named **tutorial_02**.

The path you have created is *c:\tutorials\fm8dita\tutorial_02*.

```
☐ 💿 Local Disk (C:)
   ☐ 📁 tutorials
      ☐ 📁 fm8dita
            📁 tutorial_01
            📁 tutorial_02
```

6.   Open the *tutorial_02* folder.

This will be the location the file is saved to.

7.   If required, under File name, type **c_PrintingFiles.xml**.

8.   Click Save .

Set up the Structure View and Element Catalog

In this section you open the Structure View and the Element Catalog and properly position them for use.

1. Select ⏚ from the sidebar.

   The Structure View is displayed.

2. Click [] in the sidebar.

   The Element Catalog is displayed.

3. Move and resize the Structure View and the Element Catalog until they are roughly positioned as seen below.

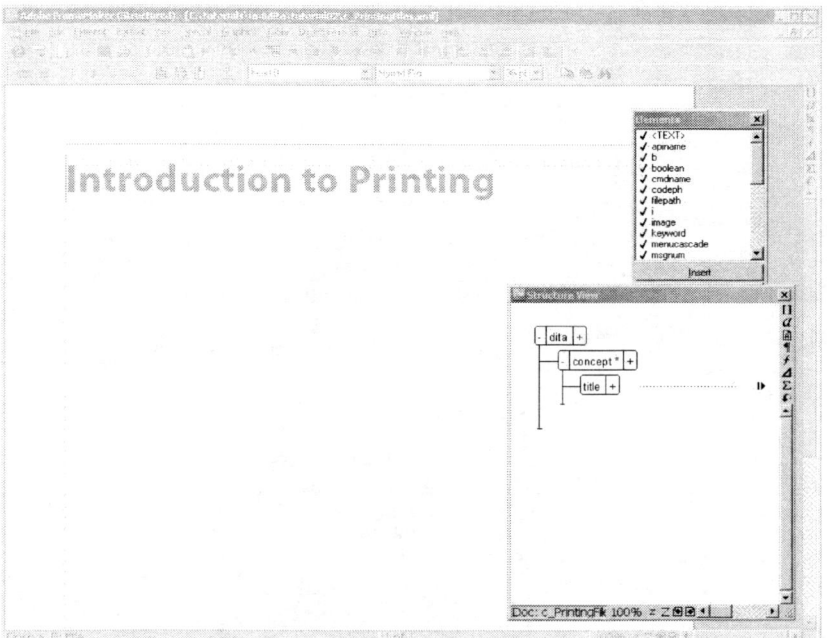

Add a short description

In this section you learn how to add a short description element.

1. In the Structure View, click immediately below the element *title*.

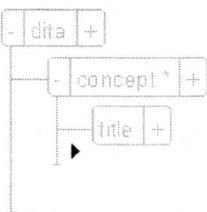

 **Note**

In subsequent tutorials, you may see this procedural information simplified to something similar to: *Insert the following short description:* (**text**)

2. In the Element Catalog, double click shortdesc.

    The element shortdesc is inserted. Do not click any other location since the insertion point is automatically placed in the shortdesc.

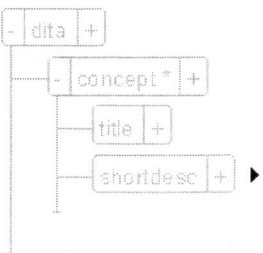

3. Type the following content: **Printing your photos is a great way to share images with people who do not have access to a computer.**

Insert the concept body

In this section you insert the body for the concept and add content to a paragraph.

1. In the Structure View, click immediately below the element *shortdesc*.

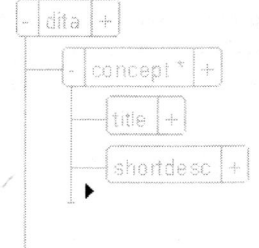

2.   In the Element Catalog, double click conbody.

The element conbody is inserted. The nested child p is also automatically inserted. Do not click any other location since the insertion point is automatically placed in the p.

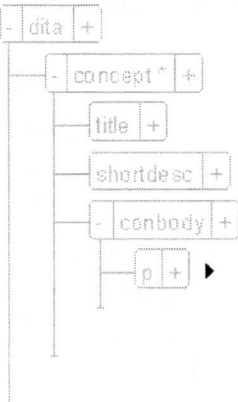

3.   Type the following content: **A wide variety of photo printing options exist. You can print on photo quality paper with high quality inkjet printers to create photographs that appear very similar to the printouts from many professional printing outlets.**

Add a new paragraph

In this section, you learn how to add another paragraph element.

1.   In the Structure View, click immediately below the element *p*.

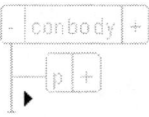

2.   In the Element Catalog, double click p.

A second element p is inserted. Do not click any other location since the insertion point is automatically placed in the p.

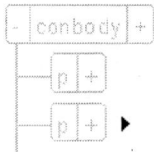

3. Type the following content: **Many companies provide excellent photo printers. A short list includes:**

Do not click elsewhere or reposition the cursor in any way.

Add an unordered list

In this section, you learn how to add an unordered list element. The list will be added within a paragraph. This ensures that both the list and the paragraph would be selected as one object.

1. Ensure that the insertion point is still at the end of the content of the element paragraph (before the tag) that contains the following text: *Many companies provide excellent photo printers. A short list includes:*

2. In the Element Catalog, double click ul.

A bulleted list is inserted and the nested child ul is added as is the nested child p.

3. Type following content: **Howitz Pictured**

4. Click the minus sign to the left of the *li* to collapse the element.

5. Click below the *li*.

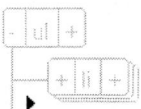

6. In the Element Catalog, double click li.

   A list item and nested child p are inserted.

7. Complete the list to appear as seen below:

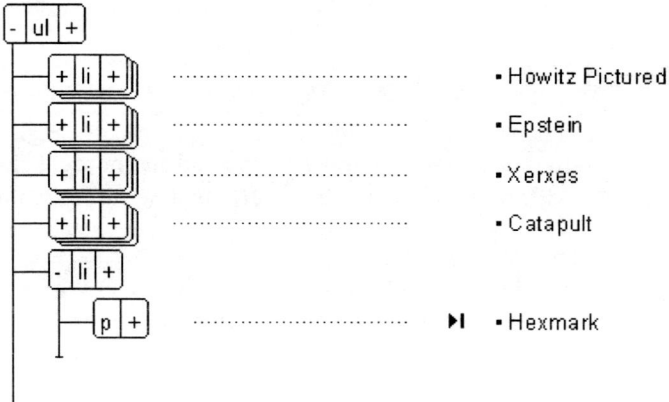

8. Save and close the file.

Tutorial 3

Work with structure

Overview

This tutorial teaches you the basics of working with structured documents.

This section contains the following topics:

- *Tutorial overview*
- *Opening a previously created DITA concept*
- *Save the file*
- *Convert an unordered list to an ordered list*
- *Add a new paragraph*
- *Wrap content in tags*
- *Remove tags*
- *Change a paragraph to a note*
- *Delete an element*
- *Convert an unordered list to an ordered list*

Tutorial overview

This tutorial guides you through the ongoing structural development of a basic DITA concept. It reviews several of the basic ideas related to working with structure and identifying elements in their relationships with each other.

The tutorial assumes a default installation of Adobe FrameMaker 8.0. If your product has been customized, some of the default options may not be available.

As the third tutorial, some of the detailed information in earlier tutorials is set aside and procedures are simplified in the way they are written.

Opening a previously created DITA concept

In this section, you open an existing DITA concept. It is stored in a default location. If you are not placing your tutorial files on the root of your local hard drive, some of the following steps may differ.

Information on "Open samples from the previous tutorial" can be found on page 232. Information on "Open a standalone sample" can be found on page 232.

Open samples from the previous tutorial

If you have not completed the previous tutorial, proceed to *Open a standalone sample*. If you have completed the previous tutorial proceed with the following steps.

1. If required, launch FrameMaker.
2. Select File > Open.
3. Navigate to *c:\tutorials\fm8dita\tutorial_02*.
4. Select the file *c_PrintingFiles.xml*, which was created in the previous tutorial.
5. Click Open .

Open a standalone sample

If you have completed the previous tutorial do not perform the following steps.

1. If required, launch FrameMaker.
2. Select File > Open.
3. Navigate to *c:\tutorials\fm8dita\tutorial_03*.
4. Select the file *Tutorial_03_Start.xml*.
5. Click Open .

Save the file

1. Navigate to your hard drive root directory.
   In this tutorial, the location is assumed to be c:\.
2. Open the folder named *tutorials*.
3. Within the *tutorials* folder open the folder named *fm8dita*.

4. If required, within the *fm8dita* folder create a new folder named **tutorial_03**.

    The path you have created is *c:\tutorials\fm8dita\tutorial_03*.

5. Open the *tutorial_03* folder.

    This will be the location the file is saved to.

6. If required, under File name, type **c_PrintingFiles.xml**.

7. Click [Save] .

Convert an unordered list to an ordered list

In this section, you learn how to modify one type of list element to another type.

1. If required, open the Structure View and the Element Catalog.

2. Select the *ul* element.

3. In the Element Catalog, select *ol*.

4. Click [Change...] .

    The list type is changed.

    1)   Howitz Pictured

    2)   Epstein

    3)   Xerxes

    4)   Catapult

    5)   Hexmark

5. Collapse the list.

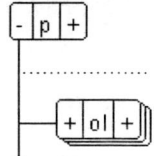

6. Collapse the paragraph.

Add a new paragraph

In this section, you add a paragraph.

1. In the Structure View, click immediately below the element *p*.

2. In the Element Catalog, double click p.

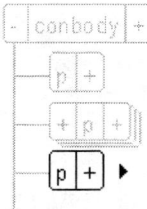

3. Type the following content: **Before buying a printer evaluate the total costs including paper stock, inkjet cartridges and regular maintenance. The least (or the most) expensive printer may not be the best printer.**

Wrap content in tags

In this section, you learn how to tag text content so that it is contained in an element.

1. Select the text: *evaluate the total costs*

    > Before buying a printer evaluate the total costs including paper stock, inkjet cartridges and regular maintenance. The least (or the most) expensive printer may not be the best printer.

2. In the Element Catalog, double click the element *b*.

    The content is wrapped in the tags for bold and is automatically formatted.

3. Select the text: *paper stock, inkjet cartridges and regular maintenance*

> Before buying a printer **evaluate the total costs** including paper stock, inkjet cartridges and regular maintenance. The least (or the most) expensive printer may not be the best printer.

4. In the Element Catalog, double click the element *i*.

The content is wrapped in the tags for italic and is automatically formatted.

Remove tags

1. Select the *i* element.

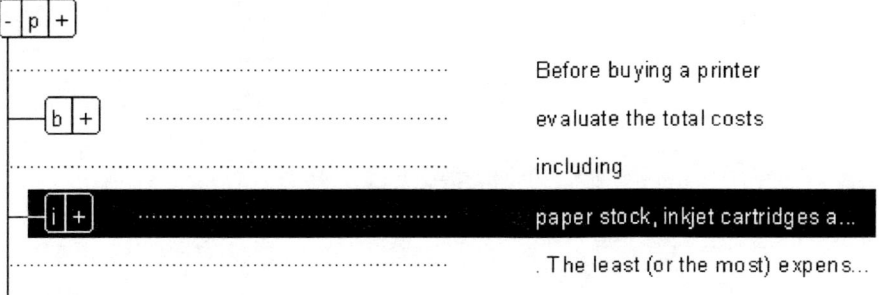

2. Select Element > Unwrap.

The italic element is removed but the untagged text remains.

3. Click the secondary mouse button in the *b* element.

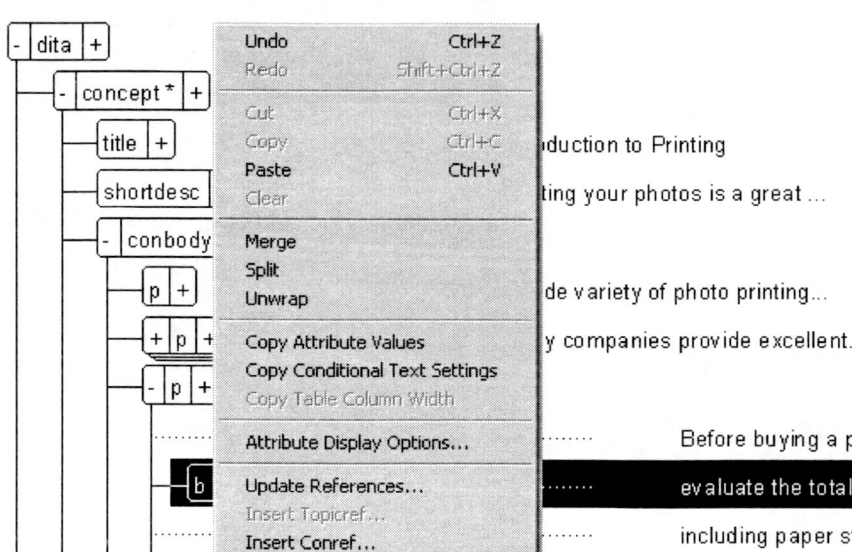

4. Select Unwrap.

Change a paragraph to a note

1. Select the element *p* that contains the text: *Before buying a printer...the best printer.*

2. In the Element Catalog select *note*.

3. Click **Change...** .

   The paragraph is changed to a <note> element and prefixed with the text *Note:* automatically.

---

4) Catapult

5) Hexmark

NOTE: *Before buying a printer evaluate the total costs including paper stock, inkjet cartridges and regular maintenance. The least (or the most) expensive printer may not be the best printer.*

Delete an element

1.   Select the *note* element.

2.   Press *Delete*.

Convert an unordered list to an ordered list

1.   Change the list back to an unordered list.

   This can be done by selecting the element *ol* and using the Element Catalog to select the *ul* and applying the change.

2.   Save and close the file.

Tutorial 4

Work with topics

Overview

This tutorial teaches you the basics of working with structured documents.

This section contains the following topics:

- *Tutorial overview*
- *Create a new topic*
- *Close a topic*

Tutorial overview

This tutorial guides you through working with DITA topics.

The tutorial assumes a default installation of Adobe FrameMaker 8.0. If your product has been customized, some of the default options may not be available.

As the fourth tutorial, much of the step-by-step information in earlier tutorials is not detailed and procedures are simplified in the way they are written.

Create a new topic

In this section, you learn the basics of creating the DITA topic.

Note

In subsequent tutorials, you may see this procedural information simplified to something similar to: *Create a new concept titled* **Introduction to Printing**.

1. Launch FrameMaker.

2. Select DITA > New DITA File > New <topic>.
   The Enter a new DITA topic file name dialog box displays.

3. Navigate to your hard drive root directory.
   In this tutorial, the location is assumed to be c:\.

4. Open the folder named *tutorials*.

5. Within the *tutorials* folder open the folder named *fm8dita*.

6. If required, within the *fm8dita* folder create a new folder named **tutorial_04**.
   The path you have created is *c:\tutorials\fm8dita\tutorial_04*.

7. Open the *tutorial_04* folder.
   This will be the location the file is saved to.

8. If required, under File name, type **FAQ.xml**.

9. Click [Select].
   A new topic is created and automatically populated with placeholder content for the title element.

10. Replace the placeholder content *Topic Title* with **Frequently Asked Questions**.

11. Using the Structure View and the Element Catalog insert a *shortdesc*.

12. Type the following content: **This topic lists a collection of questions we are often asked about our software.**

13. Using the Structure View and the Element Catalog insert a *body* and a nested *p*.

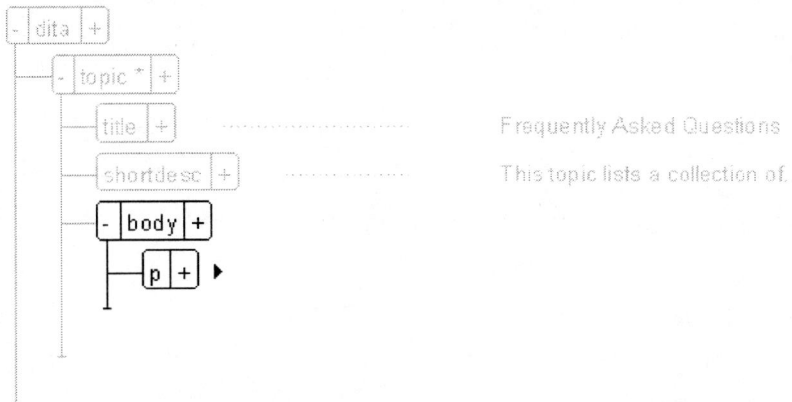

14. Type the following content: **The FAQ is organized by operating system. Therefore, questions related to Windows, Macintosh and Linux are sorted into three categories. Within each category is more information on the specific OS. For example, Windows Vista and Windows XP questions are grouped under the Windows section.**

Close a topic

1. Select File > Close.

2. When prompted, save the file.

Tutorial 5

Work with concepts

Overview

This tutorial teaches you the basics of working with a DITA concept.

This section contains the following topics:

- *Tutorial overview*
- *Create a new concept*
- *Develop the short description*
- *Modify content, change views, save and close*

Tutorial overview

This tutorial guides you through working with DITA concepts and revisits ideas from Tutorial 1: Get started with FrameMaker.

The tutorial assumes a default installation of Adobe FrameMaker 8.0. If your product has been customized, some of the default options may not be available.

As the fifth tutorial, much of the step-by-step information in earlier tutorials is not detailed and procedures are simplified in the way they are written.

Create a new concept

In this section, you learn the basics of creating the DITA concept.

1. Launch FrameMaker.

2. Using the DITA menu, create a new concept.

3. Navigate to the tutorials folder.

4. If required, within the *fm8dita* folder, create a new folder named **tutorial_05**.

5. Open the *tutorial_05* folder.
   This is the location the file is to be saved to.

6. Under File name, type **c_SavingFiles.xml**.

7. Click [Select].
   A new concept is created and automatically populated with placeholder content for the title element.

8. Replace the placeholder content Topic Title with **Saving Files**.

> **Note**
>
> The tutorials folder will be c:\tutorials\fm8dita\ with an appropriate subfolder for the tutorial number for all subsequent tutorials.

Develop the short description

1. Using the Structure View and the Element Catalog insert a *shortdesc*.

2. Type the following short description: **Saved files are stored on a server, hard drive, online or other location for later retrieval.**

Modify content, change views, save and close

In this section, you learn how to modify the paragraph placeholder.

1. Using the Structure View and the Element Catalog insert a *conbody* and a nested *p*.

2. Type the following content: **When saving files there are a variety of decisions that need to be made in regards to the location to save to. In addition, most software tools allow you to select from a variety of file formats when saving.**

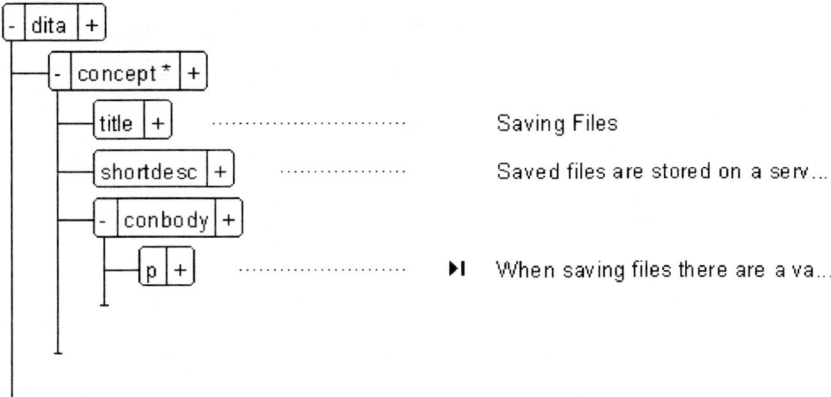

3. Select and deselect View > Element Boundaries (As Tags) to see the content with and without the structural tags.

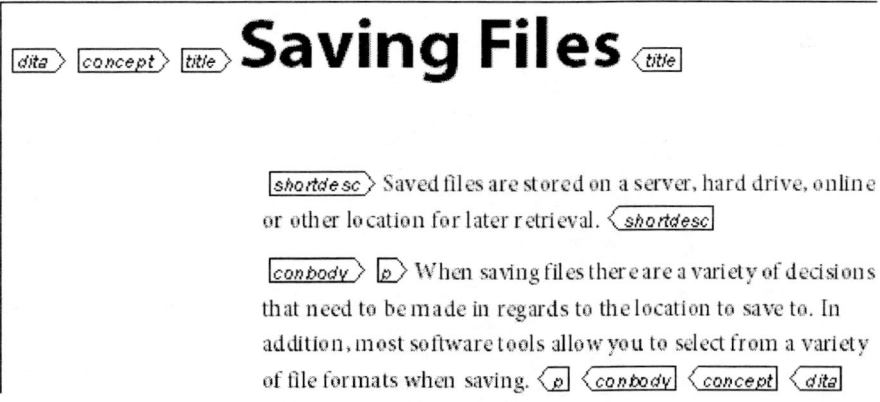

4. Select and deselect View > Element Boundaries to see the content with and without the square brackets.

5. Save and close the file.

Tutorial 6

Work with metadata

Overview

This tutorial teaches you the basics of working with DITA metadata in the prolog.

This section contains the following topics:

- *Tutorial overview*
- *Opening a previously created DITA concept*
- *Save the concept*
- *Adding initial metadata information*
- *Adding additional metadata information*

Tutorial overview

This tutorial guides you through working with DITA to create metadata in the prolog.

The tutorial assumes a default installation of Adobe FrameMaker 8.0. If your product has been customized, some of the default options may not be available.

As the sixth tutorial, most of the step-by-step information in earlier tutorials is not detailed and procedures are simplified in the way they are written.

Opening a previously created DITA concept

In this section, you open an existing DITA concept. It is stored in a default location. If you are not placing your tutorial files on the root of your local hard drive, some of the following steps may differ.

Information on "Open samples from a previous tutorial" can be found on page 248. Information on "Open a standalone sample" can be found on page 248.

Open samples from a previous tutorial

If you have not completed the previous tutorials, proceed to *Open a standalone sample*. If you have completed the previous tutorials proceed with the following steps.

1. If required, launch FrameMaker.

2. Select File > Open.

3. Navigate to *c:\tutorials\fm8dita\tutorial_05*.

4. Select the file *c_SavingFiles.xml*.

5. Click Open .

6. If required, select DITA-Topic-FM and click Continue .

Open a standalone sample

If you have completed the previous tutorial do not perform the following steps.

1. If required, launch FrameMaker.

2. Select File > Open.

3. Navigate to *c:\tutorials\fm8dita\tutorial_06*.

4. Select the file *Tutorial_06_Start.xml*.

5. Click Open .

6. If required, select DITA-Topic-FM and click Continue .

Save the concept

In this section, you save the file as c_PrintingFilesWithProlog.xml in the tutorials folder.

1. Select File > Save As.

   The Save As dialog box displays.

2. Navigate to the tutorials folder.

3. If required, within the *fm8dita* folder, create a new folder named **tutorial_06**.

4. Open the *tutorial_06* folder.

   This is the location the file is to be saved to.

5. Under File name, type **c_SavingFilesWithProlog.xml**.

6. Click [Save].

Adding initial metadata information

In this section you create a variety of metadata for the concept.

Not all types of metadata are added, but enough variety is inserted to explain in general terms how to modify metadata.

Add author metadata

1. Display the Structure View and the Element Catalog.

2. Click between the *shortdesc* and *conbody* elements.

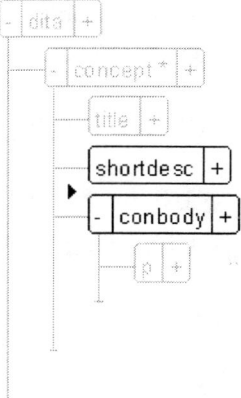

3. Using the Structure View and the Element Catalog insert a *prolog* and a nested *author*.

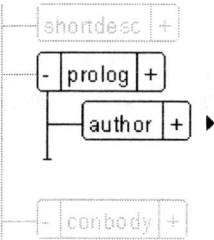

4. Type your full name.

   For example, type Noah Macleander or Vicky Lee.

5. Click below the *author* element.

6. Type another full name for an additional author.

   Notice that the first author is prefixed by the phrase Author: and the each subsequent author is separated from the first with a comma.

7. Repeat step 5 through step 6 as required if you would like to add other authors.

8. Using the Structure View, rearrange the *author* elements by dragging and dropping one above the other.

   The prefix automatically changes based on the order of the *author* elements.

Saved files are stored on a server, hard drive, online or other location for later retrieval.

AUTHOR: VICKY LEE, NOAH MACLEANDER

When saving files there are a variety of decisions that need to be made in regards to the location to save to. In addition, most software tools allow you to select from a variety of file formats when saving.

Add audience metadata

1. In the Structure View, click below the last *author*.

2. Using the Element Catalog insert a *metadata* and a nested *audience*.

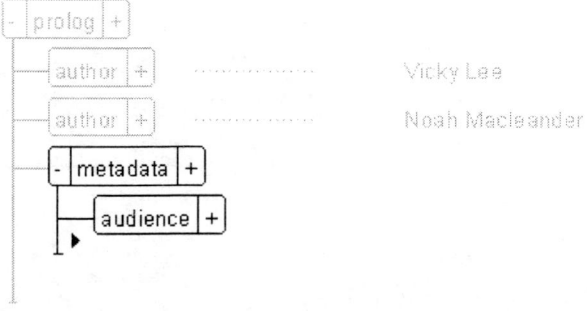

3. Click the plus sign to the right of the element *audience*.

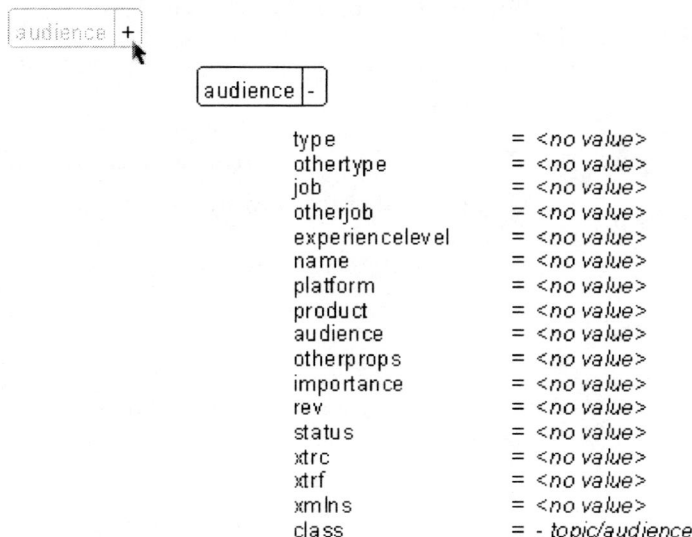

4. Double click the attribute *type*.

5. From the attribute choice popup select user.

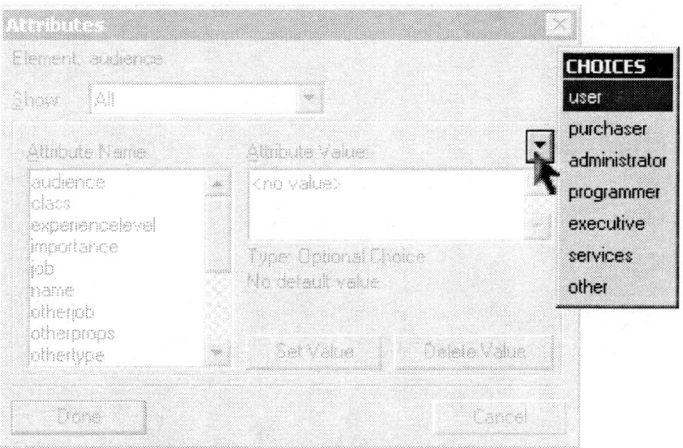

6. Click [Set Value].

7. Under Attribute Name, select job.

8. From the attribute choice popup select using.

9. Click [Set Value].

10. Set the attribute experiencelevel to novice and click [Set Value].

11. Click [Done].

    The document prolog display is updated.

12. Click the minus sign to the right of the element *audience*.

    All attributes are hidden.

13. Click the plus sign to the right of the element *audience*.

    Only required or specified attributes are displayed.

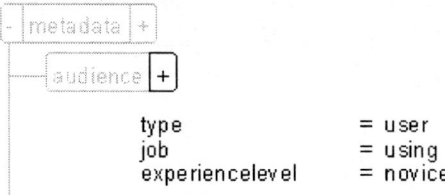

Add indexterms metadata

1. In the Structure View, click below the *audience*.

2. Using the Element Catalog insert a *keywords* and a nested *keyword*.

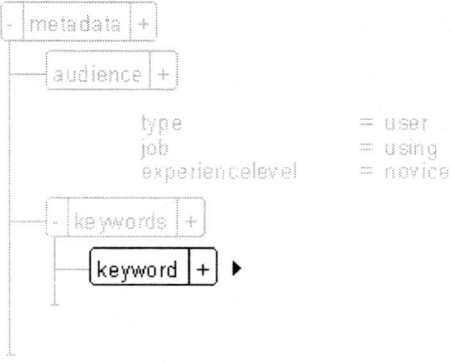

3. Type **Saving**.

    The document prolog display is updated with each new keyword.

4. Click below the *keyword* element.

5. Using the Element Catalog insert another *keyword*.

6. Type **Storing**.

7. Add *keyword* elements for the following words: **Server** and **Hard drive**.

Notice that the first keyword is prefixed by the phrase Keywords: and each subsequent keyword is separated from the first with a comma.

8. Collapse the element metadata.

Add permissions metadata

1. Display the Structure View click between the last *author* and *metadata* elements.

2. Using the Element Catalog insert *permissions*.

3. Set the attribute view to all and click [Set Value].

4. Click [Done].

The document prolog display is updated.

Adding additional metadata information

In this section you add additional metadata to the concept.

1. Add the authors **Lionel Eduardo** and **Nadia Riley** to the metadata.

AUTHOR: VICKY LEE, NOAH MACLEANDER, LIONEL EDUARDO, NADIA RILEY
FREELY DISTRIBUTABLE.
INTENDED AUDIENCE: USER
KEYWORDS: SAVING, STORING, SERVER, HARD DRIVE

2. In the element *permissions*, set the attribute view to entitled.

AUTHOR: VICKY LEE, NOAH MACLEANDER, LIONEL EDUARDO, NADIA RILEY
CONTENT PROVIDED FOR REVIEW BY A SPECIFIC AUDIENCE. CONTACT THE AUTHOR FOR DETAILS. DO NOT DISTRIBUTE, EVEN INTERNALLY.
INTENDED AUDIENCE: USER
KEYWORDS: SAVING, STORING, SERVER, HARD DRIVE

3. Toggle between View Element Boundaries (as Tags) to see the content with and without the structural tags.

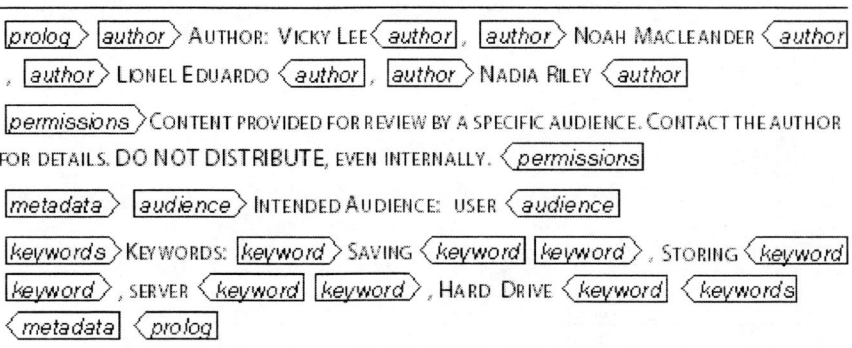

4. Save and close the file.

Tutorial 7

Publish topics

Overview

This tutorial teaches you the basics of publishing DITA topics to various outputs.

This section contains the following topics:

- *Tutorial overviewc*
- *Opening a previously created DITA concept*
- *Save the concept*
- *Publish a topic to HTML*
- *Publish a topic to PDF*

Tutorial overview

This tutorial guides you through working with DITA to create both HTML and PDF output from a single topic.

The tutorial assumes a default installation of Adobe FrameMaker 8.0. If your product has been customized, some of the default options may not be available.

Most of the step-by-step information in earlier tutorials is not detailed and procedures are simplified in the way they are written.

Opening a previously created DITA concept

In this section, you open an existing DITA concept. It is stored in a default location. If you are not placing your tutorial files on the root of your local hard drive, some of the following steps may differ.

Information on "Open samples from a previous tutorial" can be found on page 256.
Information on "Open a standalone sample" can be found on page 256.

Open samples from a previous tutorial

If you have not completed the previous tutorials, proceed to *Open a standalone sample*.
If you have completed the previous tutorials proceed with the following steps.

1. If required, launch FrameMaker.
2. Select File > Open.
3. Navigate to *c:\tutorials\fm8dita\tutorial_05*.
4. Select the file *c_SavingFiles.xml*.
5. Click Open .
6. If required, select DITA-Topic-FM and click Continue .

Open a standalone sample

If you have completed the previous tutorial do not perform the following steps.

1. If required, launch FrameMaker.
2. Select File > Open.
3. Navigate to *c:\tutorials\fm8dita\tutorial_07*.
4. Select the file *Tutorial_07_Start.xml*.
5. Click Open .
6. If required, select DITA-Topic-FM and click Continue .

Save the concept

In this section, you save the file as c_SavingFiles.xml in the tutorials folder.

1. Select File > Save As.
   The Save As dialog box displays.
2. Navigate to the tutorials folder.
3. If required, within the *fm8dita* folder, create a new folder named **tutorial_07**.
4. Open the *tutorial_07* folder.
   This is the location the file is to be saved to.

5. Under File name, type **c_SavingFiles.xml**.

6. Click [_Save_] .

Publish a topic to HTML

In this section you publish a topic to an HTML page.

1. Select File > Save As.

2. Under Save as type, select HTML.

3. If required, navigate to the *tutorial_07* folder.

4. Click [_Save_] .
    FrameMaker generates the file(s).

5. Use the Windows Explorer to navigate to the *tutorial_07* folder to view the generated file.

6. Close the generated file.

Publish a topic to PDF

In this section you publish a topic to a PDF page.

1. Select File > Save as PDF.

2. If required, navigate to the *tutorial_07* folder.

3. Click [_Save_] .
    The PDF Setup dialog is displayed.

4. Click [_Set_] .
    FrameMaker generates the file(s).

5. Use the Windows Explorer to navigate to the *tutorial_07* folder to view the generated file.

6. Close the generated file.

7. Close *c_SavingFiles.xml*.

Tutorial 8

Work with paragraphs

Overview

This tutorial teaches you the basics of working with a variety of paragraph content in a DITA concept.

This section contains the following topics:

- *Tutorial overview*
- *Create a new concept*
- *Develop the short description*
- *Develop initial paragraph content*
- *Insert notes*
- *Insert quotations*
- *Modify an existing paragraph*

Tutorial overview

This tutorial guides you through creating a DITA concept and populating it with a variety of text based content.

The tutorial assumes a default installation of Adobe FrameMaker 8.0. If your product has been customized, some of the default options may not be available.

Most of the step-by-step information in earlier tutorials is not detailed and procedures are simplified in the way they are written.

Create a new concept

In this section, you learn the basics of creating the DITA concept.

1. Launch FrameMaker.

2. Using the DITA menu, create a new concept.

3. Navigate to the tutorials folder.

> **✎ Note**
>
> The tutorials folder will be c:\tutorials\fm8dita\ with an appropriate subfolder for the tutorial number for all subsequent tutorials.

4. If required, within the *fm8dita* folder, create a new folder named **tutorial_08**.

5. Open the *tutorial_08* folder.
   This is the location the file is to be saved to.

6. Under File name, type **c_OpeningFiles.xml**.

7. Click **Select** .
   A new concept is created and automatically populated with placeholder content for the title element.

8. Replace the placeholder content Topic Title with **Opening Files**.

Develop the short description

1. Using the Structure View and the Element Catalog insert a *shortdesc*.

2. Type the following short description: **Files stored on a server, hard drive, online or other location can be opened for editing using a variety of tools.**

Develop initial paragraph content

In this section, you learn how to modify the paragraph placeholder.

1. Using the Structure View and the Element Catalog insert a *conbody* and a nested *p*.

2. Type the following content: **When opening files there are a variety of decisions that need to be made in regards to the software to use. Decisions related to software costs, features and support all play an important factor in deciding on the right tools to use.**

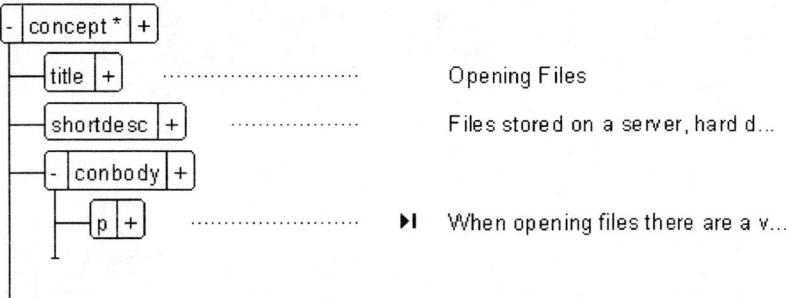

3. Click below the element *p* that contains the following text: *When opening files…right tools to use.*

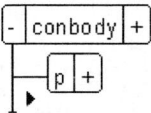

4. Using the Element Catalog insert a *p*.

5. Type the following content: **Once files have been opened a variety of options are available in regards to modifying the files. In many cases files are simply opened for printing or to review content. However, files can also be opened to modify content as needed.**

6. Press *Enter*.

    Notice that a new *p* element is inserted.

7. Type the following content: **XML files can be opened with a variety of software for editing or creation of content or for displaying content. Additionally, XML files can be transformed programmatically into other types of content.**

8. Add another *p*.

9.   Type the following content: **Software tools vary in price, but good visual editors of XML content can be purchased for under $1000. These tools often have stylesheets or templates that can be used to format content for both editing and for output to online or print deliverables.**

Insert notes

1.   Click below the element that contains the following text: *Software tools vary...online or print deliverables.*

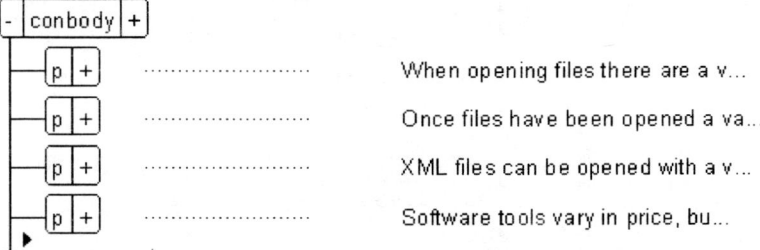

2.   Using the Element Catalog insert a *note* and a nested *p*.

3.   Type the following content: **Do not let the price alone be the deciding factor in your tools decision.**

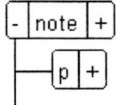

     NOTE: *Do not let the price alone be the deciding factor in your tools decision.*

4.   Collapse the *note* element.

Insert quotations

1. In the Structure View, click below the *p* containing the following text: *When opening files…right tools to use.*

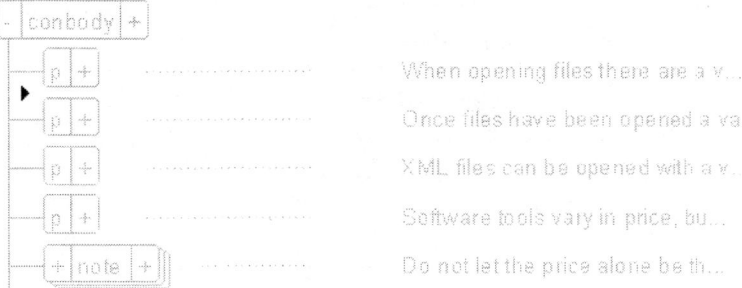

2. Using the Element Catalog insert an *lq* and a nested *p*.

3. Type the following content: **Many companies approach software purchasing in a dangerous fashion with the mistaken belief that a purchase should be done based on only price or familiarity, not the total cost of ownership, and this can result in far greater problems in the long term.**

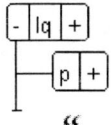

"

Many companies approach software purchasing in a dangerous fashion with the mistaken belief that a purchase should be done based on only price or familiarity, not the total cost of ownership, and this can result in far greater problems in the long term.

"

4. Collapse the *lq* element.

Modify an existing paragraph

The default paragraph can be wrapped into a variety of containers, including a note or a long quote.

1. In the Structure View, click below the *p* containing the following text: *When opening files…right tools to use.*

2. Using the Element Catalog select *note*.

3. Click [Wrap].

4. Select the element *note*.

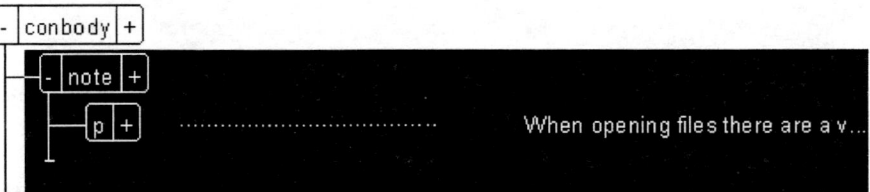

5. Using the Element Catalog select *lq*.

6. Click [Change...].

7. Select the element *lq*.

8. Select **Element > Unwrap**.

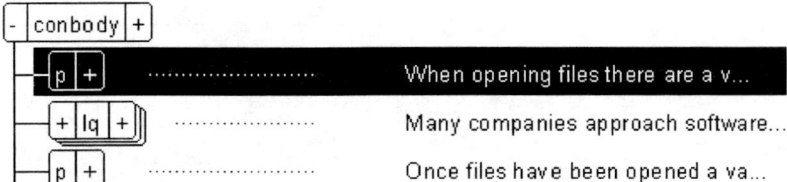

9. Save and close the file.

Tutorial 9

Work with lists

Overview

This tutorial teaches you the basics of working with a variety of paragraph content in a DITA concept.

This section contains the following topics:

- *Tutorial overview*
- *Opening a previously created DITA concept*
- *Save the concept*
- *Insert an ordered list*
- *Work with an unordered list*
- *Work with an ordered list*
- *Work with list items*
- *Work with a definition list*

Tutorial overview

This tutorial guides you through working with DITA concepts and revisits ideas from previous tutorials. It further expands on those ideas by having you develop a variety of list based content.

The tutorial assumes a default installation of Adobe FrameMaker 8.0. If your product has been customized, some of the default options may not be available.

Most of the step-by-step information in earlier tutorials is not detailed and procedures are simplified in the way they are written.

Opening a previously created DITA concept

In this section, you open an existing DITA concept. It is stored in a default location. If you are not placing your tutorial files on the root of your local hard drive, some of the following steps may differ.

Information on "Open samples from a previous tutorial" can be found on page 266. Information on "Open a standalone sample" can be found on page 266.

Open samples from a previous tutorial

If you have not completed the previous tutorials, proceed to *Open a standalone sample*. If you have completed the previous tutorials proceed with the following steps.

1. If required, launch FrameMaker.

2. Select File > Open.

3. Navigate to *c:\tutorials\fm8dita\tutorial_08*.

4. Select the file *c_OpeningFiles.xml*.

5. Click Open .

6. If required, select DITA-Topic-FM and click Continue .

Open a standalone sample

If you have completed the previous tutorial do not perform the following steps.

1. If required, launch FrameMaker.

2. Select File > Open.

3. Navigate to *c:\tutorials\fm8dita\tutorial_09*.

4. Select the file *Tutorial_09_Start.xml*.

5. Click Open .

6. If required, select DITA-Topic-FM and click Continue .

Save the concept

In this section, you save the file as c_SavingFilesWithLists.xml in the tutorials folder.

1. Select File > **Save As**.

2. Navigate to the tutorials folder.

3. If required, within the *fm8dita* folder, create a new folder named **tutorial_09**.

4. Open the *tutorial_09* folder.
   This is the location the file is to be saved to.

5. Under File name, type **c_OpeningFilesWithLists.xml**.

6. Click [Save].

Insert an ordered list

In this section you add additional paragraphs in a list.

1. If required, switch to Tags On view.

2. Ensure that the insertion point is at the end of the content of the element paragraph (before the tag) that contains the following text: *XML files can be opened...other types of content.*

3. Using the Structure View and the Element Catalog insert an *ol* and a nested *li* and nested *p*.

4. Add the following content:

> [p> XML files can be opened with a variety of software for editing or creation of content or for displaying content. Additionally, XML files can be transformed programatically into other types of content.
>
> 1)   [ol> [li> [p> Convert to PDF for print or online delivery <p] <li]
>
> 2)   [li> [p> Convert to HTML for online web based delivery <p] <li] <ol] <p]

Work with an unordered list

In this section, you learn how to add entries and reorganize an unordered list element.

1. Ensure that the insertion point is at the end of the content of the element paragraph (before the tag) that contains the following text: *Once files have been opened a...can also be opened to modify content as needed.*

2. Using the Structure View and the Element Catalog insert an *ul* and a nested *li* and nested *p.*

3. Add the following content:

    > $\boxed{p}$ Once files have been opened a variety of options are available in regards to modifying the files. In many cases files are simply opened for printing or to review content. However, files can also be opened to modify content as needed.
    >
    > - $\boxed{ul}$ $\boxed{li}$ $\boxed{p}$ Open for printing $\boxed{p}$ $\boxed{li}$
    > - $\boxed{li}$ $\boxed{p}$ Open for editing $\boxed{p}$ $\boxed{li}$ $\boxed{ul}$ $\boxed{p}$

Work with an ordered list

In this section, you modify an ordered list element.

1. Select the unordered list that contains the following text: *Open for printing...Open for editing.*

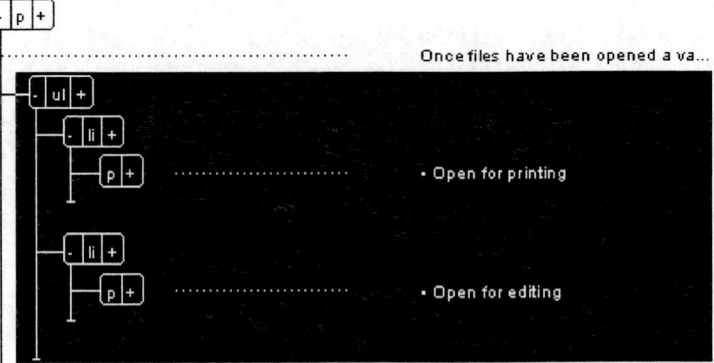

2. Delete the list.

3.   Using the Structure View and the Element Catalog insert an *ol* and a nested *li* and nested *p*.

4.   Add the following content:

5.   Click the – to the left of each *li* to collapse them.

6.   Press and hold Shift, then click the + to left of the first li to expand both of them.

7.   Press and hold Shift, then click the – to left of the first li to collapse both of them.

8.   Drag and drop the list items to reverse their order.

Work with list items

In this section you add additional elements to items in an existing list.

1.   Expand the li that contains the following text: *Open to edit*

2.   Click below the *p* element.

3.   Using the Element Catalog, add another *p* element.

4. Type the following content: **Some files can only be opened with the software used to create them.**

5. Press *Enter* to add another paragraph.

6. Type the following content: **Many file formats are proprietary to a software vendor, but XML is not.**

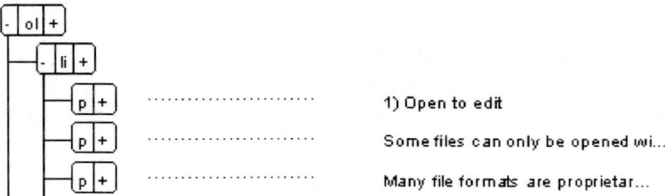

Work with a definition list

In this section you develop a definition list with terms and descriptions.

1. Ensure that the insertion point is at the end of the content of the element paragraph (before the tag) that contains the following text: *When opening files there are a...on the right tools to use.*

2. Using the Structure View and the Element Catalog insert a *dl* and a nested *dlentry* and nested *dt*.

3. Type the following content: **Costs**

4. Insert a *dd* immediately after the *dt*.

5. Type the following content: **May include initial purchase price as well as the cost of support, training and legacy file conversion.**

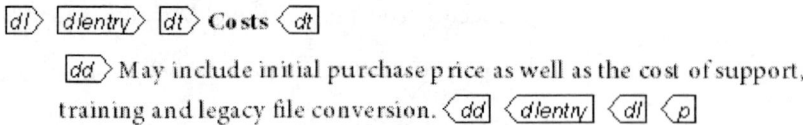

6. In the Structure View, collapse the *dlentry*.

7. Click below the *dlentry* and add another *dlentry* and nested *dt*.

8. Type the following content: **Features**

9. Insert a *dd* immediately after the *dt*.

10. Type the following content: **May include the ability to open other file formats, display content in both source and finished views, convert to other files formats or to provide restricted rights to specific users.**

`dl >` `dlentry >` `dt >` **Costs** `< dt`

> `dd >` May include initial purchase price as well as the cost of support, training and legacy file conversion. `< dd` `< dlentry`

`dlentry >` `dt >` **Features** `< dt`

> `dd >` May include the ability to open other file formats, display content in both source and finished views, convert to other files formats or to provide restricted rights to specific users. `< dd` `< dlentry` `< dl` `< p`

11. In the Structure View, collapse the *dlentry*.

12. Develop the definition list until it appears as seen below:

`dl >` `dlentry >` `dt >` **Costs** `< dt`

> `dd >` May include initial purchase price as well as the cost of support, training and legacy file conversion. `< dd` `< dlentry`

`dlentry >` `dt >` **Features** `< dt`

> `dd >` May include the ability to open other file formats, display content in both source and finished views, convert to other files formats or to provide restricted rights to specific users. `< dd` `< dlentry`

`dlentry >` `dt >` **Support** `< dt`

> `dd >` May include support provided by the software tool vendor, the user community, or internal IT teams. `< dd` `< dlentry` `< dl` `< p`

13. In the Structure View, collapse all three *dlentry* elements.

14. Save and close *c_SavingFilesWithLists.xml*.

Tutorial 10

Work with domains

Overview

This tutorial teaches you the basics of working with a variety of domain content in a DITA concept.

This section contains the following topics:

- *Tutorial overview*
- *Opening a previously created DITA topic*
- *Save the topic*
- *Work with typographic formats*
- *Work with code phrase and codeblock*
- *Work with software elements*
- *Work with user interface elements*

Tutorial overview

This tutorial guides you through working with DITA topics and revisits ideas from previous tutorials. It further expands on those ideas by having you develop a variety of domain based content.

The tutorial assumes a default installation of Adobe FrameMaker 8.0. If your product has been customized, some of the default options may not be available.

Most of the step-by-step information in earlier tutorials is not detailed and procedures are simplified in the way they are written.

Opening a previously created DITA topic

In this section, you open an existing DITA topic. It is stored in a default location. If you are not placing your tutorial files on the root of your local hard drive, some of the following steps may differ.

Information on "Open samples from the previous tutorial" can be found on page 274. Information on "Open a standalone sample" can be found on page 274.

Open samples from the previous tutorial

If you have not completed the previous tutorials, proceed to *Open a standalone sample*. If you have completed the previous tutorials proceed with the following steps.

1. If required, launch FrameMaker.

2. Select **File > Open**.

3. Navigate to *c:\tutorials\fm8dita\tutorial_04*.

4. Select the file *FAQ.xml*.

5. Click | **Open** | .

6. If required, select DITA-Topic-FM and click | **Continue** | .

Open a standalone sample

If you have completed the previous tutorial do not perform the following steps.

1. If required, launch FrameMaker.

2. Select **File > Open**.

3. Navigate to *c:\tutorials\fm8dita\tutorial_10*.

4. Select the file *Tutorial_10_Start.xml*.

5. Click | **Open** | .

6. If required, select DITA-Topic-FM and click | **Continue** | .

Save the topic

In this section, you save the topic as FAQ.xml in the tutorials folder.

1.   Select File > Save As.

2.   Navigate to the tutorials folder.

3.   If required, within the *xmad* folder, create a new folder named *tutorial_10*.

4.   Open the *tutorial_10* folder.
     This is the location the file is to be saved to.

5.   Under File name, type *FAQ.xml*.

6.   Click [Save] .

Work with typographic formats

In this section you apply typographic formatting to make words appear in bold, italic or underlined format.

1.   Display the Structure View and the Element Catalog.

2.   Select the word Windows.

3.   In the Element Catalog, double click b.

4.   Select the word Macintosh.

5.   In the Element Catalog, double click i.

6.   Select the word Linux.

7.   In the Element Catalog, double click u.

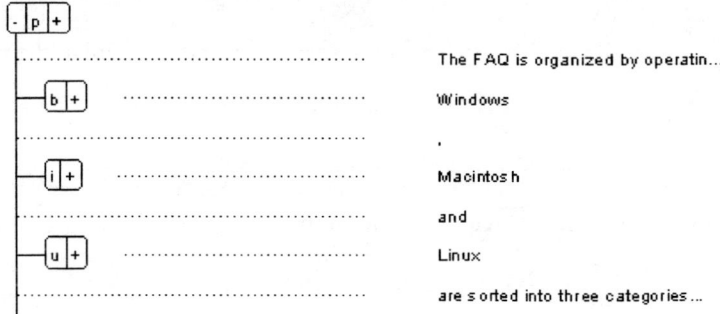

8.   Select the element *b*.

9.   Select Element > Unwrap.

10. Click the secondary mouse button in the element *i*.

11. Select Unwrap.

12. Remove the tags from the underlined text.

Work with code phrase and codeblock

The representation of a code phrase is usually inline as a text range. A codeblock is usually multiple lines of code.

1.   In the Structure View, click below the element *p*.

2.   Using the Structure View and the Element Catalog insert a *section* and a nested *title*.

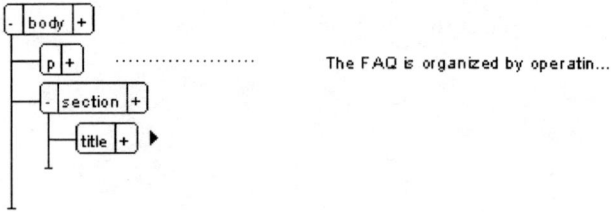

3.   Type the following content: **Windows**

4.   Below the *title*, insert a *p*.

5.   Type the following content: **Q: How can I exit the Windows command prompt?**

6.   Add another paragraph and type the following content: **A: Type**

7. Add a single space and double click codeph in the Element Catalog.

8. Type the word **exit** in the code phrase.

9. In the Structure View, click below the *codeph* element.

10. Press *Spacebar* once and type the following content: **and press Enter.**

11. Select View > Element Boundaries (as Tags).

12. Add another paragraph with the following content: **Q: What does the content of a batch file look like?**

13. Add another paragraph with the following content: **A: Batch files contain numerous lines of code and may appear as follows:**

14. Using the Element Catalog, insert a *codeblock*.

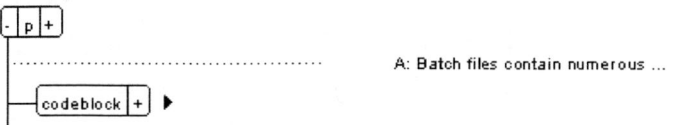

15. Type the following content. Note the line breaks and recreate them by pressing *Ctrl+Enter* at the end of the code lines:

pause
dir c:
pause
dir c:\windows

16. Collapse the element *p* that contains the *codeblock*.

Work with software elements

In this section you add a variety of software elements to a document.

1. Add another paragraph with the following content: **Q: How can I set the time using the command prompt?**

2. Add another paragraph with the following content: **A: Type**

3. Add a single space and double click userinput in the Element Catalog.

4. Type the word **time** in the user input.

5. In the Structure View, click below the *userinput* element.

6. Press *Spacebar* once and type the following content: **and press Enter.**

7. Add another paragraph and replace the placeholder text with the following content: **The system displays the current time, for example: The current time is: 23:01:10.11**

8. Select the content **The current time is: 23:01:10.11**

9. Using the Element Catalog, double–click *systemoutput*.

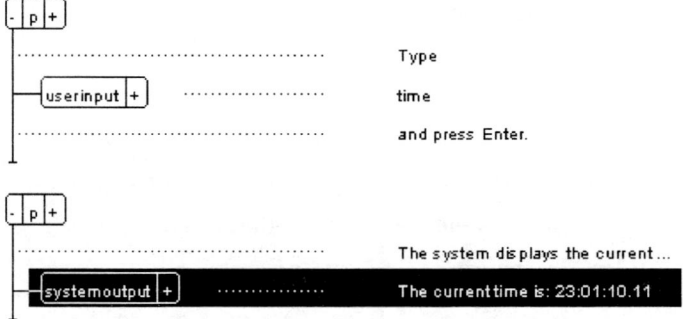

10. Collapse both *p* elements.

Work with user interface elements

In this section you add a variety of user interface elements to a document.

1. Add another paragraph with the following content: **Q: How can I print a file?**

2. Add another paragraph with the following content: **A: Click the Print icon.**

3. Select the word *Print*.

4. Using the Element Catalog, double–click *uicontrol*.

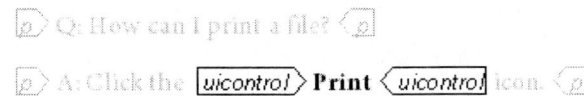

5. Add another paragraph and replace the placeholder text with the following content:
You can also use the menu. To do so, select File Print.

6. Select the word *File*.

7. Using the Element Catalog, double–click *uicontrol*.

8. Wrap the word *Print* in *uicontrol*.

9. Delete the space between the two elements.
This is represented by <whitespace> in the Structure View.

10. Select both *uicontrol* elements.
This can be done by clicking one element and pressing and holding *Shift* while clicking in the second element and then releasing *Shift* or, in the document view, drag from one *uicontrol* element into the next.

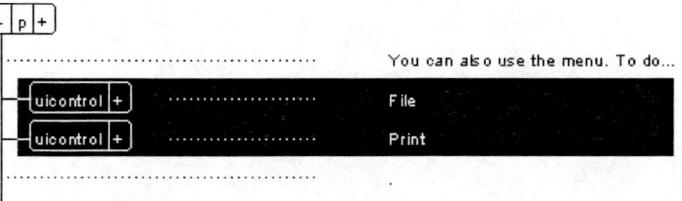

11. Using the Element Catalog, double–click *menucascade*.

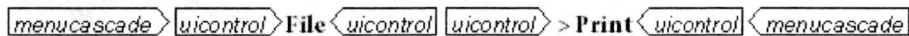

12. Save and close *FAQ.xml*.

Tutorial 11

Work with footnotes

Overview

This tutorial teaches you the basics of working with footnotes in a DITA concept.

This section contains the following topics:

- *Tutorial overview*
- *Opening a previously created DITA topic*
- *Save the topic*
- *Work with footnotes*

Tutorial overview

This tutorial guides you through working with DITA to create footnotes.

The tutorial assumes a default installation of Adobe FrameMaker 8.0. If your product has been customized, some of the default options may not be available.

Most of the step-by-step information in earlier tutorials is not detailed and procedures are simplified in the way they are written.

Opening a previously created DITA topic

In this section, you open an existing DITA topic. It is stored in a default location. If you are not placing your tutorial files on the root of your local hard drive, some of the following steps may differ.

Information on "Open samples from a previous tutorial" can be found on page 282. Information on "Open a standalone sample" can be found on page 282.

| **Open samples from a previous tutorial** | If you have not completed the previous tutorials, proceed to *Open a standalone sample*. If you have completed the previous tutorials proceed with the following steps. |

1. If required, launch FrameMaker.

2. Select File > Open.

3. Navigate to *c:\tutorials\fm8dita\tutorial_08*.

4. Select the file *c_OpeningFiles.xml*.

5. Click Open .

6. If required, select DITA-Topic-FM and click Continue .

Open a standalone sample

If you have completed the previous tutorial do not perform the following steps.

1. If required, launch FrameMaker.

2. Select File > Open.

3. Navigate to *c:\tutorials\fm8dita\tutorial_11*.

4. Select the file *Tutorial_11_Start.xml*.

5. Click Open .

6. If required, select DITA-Topic-FM and click Continue .

Save the topic

In this section, you save the topic as Footnotes.xml in the tutorials folder.

1. Select File > Save As.

2. Navigate to the tutorials folder.

3. If required, within the *fm8dita* folder, create a new folder named *tutorial_11*.

4. Open the *tutorial_11* folder.
   This is the location the file is to be saved to.

5. Under File name, type *Footnotes.xml*.

6. Click Save .

Work with footnotes

In this section you work with footnotes in a concept.

1. Display the Structure View and the Element Catalog.

2. Ensure that the insertion point is at the end of the content and after the full stop (.) in the element *p* that contains the following text: *When opening files there are a…right tools to use.*

3. Using the Element Catalog insert an *fn* element.

4. Type the following content: **Contact us to receive a free matrix of primary XML editing tools that support DITA.**

5. In the element *note* place the insertion point after: *…in your tools decision* but before the full stop (.) in the sentence.

6. Using the Element Catalog insert an *fn* element.

7. Replace the placeholder text with the following content: **Not all software tools may have support for features you need, or plan to use. First decide on what you need, then evaluate tools and review pricing for tools that meet your needs.**

8. Review the structure noting the two *fn* elements.

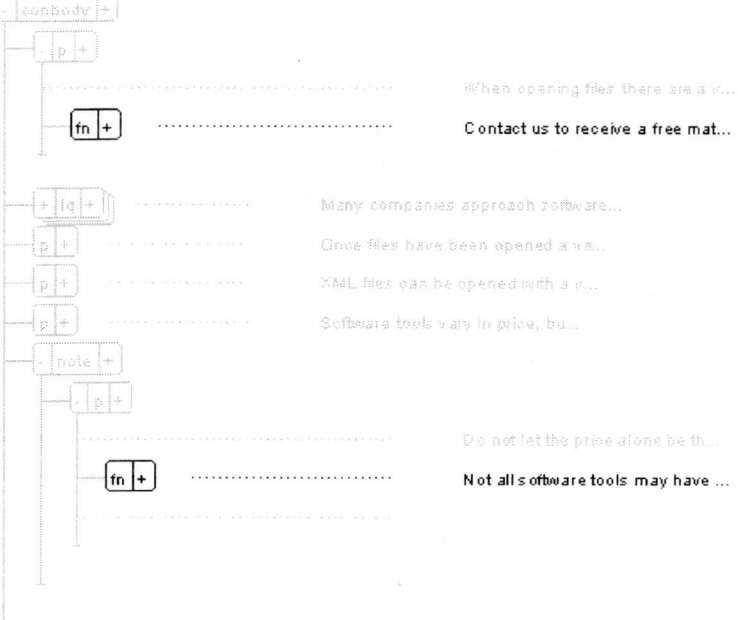

9. Save and close *Footnotes.xml*.

Tutorial 12

Work with indices

Overview

This tutorial teaches you the basics of indexing in a DITA concept.

This section contains the following topics:

- *Tutorial overview*
- *Opening a previously created DITA topic*
- *Save the topic*
- *Work with single-level index entries*
- *Generate a standalone index*
- *Modify existing index entries*

Tutorial overview

This tutorial guides you through working with DITA to create index entries.

The tutorial assumes a default installation of Adobe FrameMaker 8.0. If your product has been customized, some of the default options may not be available.

Most of the step-by-step information in earlier tutorials is not detailed and procedures are simplified in the way they are written.

Opening a previously created DITA topic

In this section, you open an existing DITA topic. It is stored in a default location. If you are not placing your tutorial files on the root of your local hard drive, some of the following steps may differ.

Information on "Open samples from a previous tutorial" can be found on page 286. Information on "Open a standalone sample" can be found on page 286.

Open samples from a previous tutorial

If you have not completed the previous tutorials, proceed to *Open a standalone sample*. If you have completed the previous tutorials proceed with the following steps.

1. If required, launch FrameMaker.

2. Select File > Open.

3. Navigate to *c:\tutorials\fm8dita\tutorial_08*.

4. Select the file *c_OpeningFiles.xml*.

5. Click [Open] .

6. If required, select DITA-Topic-FM and click [Continue] .

Open a standalone sample

If you have completed the previous tutorial do not perform the following steps.

1. If required, launch FrameMaker.

2. Select File > Open.

3. Navigate to *c:\tutorials\fm8dita\tutorial_12*.

4. Select the file *Tutorial_12_Start.xml*.

5. Click [Open] .

6. If required, select DITA-Topic-FM and click [Continue] .

Save the topic

In this section, you save the topic as Footnotes.xml in the tutorials folder.

1. Select File > Save As.

2. Navigate to the tutorials folder.

3. If required, within the *fm8dita* folder, create a new folder named **tutorial_12**.

4. Open the *tutorial_12* folder.

This is the location the file is to be saved to.

5. Under File name, type *Index.xml*.

6. Click ⟨ <u>S</u>ave ⟩.

Work with single-level index entries

In this section you work with index entries in a concept.

1. Ensure that the insertion point is at the start of the word *opening* in the element *p* that contains the following text: *When opening files there are a...right tools to use.*

    When opening files there are a variety of decisions that need to be made in regards to the software to use. Decisions related to software costs, features and support all play an important factor in deciding on the right tools to use.

2. Using the Element Catalog, insert an *indexterm*.

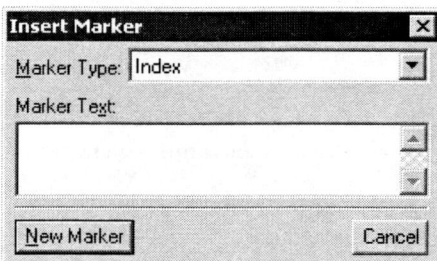

3. Under Marker Text type the words **opening files**.

4. Click ⟨ <u>N</u>ew Marker ⟩.

5. Click at the end of the word *software costs* in the first paragraph.

6. Using the Element Catalog, insert an *indexterm*.

7. Under Index entry type the word **software costs**.

8. Click ⟨ <u>N</u>ew Marker ⟩.

9. Continue to index the first paragraph for the words *features*, *support* and *tools* have *indexterms* associated with them.

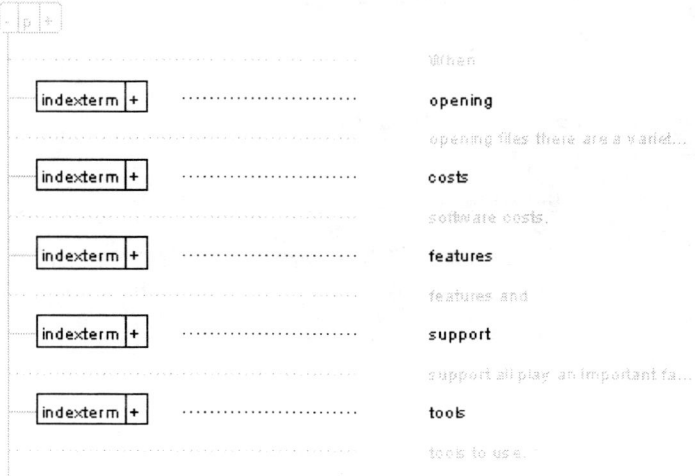

Generate a standalone index

In this section you create a standalone generated file listing indexterms alphabetically.

1. Select **Special > Standard Index.**

2. Click **Yes** to create a standalone index.

3. Click **Set** .

4. Review the default appearance of the content in the generated file.

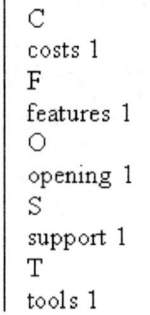

```
C
costs 1
F
features 1
O
opening 1
S
support 1
T
tools 1
```

5. Close the generated file but do not save it.

Modify existing index entries

In this section you modify index entries in a concept.

1. Using the Structure View, find the first indexterm that contains the words *opening files*.

2. Single-click the indexterm.

3. Select Special > Marker.

4. Modify the content to read **files, opening**.

1. Find the first indexterm that contains the word *tools*.

2. Double-click the entry.

3. Under Index entry modify the content to read **tools, software**.

1. Select Special > Standard Index.

2. Click [Yes] to create a standalone index.

3. Click [Set].

4. Review the appearance of the content in the generated file.

5. Close the generated file but do not save it.

6. Save and close *Index.xml*.

Tutorial 13

Work with attributes

Overview	This tutorial teaches you the basics of working with attributes in a DITA concept.
	This section contains the following topics:

- *Tutorial overview*
- *Opening a previously created DITA topic*
- *Save the topic*
- *Work with attributes*
- *Change the note type*

Tutorial overview

This tutorial guides you through working with DITA to modify attributes.

The tutorial assumes a default installation of Adobe FrameMaker 8.0. If your product has been customized, some of the default options may not be available.

Most of the step-by-step information in earlier tutorials is not detailed and procedures are simplified in the way they are written.

Opening a previously created DITA topic

In this section, you open an existing DITA topic. It is stored in a default location. If you are not placing your tutorial files on the root of your local hard drive, some of the following steps may differ.

Information on "Open samples from a previous tutorial" can be found on page 292.
Information on "Open a standalone sample" can be found on page 292.

Open samples from a previous tutorial

If you have not completed the previous tutorials, proceed to *Open a standalone sample*.
If you have completed the previous tutorials proceed with the following steps.

1. If required, launch FrameMaker.
2. Select File > Open.
3. Navigate to *c:\tutorials\fm8dita\tutorial_08*.
4. Select the file *c_OpeningFiles*.
5. Click Open .
6. If required, select DITA-Topic-FM and click Continue .

Open a standalone sample

If you have completed the previous tutorial do not perform the following steps.

1. If required, launch FrameMaker.
2. Select File > Open.
3. Navigate to *c:\tutorials\fm8dita\tutorial_13*.
4. Select the file *Tutorial_13_Start.xml*.
5. Click Open .
6. If required, select DITA-Topic-FM and click Continue .

Save the topic

In this section, you save the topic as Footnotes.xml in the tutorials folder.

1. Select File > Save As.
2. Navigate to the tutorials folder.
3. If required, within the *fm8dita* folder, create a new folder named *tutorial_13*.
4. Open the *tutorial_13* folder.
   This is the location the file is to be saved to.

5. Under File name, type **Attributes.xml**.

6. Click [Save] .

Work with attributes

In this section you work with attributes in a concept.

1. Display the Structure View and the Element Catalog.

2. Select Elements > Edit Attributes.

3. Select the element named *concept*.

4. In the Attributes dialog, click the attribute named *id*.

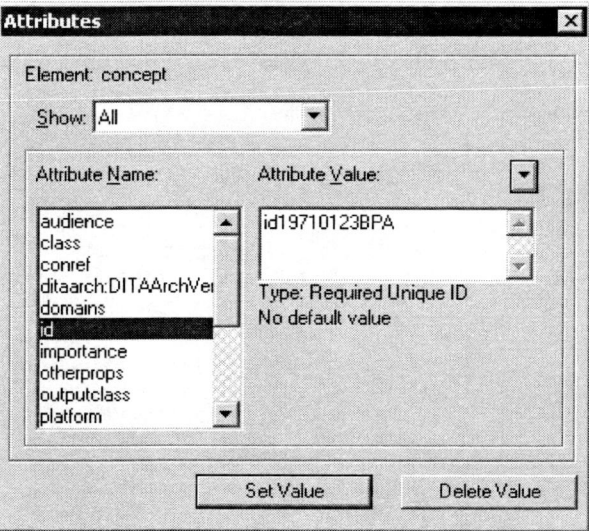

5. Review the value of the *id*.

6. In the Structure View, click the + to the right of the element named *concept*.

7. Review the value of the *id* noting it is the same as the id in the Attributes dialog.

8. In the document, scroll down to the element *note*.

    The format of the note is configured to display the word *Note* by default.

9. Expand the attribute values of the element *note*.

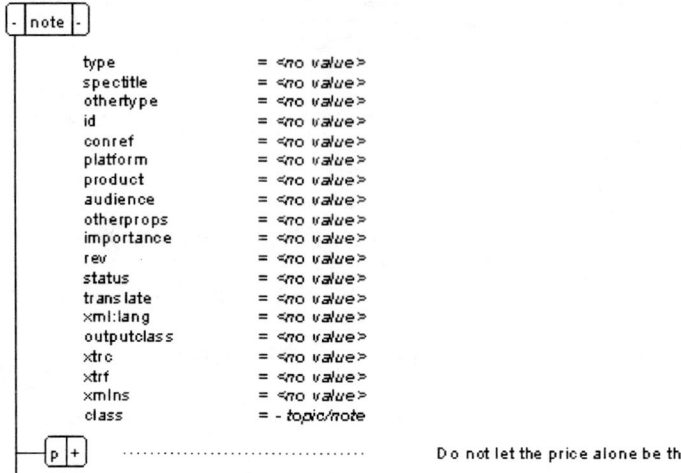

10. Review the attributes *othertype* and *type* in the Attributes dialog and in the Structure view noting that they are currently set to <no value>.

Change the note type

1. Click the plus sign to the right of the note to display its attributes.

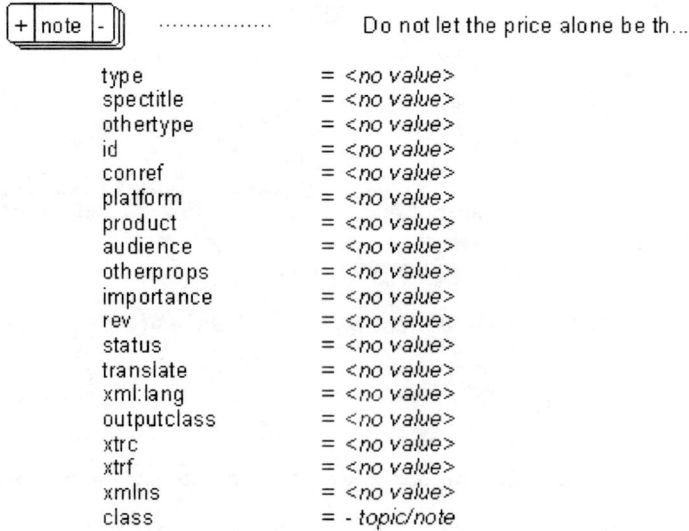

2. In the Attributes dialog, select *type*.

3. From the attribute choice popup select remember.

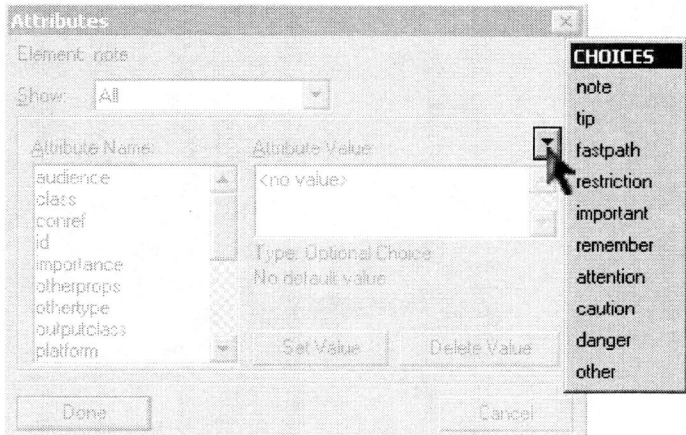

4. Click [Set Value].
   The value is modified and the note is prefixed with the word **Remember**.

5. Close the Attributes dialog.

6. Click the minus sign to the right of the element *note*.
   All attributes are hidden.

7. Click the plus sign to the right of the element *note*.
   Only required or specified attributes are displayed.

8. Double click the attribute *type*.

9. From the attribute choice popup select other.

10. Click [Set Value].

11. Click [Done].
    The *note* is updated with a message that the *othertype* value must be set.

12. Click the plus sign to the right of the element *note*.
    All attributes are displayed.

13. Double click the attribute *othertype*.

14. Under Attribute Value, type **Planning Ahead**.

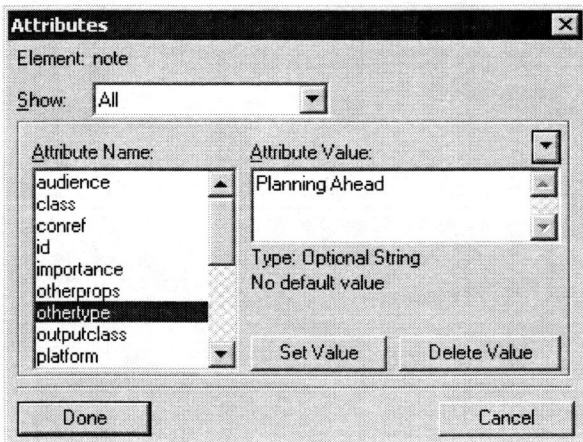

15. Click Set Value .

16. Click Done .

The *note* is updated with a message to set the *othertype* value.

17. Save and close the file.

Tutorial 14

Work with tables

Overview

This tutorial teaches you the basics of working with tables in a DITA concept.

This section contains the following topics:

- *Tutorial overview*
- *Opening a previously created DITA topic*
- *Save the topic*
- *Insert a basic table*
- *Add, move and delete content in a table*
- *Modify table properties*
- *Modify column widths*
- *Modify cell properties*
- *Merge and split cell content*

Tutorial overview

This tutorial guides you through working with DITA to develop and modify tables.

The tutorial assumes a default installation of Adobe FrameMaker 8.0. If your product has been customized, some of the default options may not be available.

Most of the step-by-step information in earlier tutorials is not detailed and procedures are simplified in the way they are written.

Opening a previously created DITA topic

In this section, you open an existing DITA topic. It is stored in a default location. If you are not placing your tutorial files on the root of your local hard drive, some of the following steps may differ.

Information on "Open samples from a previous tutorial" can be found on page 298. Information on "Open a standalone sample" can be found on page 298.

Open samples from a previous tutorial

If you have not completed the previous tutorials, proceed to *Open a standalone sample*. If you have completed the previous tutorials proceed with the following steps.

1. If required, launch FrameMaker.

2. Select File > Open.

3. Navigate to *c:\tutorials\fm8dita\tutorial_05*.

4. Select the file *c_SavingFiles.xml*, which was created in an earlier tutorial.

5. Click Open .

6. If required, select DITA-Topic-FM and click Continue .

Open a standalone sample

If you have completed the previous tutorial do not perform the following steps.

1. If required, launch FrameMaker.

2. Select File > Open.

3. Navigate to *c:\tutorials\fm8dita\tutorial_14*.

4. Select the file *Tutorial_14_Start.xml*.

5. Click Open .

6. If required, select DITA-Topic-FM and click Continue .

Save the topic

In this section, you save the topic as Footnotes.xml in the tutorials folder.

1. Select File > Save As.

2. Navigate to the tutorials folder.

3. If required, within the *fm8dita* folder, create a new folder named *tutorial_14*.

4. Open the *tutorial_14* folder.
    This is the location the file is to be saved to.

5. Under File name, type **Tables.xml**.

6. Click [Save].

Insert a basic table

In this section you insert a basic table in a concept.

1. Display the Structure View and the Element Catalog.

2. Ensure that the insertion point is at the end of the paragraph that contains the following text: *When saving files there are a...file formats when saving.*

3. Using the Element Catalog, insert an *indexterm*.
    The *Insert Table* dialog displays.

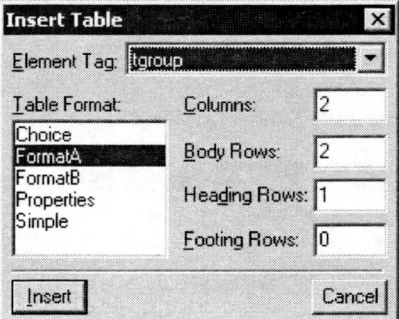

4. Under Table Format, select FormatA.

5. Under Columns, enter **2**.

6. Under Body Rows, enter **3**.

7. Under Heading Rows, select **1**.

8. Click Insert

9. Complete the table as seen below by typing content and pressing *Tab* to move from one cell to the next.

Format	Purpose
.html	Used by web pages.
.doc	Proprietary Microsoft Word files.
.xml	Non-proprietary coded content.

10. Click anywhere in the second column.

11. Select Table > Resize Columns.

12. Under To Width, enter **2.5"**.

13. Click Resize .

Add, move and delete content in a table

In this section you modify content in a basic table in a concept.

1. Place the insertion point anywhere in the row related to the *.doc* extension.

2. Select Table > Add Rows or Columns.

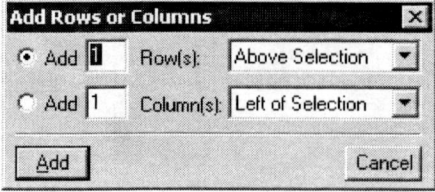

3. Under Row(s) select Below Selection.

4. Under Add, enter 2.

5. Click [Add].

6. In the first row, enter the values **.jpg** and **Web based graphics**.

7. In the second row, enter the values **.mp3** and **Music and sound files**.

8. In the Structure View, collapse the *thead*.

9. In the Structure View, collapse all *row* elements for the *tbody*.

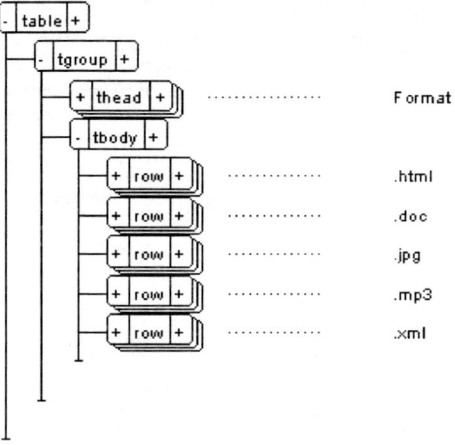

10. In the Structure View, drag and drop the first row element (.html) below the second row element (.doc).

 Tip

Look for the bold checkmark next to the row element to indicate a valid location to drop the element.

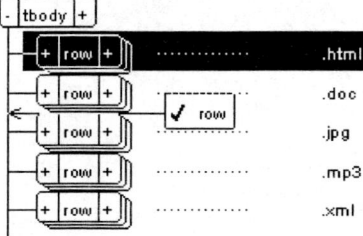

11. Select the row related to the *.doc* extension.

12. Press *Delete*.

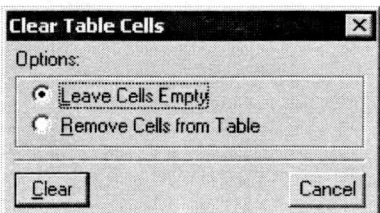

13. Select Remove Cells from Table.

14. Click Clear .

15. In the document view, place the insertion point anywhere in the row related to the *.html* extension.

16. Press *Ctrl+Enter*.

17. Modify the table by adding and rearranging content until it appears as seen below:

Format	Purpose
.html	Used by web pages.
.css	
.jpg	Web based graphics
.gif	
.png	
.mp3	Movies and sound files
.xml	Non-proprietary coded content.

Modify table properties

1. Click anywhere in the table.

2. Select Table > Table Designer.
   The Table Designer displays.

3.   Under Table Tag, select FormatB.

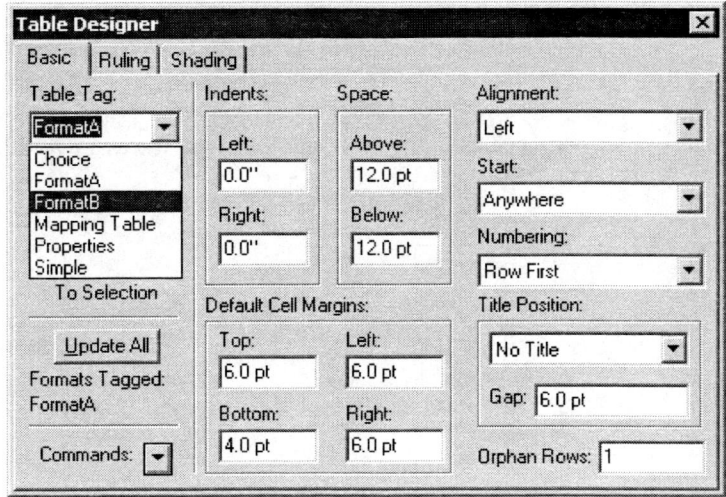

4.   Click [Apply].

Modify column widths

1.   Click anywhere in the first column.

2.   Select **Table > Resize Columns**.

3.   Under **To Width of Column Number**, enter **1**.

4.   Click [Resize].

5.   Select **Table > Resize Columns**.

6.   Under **To Width**, enter **1.0"**.

7.   Click [Resize].

8.   Resize the second column to exactly **1.5"**.

Modify cell properties

1. Change the text in the heading cell from *Purpose* to **What this format is primarily used for**.

2. Click in the first cell containing the text *Format*.

3. In the Structure View, expand the attributes for the element *entry*.

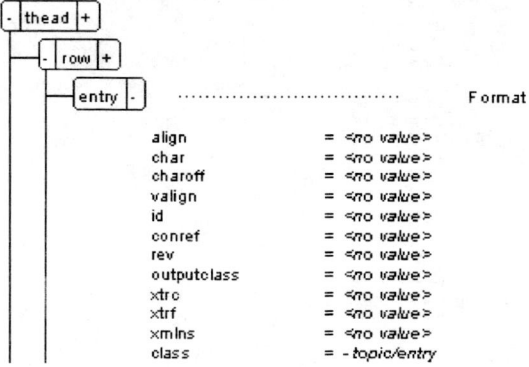

4. Double click the attribute *align*.

5. From the attribute choice popup select left.

6. Click [Set Value].

7. Select the attribute *valign*.

8. From the attribute choice popup select top.

9. Click [Set Value].

10. Click [Done].

Merge and split cell content

1. Select the cell containing the text *Used by web pages* and the blank cell below it.

Format	What this format is primarily used for
.html	Used by web pages.
.css	
.jpg	Web based graphics

2. Select **Table** > **Straddle**.

3. Straddle content to appear as seen below:

Format	What this format is primarily used for
.html	Used by web pages.
.css	
.jpg	Web based graphics
.gif	
.png	
.mp3 .xml	Movies and sound files
	Non-proprietary coded content.

4. Click in the cell containing *.mp3 .xml*.

5. Select **Table** > **Unstraddle**.

6. Reorganize the text content so that the Format column is correctly configured with both *.mp3* and *.xml* in the correct cells.

7. Save and close *Tables.xml*.

Tutorial 15

Work with images

Overview

This tutorial teaches you the basics of working with images in a DITA concept.

This section contains the following topics:

- *Tutorial overview*
- *Opening a previously created DITA topic*
- *Save the topic*
- *Insert an image*
- *Modify image properties*
- *Insert an image with a title*

Tutorial overview

This tutorial guides you through working with DITA and images and multimedia.

The tutorial assumes a default installation of Adobe FrameMaker 8.0. If your product has been customized, some of the default options may not be available.

Most of the step-by-step information in earlier tutorials is not detailed and procedures are simplified in the way they are written.

Opening a previously created DITA topic

In this section, you open an existing DITA topic. It is stored in a default location. If you are not placing your tutorial files on the root of your local hard drive, some of the following steps may differ.

Information on "Open samples from a previous tutorial" can be found on page 308. Information on "Open a standalone sample" can be found on page 308.

Open samples from a previous tutorial

If you have not completed the previous tutorials, proceed to *Open a standalone sample*. If you have completed the previous tutorials proceed with the following steps.

1. If required, launch FrameMaker.

2. Select File > Open.

3. Navigate to *c:\tutorials\fm8dita\tutorial_05*.

4. Select the file *c_SavingFiles.xml*, which was created in an earlier tutorial.

5. Click Open .

6. If required, select DITA-Topic-FM and click Continue .

Open a standalone sample

If you have completed the previous tutorial do not perform the following steps.

1. If required, launch FrameMaker.

2. Select File > Open.

3. Navigate to *c:\tutorials\fm8dita\tutorial_15*.

4. Select the file *Tutorial_15_Start.xml*.

5. Click Open .

6. If required, select DITA-Topic-FM and click Continue .

Save the topic

In this section, you save the concept as Images.xml in the tutorials folder.

1. Select File > Save As.

2. Navigate to the tutorials folder.

3. If required, within the *fm8dita* folder, create a new folder named **tutorial_15**.

4. Open the *tutorial_15* folder.

    This is the location the file is to be saved to.

5. Under File name, type **Images.xml**.

6. Click [Save].

Insert an image

In this section you insert an image in a concept.

1. Display the Structure View and the Element Catalog.

2. Ensure that the insertion point is at the end of the paragraph that contains the following text: *When saving files there are a...file formats when saving.*

3. Using the Element Catalog, insert an *image*.

4. Navigate to the images folder in *tutorial_15*.

5. Select the jpg named *SaveAsDialog.jpg*

6. Click [Import].

7. Click [Set].
   The image is inserted and placed immediately below the text.

Modify image properties

1. Expand the attributes for the *SaveAsDialog* image.

2. Double click the attribute *placement*.

3. Set the attribute choice *popup* to break.

4. Modify the attribute for the *alt* to the typed text string: **Save As Dialog**.

5. Click Done .

Insert an image with a title

In this section you insert an image in a concept.

1. Ensure that the insertion point is at the end of the *p* that contains the image and the following text:

    When saving files there are a…file formats when saving.

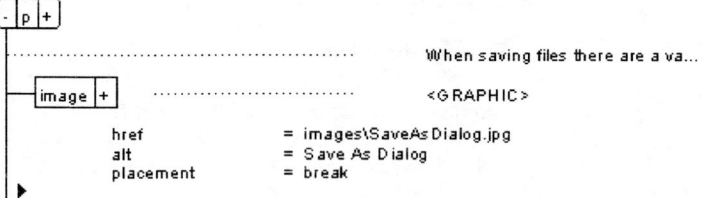

2. Press *Enter.*

3. Type the following content: **XML files can be opened with a variety of software for editing or creation of content or for displaying content.**

4. Using the Element Catalog, insert a *fig.*

5. Navigate to the images folder in *tutorial_15.*

6. Select the jpg named *OpenWithApplication.jpg*

7. Click [Import].

8. Click [Set].

9. In the Structure View, click above the image.

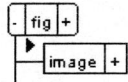

10. Using the Element Catalog, insert a *title* with the following content: **Using many tools to open XML**

11. Save and close *Images.xml*.

Tutorial 16

Work with references

Overview	This tutorial teaches you the basics of working with a DITA reference.

This section contains the following topics:

- *Tutorial overview*
- *Create a new reference*

Tutorial overview

This tutorial guides you through working with DITA to create references.

The tutorial assumes a default installation of Adobe FrameMaker 8.0. If your product has been customized, some of the default options may not be available.

Most of the step-by-step information in earlier tutorials is not detailed and procedures are simplified in the way they are written.

Create a new reference

In this section, you learn the basics of creating the DITA reference.

1. Launch FrameMaker.

2. Using the DITA menu, create a new reference.

3. Navigate to the tutorials folder.

4. If required, within the *fm8dita* folder, create a new folder named **tutorial_16**.

5. Open the *tutorial_16* folder.

   This is the location the file is to be saved to.

6. Under File name, type **r_BEMLogon.xml**.

7. Click [Select].

   A new reference is created and automatically populated with placeholder content for the title element.

8. Replace the placeholder content Topic Title with **BEM Logon**.

9. Insert a *refbody* and delete the default *section*.

10. Insert a refsyn as seen below:

    refbody⟩ refsyn⟩ extern LIBBE_API int bem_logon(bem_handle_t*, char*, char*, char**); ⟨refsyn ⟨refbody ⟨reference ⟨dita

11. Save and close the file.

Tutorial 17

Work with sections and examples

Overview

This tutorial teaches you the basics of working with DITA sections and examples in a variety of elements.

This section contains the following topics:

- *Tutorial overview*
- *Create a new reference*
- *Add a section*
- *Insert a properties table*
- *Update content and develop another section*
- *Create and save a new concept*
- *Add and develop section content*
- *Add and develop example content*
- *Complete the concept with sections and examples*

Tutorial overview

This tutorial guides you through working with DITA to create sections and examples.

The tutorial assumes a default installation of Adobe FrameMaker 8.0. If your product has been customized, some of the default options may not be available.

Most of the step-by-step information in earlier tutorials is not detailed and procedures are simplified in the way they are written.

Create a new reference

In this section, you learn the basics of creating the DITA reference.

1. Launch FrameMaker.

2. Using the DITA menu, create a new reference.

3. Navigate to the tutorials folder.

4. If required, within the *fm8dita* folder, create a new folder named **tutorial_16**.

5. Open the *tutorial_16* folder.
   This is the location the file is to be saved to.

6. Under File name, type **r_ApplicationRequirements.xml**.

7. Click Select .
   A new reference is created and automatically populated with placeholder content for the title element.

8. Replace the placeholder content Topic Title with **Application Requirements**.

9. Below the *title*, add a *shortdesc* with the following content: **Minimum requirements must be met before installing the application.**

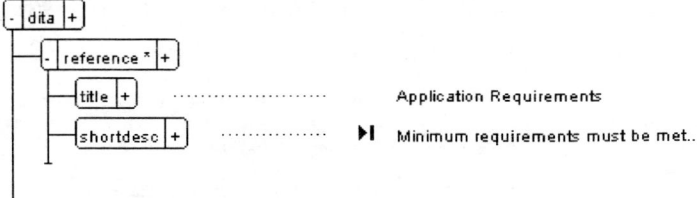

Add a section

In this section, you learn how to add a section to the reference content.

1. Below the *shortdesc*, insert a *refbody* and nested *section*.

2. In the *section*, above the *p* insert a *title* with the following text: **Hardware Requirements**.

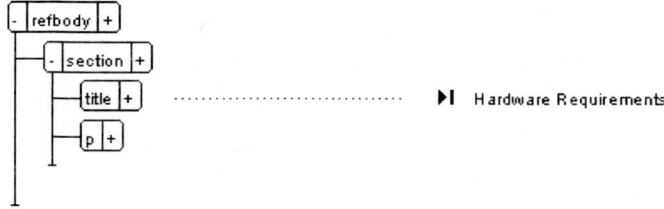

3. Enter the following content into the *p*: **Ensure that your hardware meets the following suggested minimum operating requirements.**

4. Within the *p* add a *note* with the following content:

    These suggestions are for daily use of the software and exceed the minimum installation requirements.

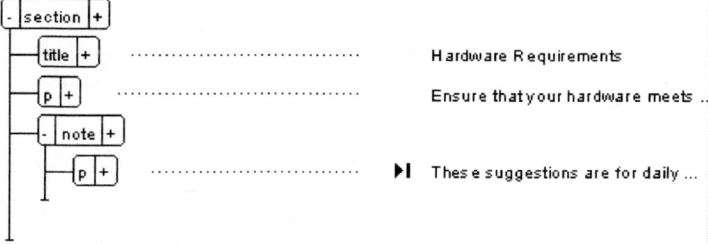

5. Click the – sign to collapse the element note.

Insert a properties table

In this section, you create and populate a properties table.

1. Click below the *note* and use the Element Catalog to insert a *table*.

2. Under Table Format, select Properties.

3. Under Columns, enter **3**.

4. Under Body Rows, enter **3**.

5. Under Heading Rows, select **1**.

6. Click Insert

7. Complete the table as seen below.

Hardware	Value	Description
RAM	1GB	Suggested if using multiple applications
HD Size	10GB	Minimum hard drive requirements for files
Video	128MB	Higher requirements if working with multimedia

8. Click and drag from Hardware to the bottom right cell to select the entire table.

9. Select Table > Resize Columns.

10. Select To Width of Selected Cells' Contents.

11. Click Resize .

Hardware	Value	Description
RAM	1GB	Suggested if using multiple applications
HD Size	10GB	Minimum hard drive requirements for files
Video	128MB	Higher requirements if working with multimedia

Update content and develop another section

In this section, you add another section.

1.   In the Structure View, collapse the *section*.

2.   Insert a *title* with the text **Software Requirements**.

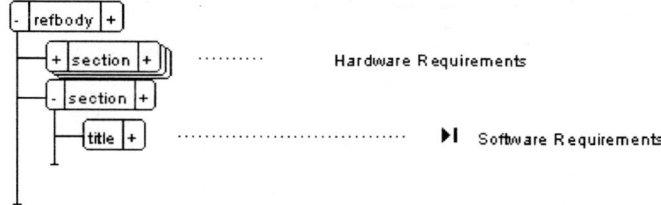

3.   Below the *title*, add a *p* with the following content: **Ensure that your software meets the following suggested minimum OS requirements.**

4.   Click below the *p* and use the Element Catalog to insert a *table*.

5.   Under Table Format, select Properties.

6.   Under Columns, enter **3**, under Body Rows, enter **3** and under Heading Rows, select **1**.

7.   Click Insert

8.   Complete the table as seen below.

Hardware	OS	Notes
Intel (PC)	Windows XP	Vista is recommended for optimal performance
Intel (Mac)	OS X	Tiger (10.4) or later
Sun	Linux	Red Hat or SuSE

9.   Click and drag from Hardware to the bottom right cell to select the entire table.

10. Select Table > Resize Columns.

11. Select To Width of Selected Cells' Contents.

12. Click Resize .

13. Save and close *r_ApplicationRequirements.xml*.

Create and save a new concept

1. Create a new concept named **c_DeliveringContent.xml** in the *tutorial_17* folder.

2. Replace the placeholder content Topic Title with **Delivering Content**.

3. Below the *title*, add a *shortdesc* with the following content: **Content can be delivered as PDF, HTML or online help depending on audience needs.**

Add and develop section content

In this section, you learn how to add a section to the content.

1. Below the *shortdesc* insert a *conbody*.

2. Delete the default *p* and insert a *section* instead.

3. Update the content to appear as seen below:

section > title > **PDF Files** < title

> p > The PDF format is ideal when content needs to be delivered as a complete and standalone file that is print ready, but also has the option of online functionality. Converting from most application to PDF is easy to do and provides consistent results. < p

> p > PDF files are generally compact, easy to share, secure and simple to create. Most tools can convert content to PDF via a transformation using a tool like Adobe Acrobat Distiller or moderately priced tools that can be found online. < p

> p > DITA based content can be converted to PDF using the DITA Toolkit or software tools. < p < section

4. Collapse the *section* element when done.

Add and develop example content

In this section, you learn how to add an example.

1.   Below the *section* insert an *example*.

2.   Update the content to appear as seen below:

| example ⟩ *EXAMPLE:*

| title ⟩ **Create and distribute PDF** ⟨ title |

| p ⟩ You create content using Microsoft Office and need to create a PDF for secure distribution. You have Microsoft Office and Adobe Acrobat installed on your computer. ⟨ p |

| p ⟩ To create the PDF documents you create content using Word, Excel or PowerPoint and select the Adobe PDF menu. Use one of the available options to convert your file. ⟨ p |

| p ⟩ Once the PDF has been created add security directly to the PDF or, if you need the same security setting often, configure the way that Acrobat Distiller works to create your PDF with default security settings. ⟨ p | ⟨ example |

3.   Collapse the *example* element when done.

Complete the concept with sections and examples

In this section, you learn how to add a section to the reference content.

1. Insert and develop the following *section* and *example*.

section ⟩ title ⟩ **HTML Files** ⟨ title

⟨p⟩ The HTML format is ideal when content needs to be deli
as part of a website. Dedicated HTML editors are available. ⟨
⟨p⟩ DITA based content can be converted to HTML using the
Toolkit or software tools. ⟨p⟩ ⟨section

example ⟩ *EXAMPLE:*

title ⟩ **Create and distribute HTML** ⟨ title

⟨p⟩ You create content using various software tools that can
HTML content. You open files and use Save As to export HTM
⟨p⟩ Manage HTML documents by importing to a site manag
tool. It should allow HTML to be created, imported, modifie
uploaded to a web server. ⟨p⟩ ⟨example

2. Insert and develop the following example.

section ⟩ title ⟩ **Online help** ⟨ title

⟨p⟩ The online help format is ideal when content needs to be
ered as a help system (either as one standalone document, or
a website) with online functionality. In many cases specific h
development tools are required. ⟨p⟩
⟨p⟩ DITA based content can be delivered as help using the [
Toolkit or software tools. ⟨p⟩ ⟨section

example ⟩ *EXAMPLE:*

title ⟩ **Create and distribute online help** ⟨ title

⟨p⟩ You create content using numerous tools and need to cr
online help system. You have numerous tools including a he
generation tool installed on your computer. You can deliver
numerous formats as well.

- ul ⟩ li ⟩ Compiled Help ⟨ li
- li ⟩ Flash based help ⟨ li
- li ⟩ Web based HTML
  help ⟨ li ⟨ ul ⟨ p ⟨ example ⟨ conbody ⟨ concept ⟨ di

3. Save and close the file.

Tutorial 18

Work with tasks

Overview

This tutorial teaches you the basics of working with a DITA reference.

This section contains the following topics:

- *Tutorial overview*
- *Create a new task*
- *Develop the cmd and stepresult*
- *Add a prerequisite*
- *Create a detailed task*

Tutorial overview

This tutorial guides you through working with DITA to create a task.

The tutorial assumes a default installation of Adobe FrameMaker 8.0. If your product has been customized, some of the default options may not be available.

Most of the step-by-step information in earlier tutorials is not detailed and procedures are simplified in the way they are written.

Create a new task

In this section, you learn the basics of creating the DITA task.

1. Launch FrameMaker.

2. Using the DITA menu, create a new task.

3. Navigate to the tutorials folder.

4. If required, within the *fm8dita* folder, create a new folder named **tutorial_18**.

5. Open the *tutorial_18* folder.

   This is the location the file is to be saved to.

6. Under File name, type **t_PrintingFiles.xml**.

7. Click [Select].

   A new task is created and automatically populated with placeholder content for the title element.

8. Replace the placeholder content Topic Title with **Printing Images**.

9. Below the *title*, add a *shortdesc* with the following content: **This task teaches you how to easily print any electronic photo image to a high quality paper copy.**

Develop the cmd and stepresult

In this section, you learn how to modify the command placeholder.

1. Below the *shortdesc* insert a *taskbody* element.

2. In the *taskbody* insert a *steps* element and nested *step* and *cmd* elements.

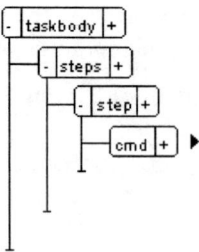

3. Type the following content: **Open an image in your image editing software.**

4. Below the *cmd* insert a *stepresult* element and nested *p* element.

5. Type the following content: **The image is displayed and ready to print.**

TASK

1.   Open an image in your image editing software.

        STEP RESULT: The image is displayed and ready to print.

Add a prerequisite

In this section, you add a prerequisite element to the task.

1. In the Structure View, click below the element *taskbody*, but before the element *steps*.

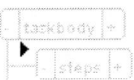

2. Using the Element Catalog, insert the *prereq* element.

3. Type the following content: **You must have image editing software (such as FotoShoppe or Carol's Photopainter) installed.**

4. Collapse the *prereq* element.

5. Collapse the *step* element.

    Ensure you do not collapse the *steps* element.

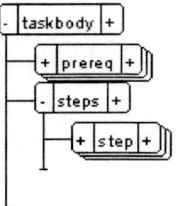

6. Click below the *step* element.

7. Insert a *step* element and nested *cmd* element with the text: **Click the Print icon.**

8. Insert a *stepresult* element and nested *p* element with the text: **The picture is printed.**

TASK

1. Open an image in your image editing software.

    STEP RESULT: The image is displayed and ready to print.

2. Click the Print icon.

    STEP RESULT: The picture is printed.

9. Collapse the *steps* element.

10. Below the *steps* element insert a *postreq* element and nested *p* element with the text: **Pick up your printed photo.**

TASK

1. Open an image in your image editing software.

    STEP RESULT: The image is displayed and ready to print.

2. Click the Print icon.

    STEP RESULT: The picture is printed.

AFTER COMPLETING THIS TASK:

Pick up your printed photo.

11. Save and close *t_PrintingFiles.xml.*

Create a detailed task

A finished sample of the following task is provided in the *tutorial_18* folder if required.

1. Create a new task, named **t_SaveFilesToServer.xml** in the *tutorial_18* folder.

2. Replace the placeholder content Topic Title with **Printing Images**.

3. Below the *title*, add a *shortdesc* with the following content: **This task guides you through saving files to a network location.**

4. Develop the *taskbody*, *prerequisite* and *context* as seen below:

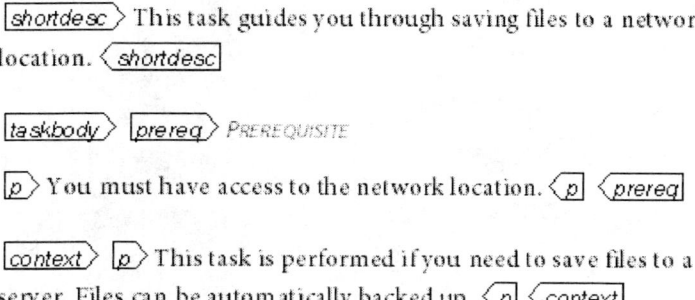

5. In the Structure View collapse the *prereq* and the *context*.

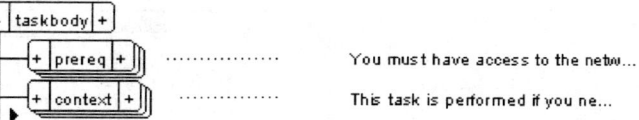

6. Below the context, insert the *steps* element.

7. Develop the *steps*, *step* and *cmd* as well as all *menucascade*, *uicontrol*, *wintitle*, *fig*, *substeps* and other elements as required to ensure the content appears as seen below:

Note that the structure to the left is correct, but incomplete, and is shown as a representation only for comparison.

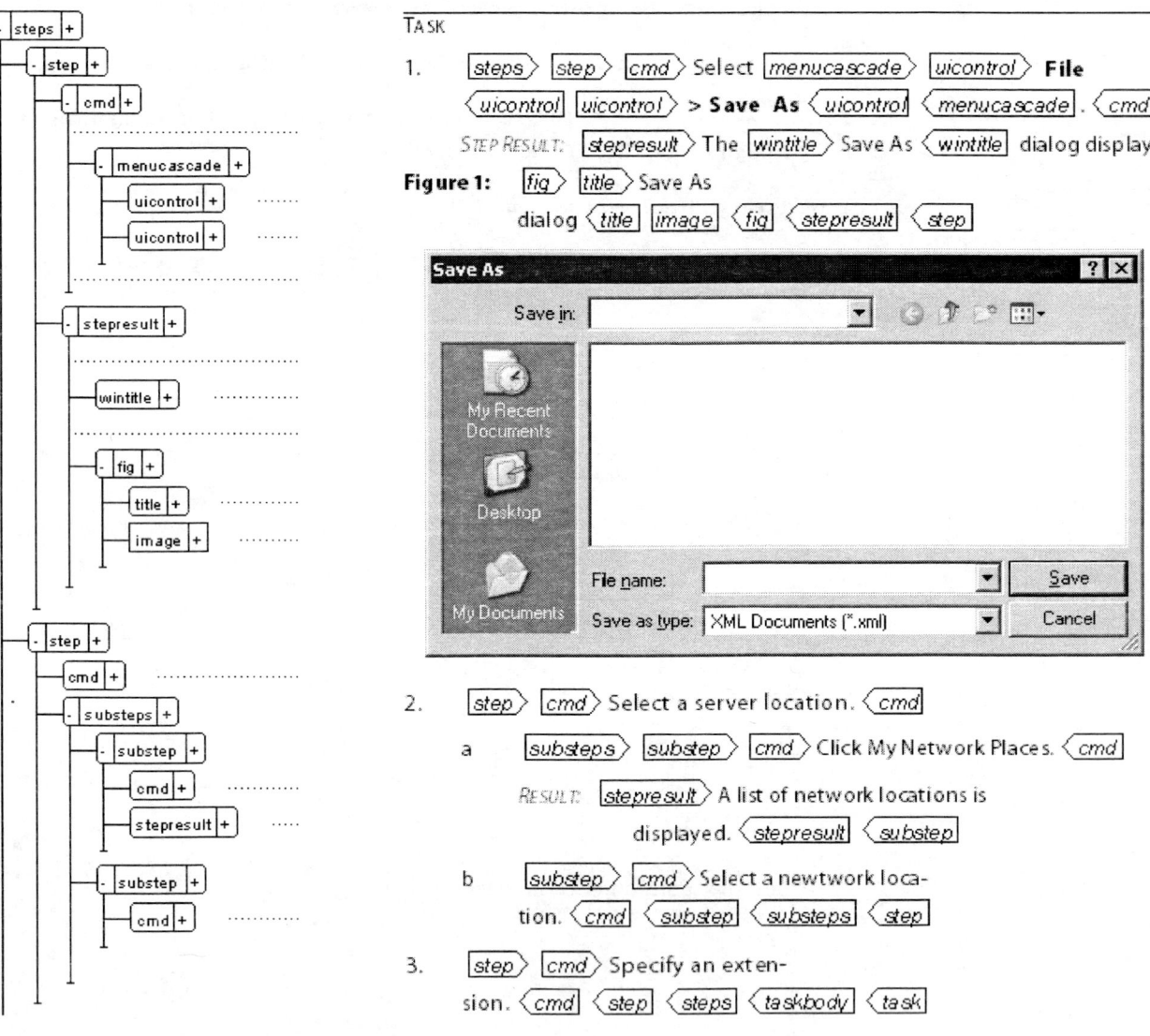

8. Save and close *t_SaveFilesToServer.xml*.

Tutorial 19

Work with track changes

Overview

This tutorial teaches you the basics of working with the track changes feature.

This section contains the following topics:

- *Tutorial overview*
- *Open a sample file*
- *Add content to a document while tracking changes*
- *Modify content in a document while tracking changes*
- *Delete content in a document while tracking changes*
- *Modify the structure in a document while tracking changes*
- *Accept or reject changes in a document*

Tutorial overview

This tutorial guides you through working with Adobe FrameMaker 8.0 to track changes.

The tutorial assumes a default installation of FrameMaker. If your product has been customized, some of the default options may not be available.

Most of the step-by-step information in earlier tutorials is not detailed and procedures are simplified in the way they are written.

Open a sample file

In this section, you open a sample file that will be modified.

1.   If required, launch FrameMaker.

2.   Select File > Open.

3.   Navigate to *c:\tutorials\fm8dita\tutorial_19*.

4.   Select the file *t_SaveFilesToServer.xml*.

5.   Click   Open   .

6.   If required, select DITA-Topic-FM and click   Continue   .

Add content to a document while tracking changes

1.   Select Special > Track Text Edits > Enable.

2.   Select View > Element Boundaries (as Tags).

3.   Add two *p* elements to the prereq as seen below.

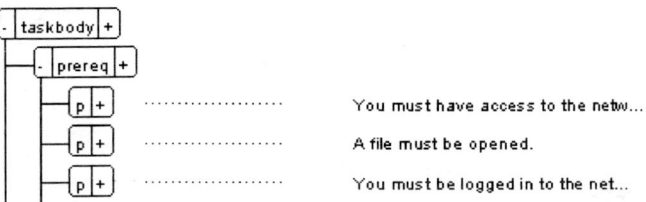

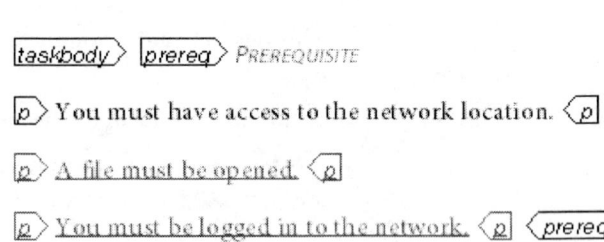

Modify content in a document while tracking changes

In this section you modify existing content in two key ways. The first part of the task is to replace a sentence of existing content with new text. This results in the existing text appearing as deleted content and new text as inserted content. Secondly, a set of additional paragraphs are added and retagged as a list. The new content is formatted with revision marking, but the change to the structure is not marked.

1. Select the first sentence in the context.

    context ⟩ p ⟩ This task is performed if you need to save files to a server. Files can be automatically backed up. ⟨ p ⟨ context

2. Type the following revised content: **By saving files to a server several immediate benefits are realized including:**

    context ⟩ p ⟩ ~~This task is performed if you need to save files to a server.~~ By saving files to a server several immediate benefits are realized including: Files can be automatically backed up. ⟨ p ⟨ context

3. Press *Enter* to split the content into two paragraphs.

4. Type the following new content: **Files can be shared by multiple users.**

    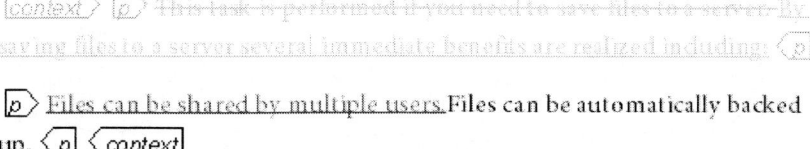

    context ⟩ p ⟩ ~~This task is performed if you need to save files to a server.~~ By saving files to a server several immediate benefits are realized including: ⟨ p

    p ⟩ Files can be shared by multiple users. Files can be automatically backed up. ⟨ p ⟨ context

5. Press *Enter* to split the content.

6. Type the following new content: **Files are more secure than local copies.**

7. Press *Enter*.

    context ⟩ p ⟩ ~~This task is performed if you need to save files to a server.~~ By saving files to a server several immediate benefits are realized including: ⟨ p

    p ⟩ Files can be shared by multiple users. ⟨ p

    p ⟩ Files are more secure than local copies. ⟨ p

    p ⟩ Files can be automatically backed up. ⟨ p ⟨ context

8. Select the second paragraph.

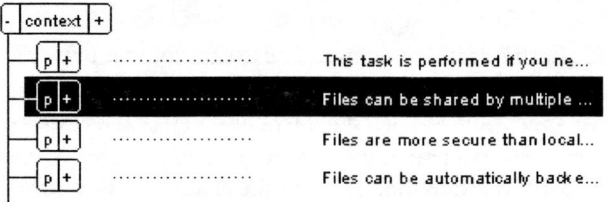

9. Using the Element Catalog, double click *ul*.

   The *p* is wrapped in a *ul* element but is invalid.

10. Select the invalid *p* element.

11. Using the Element Catalog, double click *li*.

    The *p* is wrapped in an *li* element and is valid.

12. Collapse the *li*.

13. Move the remaining two *p* elements below the *li* element.

14. Structure the remaining *p* elements into *li* elements as seen below.

Delete content in a document while tracking changes

1. Select the *stepresult* element in the first step.

2. Press *Delete*.

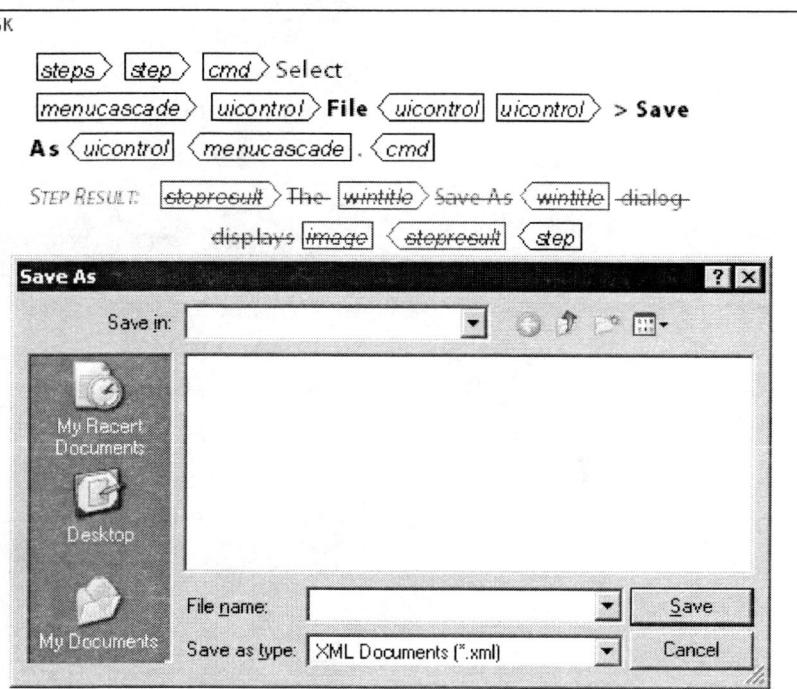

Modify the structure in a document while tracking changes

1. Select the text *My Network Places* in the first substep.

2. Using the Element Catalog wrap the text in the *uicontrol* element.
    The content is wrapped in a uicontrol, but no change is tracked.

Accept or reject changes in a document

1.   Select View > Element Boundaries (as Tags) to hide the tags.

How to Save Files to a Server

This task guides you through saving files to a network location.

PREREQUISITE

You must have access to the network location.

~~A file must be opened.~~

~~You must be logged into the network.~~

~~This task is performed if you need to save files to a server.~~ By saving files to a server several immediate benefits are realized including:

- ~~Files can be shared by multiple users.~~
- ~~Files are more secure than local copies.~~
- Files can be automatically backed up.

TASK

1.   Select **File > Save As.**

     STEP RESULT: ~~The Save As dialog displays~~

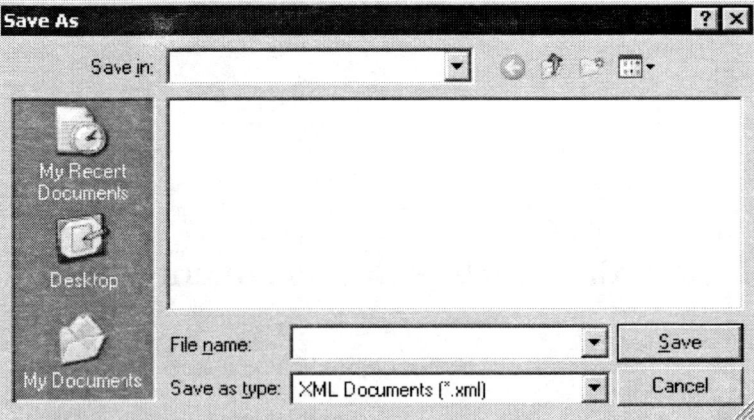

2.   Select a server location.

    a   Click **My Network Places**.

       RESULT: A list of network locations is displayed.

    b   Select a newtwork location.

3.   Specify an extension.

2.   Save the open file as **t_SaveFilesToServer_REV.xml** before continuing.

3.   Click anywhere in the title of the task.

4. Select **View > Track Text Edit Bar.**

   The Track Text Edit toolbar displays.

5. Click ⬛ to move to the first edit.

6. Click ⬛ to accept the first edit.

7. Continue to modify the document using the toolbar to do one of the following:

   - Move to the next or previous change using ⬛ or ⬛.

   - Accept or reject text edits one at a time by clicking ⬛ or ⬛.

   - Accept or reject all text edits in the document at once by clicking ⬛ or ⬛.

8. Close *t_SaveFilesToServer_REV.xml* without saving the changes.

9. Reopen *t_SaveFilesToServer_REV.xml*.

10. Repeat the accepting and rejecting of changes with different options to note the change to the document based on your selections.

11. Close *t_SaveFilesToServer.xml* without saving the file.

Tutorial 20

Work with validation

Overview

This tutorial teaches you the basics of validating structure and correcting errors.

This section contains the following topics:

- *Tutorial overview*
- *Open a sample file*
- *Perform a basic validation check*
- *Invalidate content*
- *Open content with missing elements*
- *Open content with invalid element names*

Tutorial overview

This tutorial guides you through working with Adobe FrameMaker 8.0 to validate structure in a document to ensure compliance with the DITA specification.

The tutorial assumes a default installation of FrameMaker. If your product has been customized, some of the default options may not be available.

Most of the step-by-step information in earlier tutorials is not detailed and procedures are simplified in the way they are written.

Open a sample file

In this section, you open a sample file that will be validated.

1. If required, launch FrameMaker.

2. Select File > Open.

3. Navigate to *c:\tutorials\fm8dita\tutorial_20*.

4. Select the file *c_PrintingFiles.xml*.

5. Click Open .

6. If required, select DITA-Topic-FM and click Continue .

Perform a basic validation check

1. Select Element > Validate.

2. Click Start Validating .

   The default document is valid.

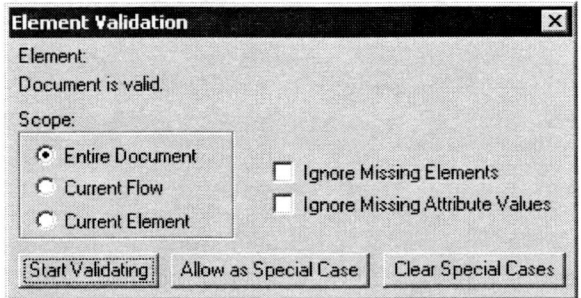

Invalidate content

In order to create an invalid document it is required to intentionally delete required elements.

1. In the Structure View, select the *title* element.

2. Press *Delete*.

   The element is deleted. Since it is required for valid DITA content the structure displays with a red box indicating a missing element.

1. Select Element > Validate.

2. Click [Start Validating].

   The modified document is invalid.

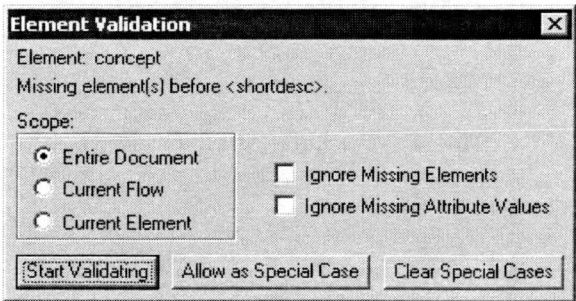

3. Close the file without saving.

Open content with missing elements

Files modified outside of FrameMaker may be invalid when opened. This is likely due to an error such as a required element being deleted.

1. Select File > Open.

2. Navigate to *c:\tutorials\fm8dita\tutorial_20*.

3. Select the file *c_SavingFiles.xml*.

4. Click [Open].

5. If required, select DITA-Topic-FM and click 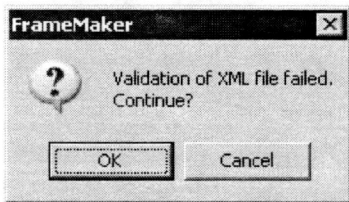 .

   Due to structural errors a dialog displays.

6. Click OK .

   SInce the file is invalid an XML Read Report Log is generated. This will be closed later.

7. Open the Structure View.

8. Select Element > Validate.

9. Click Start Validating .

The document is invalid.

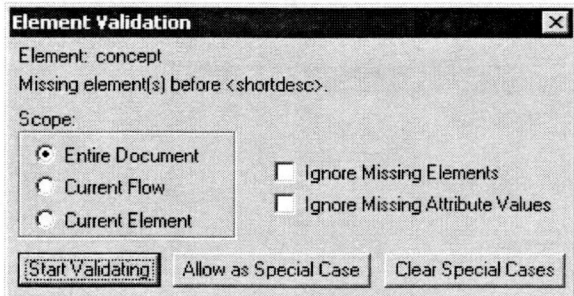

10. Using the Element Catalog insert a *title* with the text: **Saving Files**.

11. Select Tools > Validate Document.

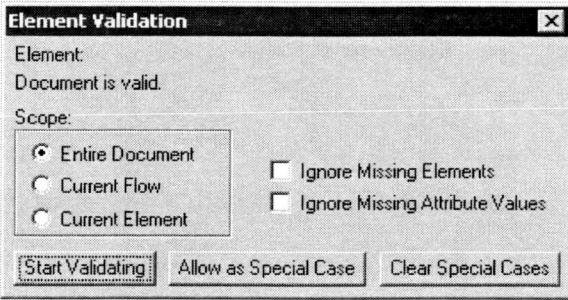

12. Close the file without saving.

The XML Read Report Log document is displayed.

13. Click ■Done .

Open content with invalid element names

Files modified outside of FrameMaker may be invalid when opened. This may also be due to errors where elements have been introduced with invalid names that do not comply with the DITA specification.

1. Select File > Open.

2. Navigate to *c:\tutorials\fm8dita\tutorial_20*.

3. Select the file *c_DeliveringContent.xml*.

4. Click [<u>O</u>pen].

5. If required, select DITA-Topic-FM and click [Continue].
   Due to structural errors a dialog displays.

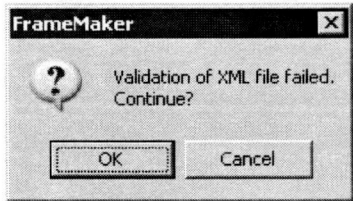

6. Click [OK].
   Since the file is invalid an XML Read Report Log is generated. This will be closed later.

7. Open the Structure View.

8. Select Element > Validate.

9. Click [Start Validating].
   The document is invalid.

10. Select the invalid *para* element.

11. Using the Element Catalog change it to a *p* element.

12. Validate the document.

13. Close the file without saving.

Tutorial 21

Work with links

Overview

This tutorial teaches you the basics of developing links within and between files as well as links to external resources (such as PDF or websites).

This section contains the following topics:

- *Tutorial overview*
- *Insert a FrameMaker cross-reference link*
- *Insert inline internal xrefs links*
- *Insert inline external xref links to DITA files*
- *Insert inline external xref links to non-DITA files*
- *Insert inline web links*
- *Insert related links to topics*
- *Insert related links to web pages*
- *Insert related links to files*

Tutorial overview

This tutorial guides you through working with Adobe FrameMaker 8.0 to develop links within and between files and ensure compliance with the DITA specification.

The tutorial assumes a default installation of FrameMaker. If your product has been customized, some of the default options may not be available.

Most of the step-by-step information in earlier tutorials is not detailed and procedures are simplified in the way they are written.

This tutorial also introduces conversion to multiple HTML files as well as conversion to a single file.

Insert a FrameMaker cross-reference link

This type of link is based on the traditional FrameMaker cross-reference. It allows links to be inserted between FrameMaker objects that support the unique ID.

1. Open the file *c:\tutorials\fm8dita\tutorial_21\t_PasteSpecial.xml* using the DITA-Topic-FM application.

2. Save the file as **t_PasteSpecialREV.xml**.

3. Open the file *t_copy.xml* in the *tutorial_21* folder using the DITA-Topic-FM application.

4. Select Window > t_PasteSpecialREV.xml to switch back to the tutorial sample document.

5. Display the document with Element Boundaries (as Tags) displayed.

6. Click at the end of the *p* element in the *prereq* element.

7. Press *Spacebar* once.

8. Using the Element Catalog, insert an *fm-xref*.

9. Under Source Type, click ▾.

10. From the Source Type drop-down list, select Elements Listed in Order.

11. Under Element Tags, select *task*.

12. Under Document, select *t_copy.xml*.

13. Under Elements (in Document Order), select *How to copy content*.

14. From the Format drop-down list, select *See_Title_and_Page*.

15. Click Insert .
    The cross-reference is inserted with automatic text.

16. Select the *fm-xref* element and press *Delete*.

Insert inline internal xrefs links

In this section, you open a sample file and convert the content of a single step to contain both text and xref elements.

1. Select the content of step 5.

5.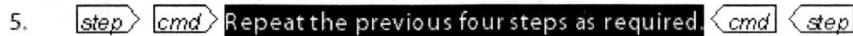

2. Type **Repeat step** and press *Spacebar* once.

3. Using the Element Catalog insert an *xref* element.

4. Under Element Tag, select step.

5. Under Element Data [id | content] select the first *step* element.

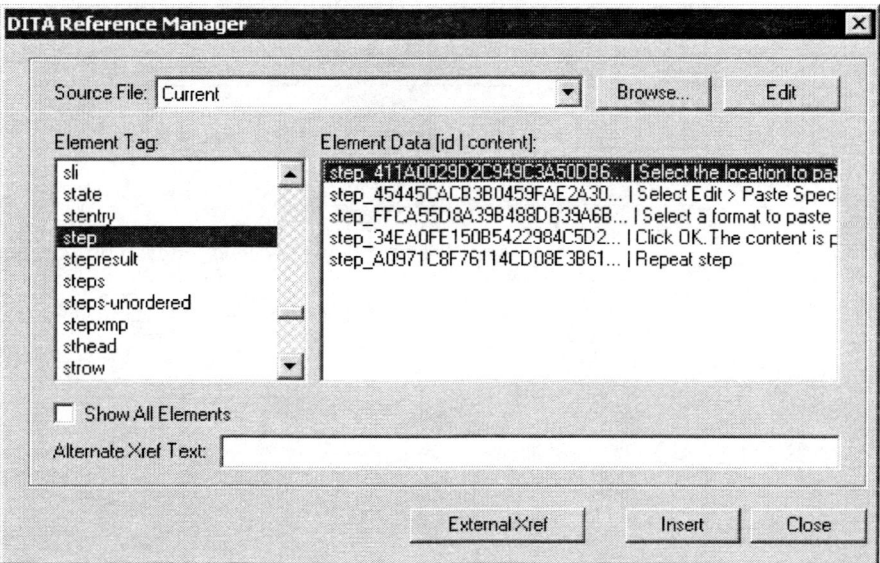

6. Under Alternate Xref Text type **1**.

7. Click [Insert].

8. After the *xref*, press *Spacebar* once, type **through** and press *Spacebar* again.

9. Using the Element Catalog insert an *xref* element.

10. Under Element Tag, select step.

11. Under Element Data [id | content] select the second last *step* element.

12. Under Target Element Type, select Task step or substep.

13. Under Select a TaskStep, click the second last task step.

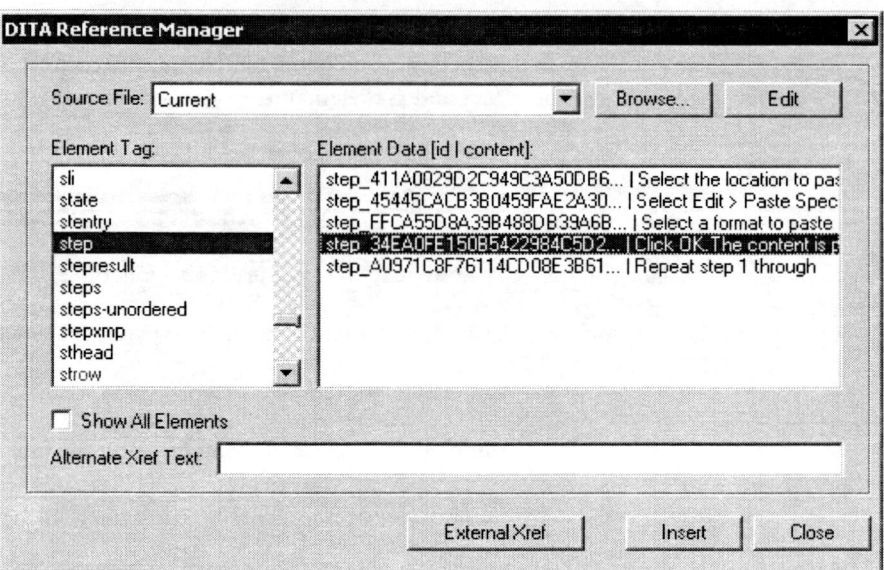

14. Under Alternate Xref Text type **4**.

15. Click Insert .

16. After the xref, press *Spacebar* once, type **as required.** to complete the cmd.

   5. step cmd Repeat step xref 1 xref through xref 4 xref a required. cmd step steps taskbody task

Insert inline external xref links to DITA files

In this section, you create a set of links to DITA topics stored in the same location as the source file.

Note

The conversion of links is handled by default using the DITA Toolkit. Not all output types convert links cleanly by default and links may not always work. This can be customized.

1. In the *prereq*, at the end of the *p* element, insert a *ul* element.

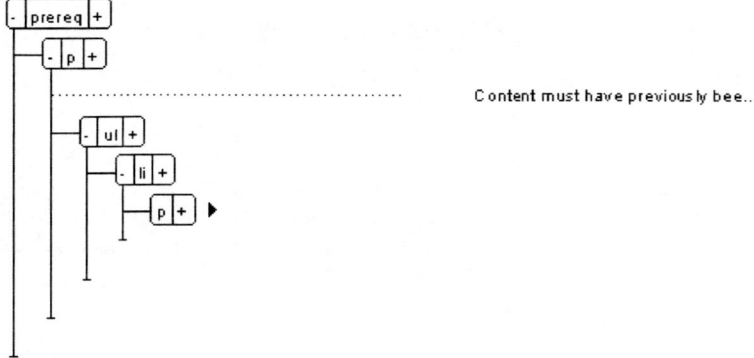

2. Using the Element Catalog insert an *xref* element.

3. Click Browse... .

4. Select the file *c:\tutorials\fm8dita\tutorial_21\t_Copy.xml*.

5. Click Select .

6. Under Element Tag, select task.

7. Under Element Data [id | content] select the *task* element.

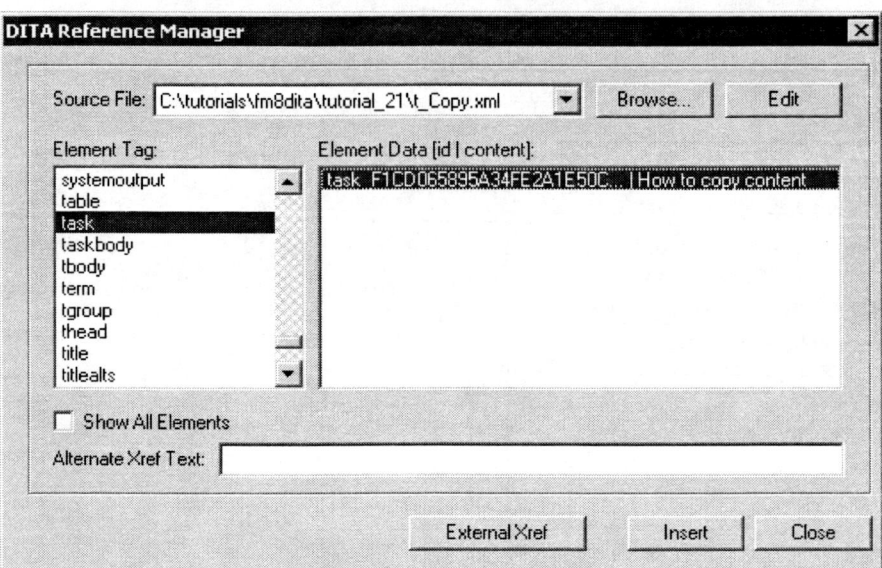

8. Click Insert .

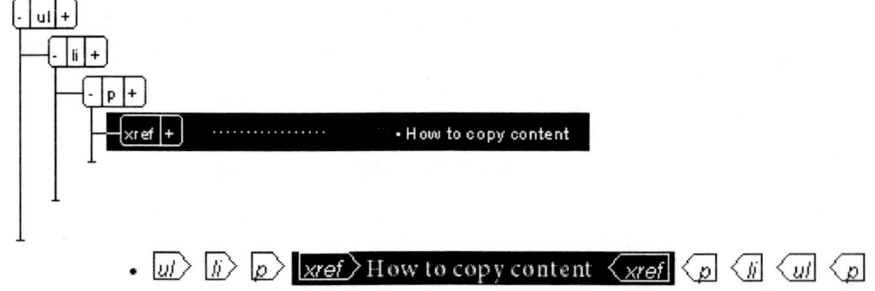

9. Develop the following *xref* to the file *t_Cut.xml*.

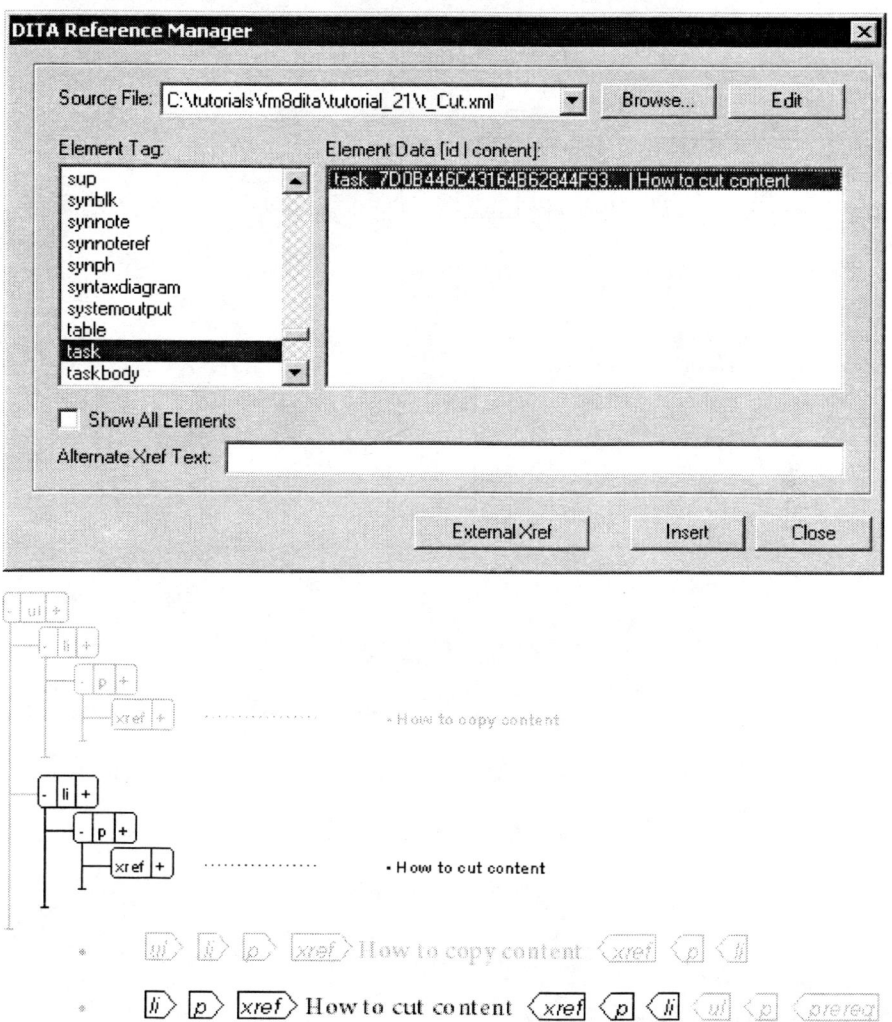

10. Collapse both *li* elements.

Insert inline external xref links to non-DITA files

In this section, you create a set of links to non-DITA files stored in the same location as the source file.

1. Add another *li*.

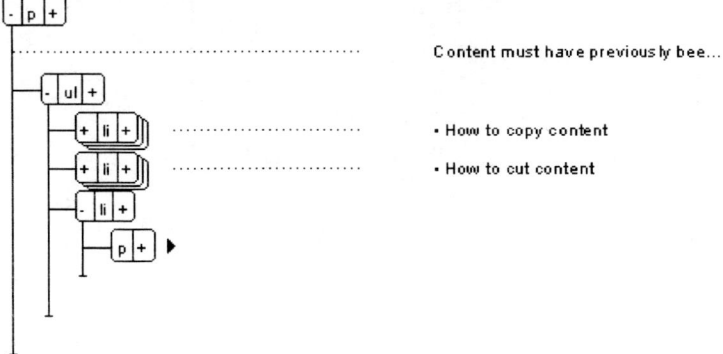

2. Using the Element Catalog insert an *xref* element.

3. Click [External Xref].

4. Under Xref Target (href) type **images/d_PasteSpecial.jpg**

5. Under Xref Link Text type **Paste Special Dialog**.

6. Click [OK].

7. Collapse the *li* element.

Insert inline web links

In this section, you create a set of links to websites.

1. Add another list item.

2. Type **You may also want to search online for more information.** and press *Spacebar*.

3. Using the Element Catalog insert an *xref* element.

4. Click [External Xref].

5. Under Xref Target (href) type **http://www.google.com**

6. Under Xref Link Text type **Search Google**.

7. Click OK .

8. Collapse the *li* element.

Insert related links to topics

In this section, you open a sample file and insert related links which automatically are grouped at the end of the topic.

Note

The conversion of links is handled by default using the DITA Toolkit. Not all output types convert links cleanly by default and links may not always work. This can be customized.

1. Collapse the *taskbody* element.

2. Insert a *related-links* element.

3. Insert a *link* element.

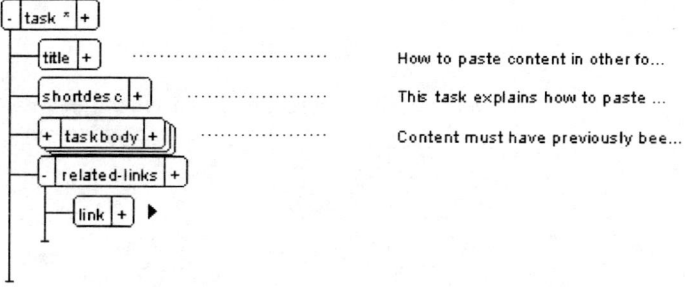

4. Expand the attributes for the *link* element.

5. Double click the attribute *href*.

6. Modify the attribute for the *href* to the typed text string: **t_Copy.xml**.

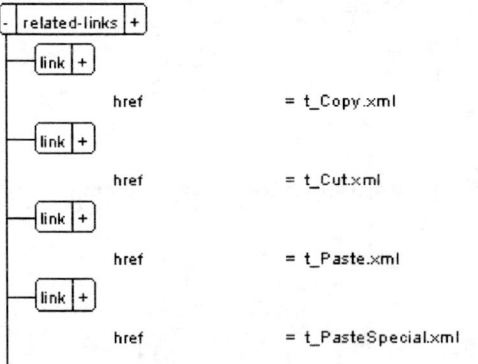

7. Click Done .

The link is inserted with default content based on the *href* attribute.

8. Expand the attribute value to show only the *href* value.

9. Develop additional related links as seen below:

Insert related links to web pages

In this section, you create a link to a website.

1. Click below the last *link* element.

2. Insert a *link* element.

3. Expand the attributes for the *link* element.

4. Double click the attribute *href*.

5. Modify the *href* value to the typed text string: **http://www.google.com**.

Insert related links to files

In this section, you create a link to a non-DITA file stored in the same location as the source file.

1. Click below the last *link* element.

2. Insert a *link* element.

3. Expand the attributes for the *link* element.

4. Double click the attribute *href*.

5. Modify the *href* value to the typed text string: **images/d_PasteSpecial.jpg**.

6. Click [Done].

7. Save and close *t_PasteSpecialREV.xml*.

8. Close other files which have been automatically opened during this tutorial.

Tutorial 22

Work with content reuse

Overview

This tutorial teaches you the basics of reusing content based on the DITA specification.

This section contains the following topics:

- *Tutorial overview*
- *Apply conditional content markup*
- *Create filter by attribute settings*
- *Configure output for conditional content*
- *Remove conditional content markup*
- *Reference other topics*
- *Modify a content reference in another topic*
- *Create a reusable component*
- *Insert a reusable component*
- *Modify a reusable component*

Tutorial overview

This tutorial guides you through working with Adobe FrameMaker 8.0 to develop reusable content within and between files and ensure compliance with the DITA specification.

The tutorial assumes a default installation of FrameMaker. If your product has been customized, some of the default options may not be available.

Most of the step-by-step information in earlier tutorials is not detailed and procedures are simplified in the way they are written.

Apply conditional content markup

In this section, you configure content to be conditional.

1. Launch FrameMaker.

2. Open the file *c:\tutorials\fm8dita\tutorial_22\c_DeliveringContent.xml* using the DITA-Topic-FM application.

3. In the *section* titled *PDF files*, display the attributes of the last *p* element.

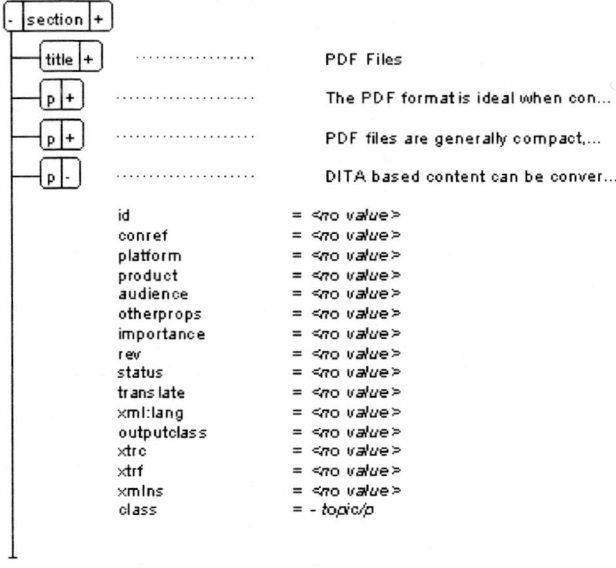

4. Double click the attribute *audience*.

5. Change the value of the *audience* to **admin**.

6. Collapse the attributes of the *p* element to show only the specified value.

7. In the *example* titled *Create and Distribute PDF*, display the attributes of *example* element.

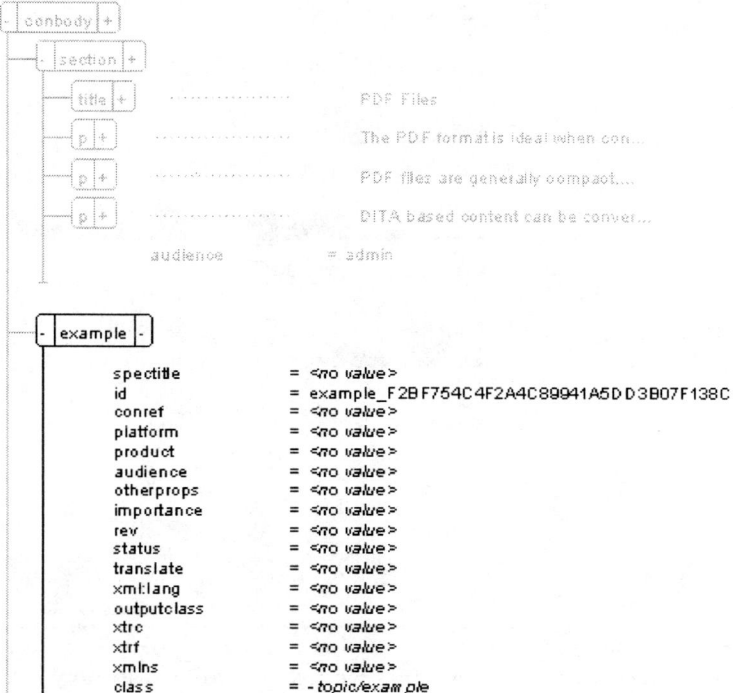

8. Double click the attribute *audience*.

9. Change the value of the *audience* to **user**.

10. Collapse the attributes of the *example* element to show only the specified values.

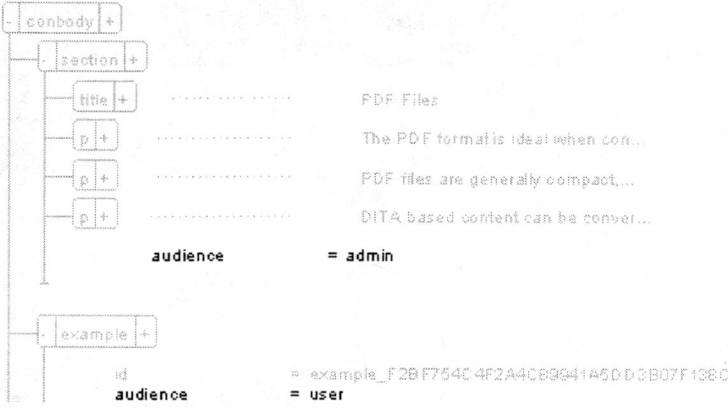

Create filter by attribute settings

This topic explains how to create a new filter by attribute setting.

1. Select Special > Filter by Attribute.

2. Click [New].

   The Build Expression dialog displays.

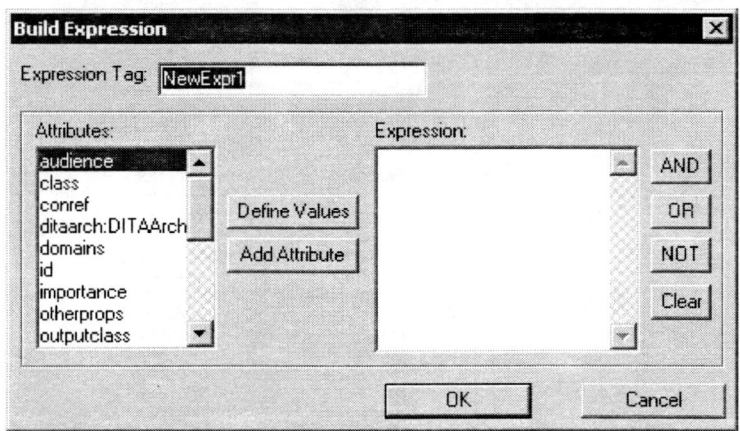

3. Under Expression Tag, type **Administrator's Guide**.

4. Under Expression, type **(audience="admin")** to specify that only the admin content should display.

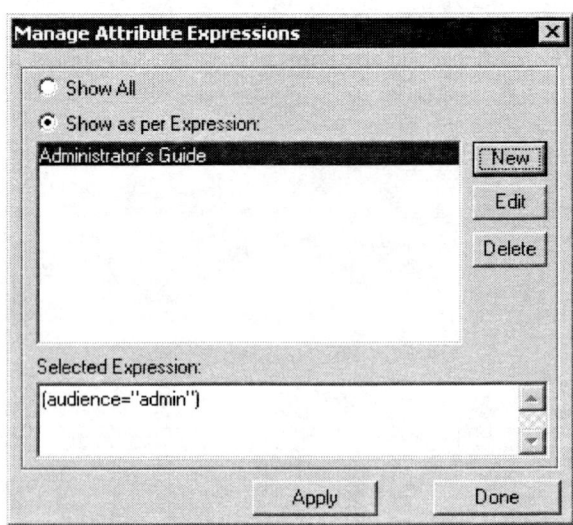

5. Click [New].

6. Under Expression Tag, type **User's Guide**.

7. Under Expression, type **(audience="user")** to specify that only the admin content should display.

8. Click [OK].

Configure output for conditional content

In this section you display or hide specific conditional information based on attributes.

1. Review the *example* titled *Create and distribute PDF*.

2. Select Special > Filter by Attribute.

3. Under Show as Per Expression select *Administrator's Guide*.

4. Click [Apply].
   Notice that the *example* is hidden.

5. Select Show All.

6. Click [Apply].
   Notice that the *example* is displayed.

7. Review the *p* containing the text *DITA based content can be converted to PDF using the DITA Toolkit or software tools*.

8. Under Show as Per Expression select *User's Guide*.

9. Click [Apply].
   Notice that the *p* is hidden.

10. Select Show All.

11. Click [Apply].
    Notice that the *p* is displayed.

12. Click [Done].

Remove conditional content markup

1. In the p element containing the text *DITA based content can be converted to PDF using the DITA Toolkit or software tools* double click the *audience* attribute.

2. Click [Delete Value].

3. Click [Done].

   The condition is removed.

4. Select the *example* element titled *Create and Distribute PDF*.

5. Delete the value of the attribute *audience*.

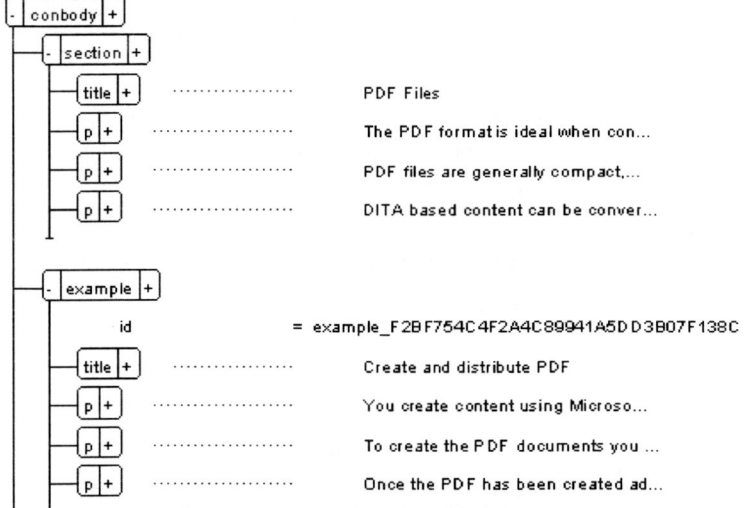

6. Close the file without saving it.

Reference other topics

In this section you insert part of an existing topic into another topic.

1. Open the file *c:\tutorials\fm8dita\tutorial_22\t_LaserRemove.xml* using the DITA-Topic-FM application.

2. Review the content of the first step.

    TASK

    1. Shut down external power to the device.

        STEP RESULT: All status lights switch to red to indicate that no external power is being consumed. The status lights are powered by battery backup that is not connected to the laser and can not be used to power the device.

3. Close the file.

4. Open the file *t_LaserClean.xml* using the DITA-Topic-FM application.

5. Click before the first *step* element in the *steps* element.

6. Select DITA > Insert Conref.

7. Click **Browse...** .

8. Select the file *t_LaserRemove.xml*.

9. Click **Select** .

10. Click Show All Elements.

11. Under Element Tag select *step*.

12. Under Element Data [id | content] select the first *step* element.

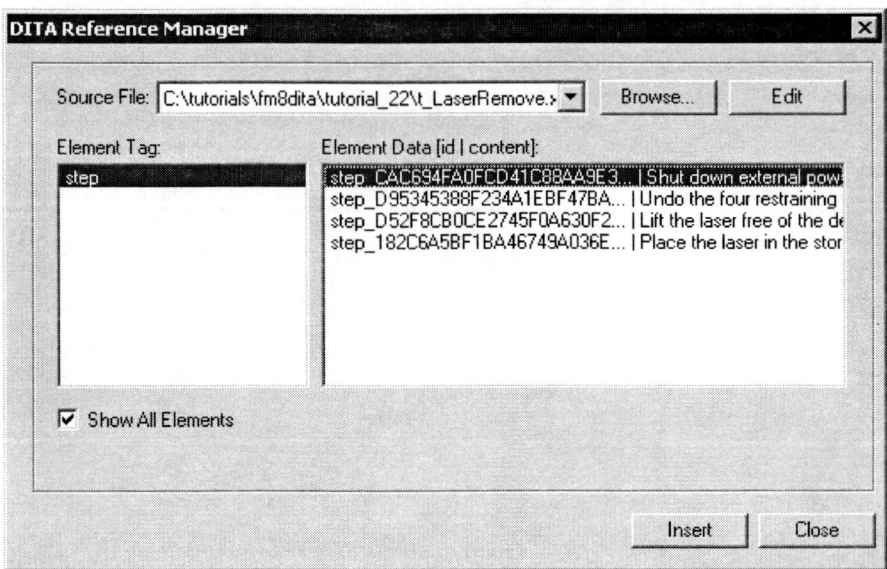

13. Click Insert .

Modify a content reference in another topic

1. Open the file *t_LaserRemove.xml* using the DITA-Topic-FM application.

2. Add the following *note* element in the *stepresult* element:

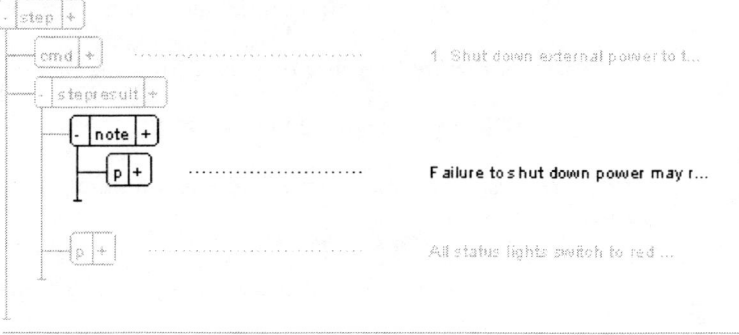

3. Select File > Save.

4. Select File > Close.

   The document is closed and you are returned to the original document.

5. Select DITA > Update References.

6. Select Update All Conrefs In File.

7. Click [OK].

8. Review the first step.

9. Save and close any open files.

Create a reusable component

In this section you create a reusable component.

1. Using the DITA menu, create a new topic.

2. Navigate to the tutorials folder.

3. If required, create a *tutorial_22/reuse* folder.

4. Open the *tutorial_22/reuse* folder.

5. Under File name, type **AudienceInfo.xml**.

6. Click [Select].

    A new topic is created and automatically populated with placeholder content for the title element.

7. Replace the placeholder content Topic Title with **Audience Information Reuse Component**.

8. Below the *title*, add a *shortdesc* with the following content: **This reuse component is related to identification of audience needs.**

9. Add a *body* element and the nested *p* element.

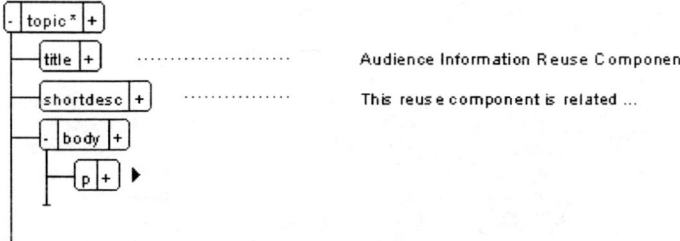

10. Type: **Identify audience needs before deciding on a file format.**

11. Display the attributes for the new *p* element.

Note that there is no value assigned to the attribute *id*. Therefore, this *p* element can not be referenced.

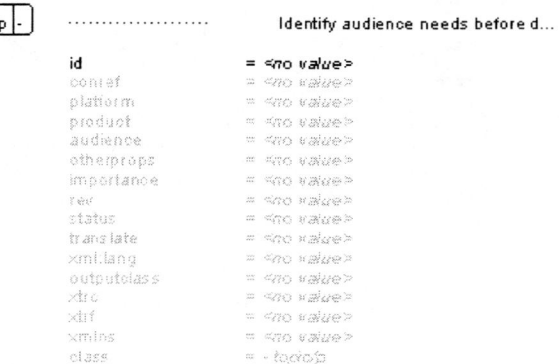

12. Select the *p* element.

13. Select DITA > Assign ID to Element.

A value is autoassigned to the *id* attribute.

14. Save and close the file.

Insert a reusable component

1. Click after the title for the section HTML Files.

2. Select DITA > Insert Conref.

3. Click **Browse...**.

4. Select the file ..*tutorial_22\reuse\AudienceInfo.xml*.

5. Click **Select**.

6. Click Show All Elements.

7. Under Element Tag select *p*.

8. Under Element Data [id | content] select the first *p* element.

9. Click Insert .

10. Insert the same content reference for *Online help* as seen below.

11. Insert the same content reference for *PDF*.

Modify a reusable component

1. Open the file the file ..*tutorial_22\reuse\AudienceInfo.xml* using the DITA-Topic-FM application.

2. Modify the content to appear as seen below.

    body〉 p〉 Prior to deciding on a file format, identify the audience needs. This may require emailing your audience, undertaking user surveys or even interviewing your audience. 〈p 〈body 〈topic 〈dita

3. Select File > Save.

4. Select File > Close.

    The document is closed and you are returned to the original document.

5. Select DITA > Update References.

6. Select Update All Conrefs In File.

7. Click OK .

8. Review the three sections.

9. Save and close any open files.

Tutorial 23

Work with maps

| Overview | This tutorial teaches you the basics of creating and publishing maps based on the DITA specification. |

Overview

This tutorial teaches you the basics of creating and publishing maps based on the DITA specification.

This section contains the following topics:

- *Tutorial overview*
-

Tutorial overview

This tutorial guides you through working with Adobe FrameMaker 8.0 to develop maps and ensure compliance with the DITA specification.

The tutorial assumes a default installation of FrameMaker. If your product has been customized, some of the default options may not be available.

Most of the step-by-step information in earlier tutorials is not detailed and procedures are simplified in the way they are written.

Open and publish an existing map

1. Launch FrameMaker.

2. Open the file *c:\tutorials\fm8dita\tutorial_23\concept_map\Concepts.ditamap* using the DITA-Map-FM application.

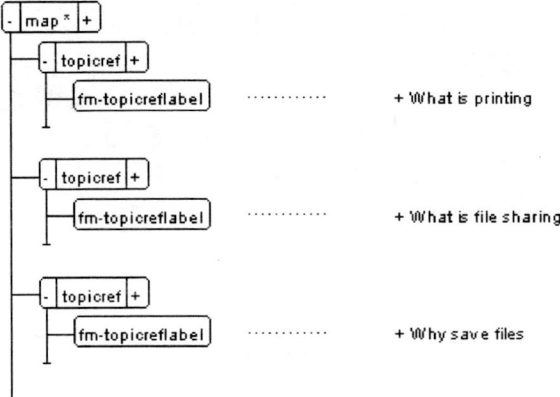

Working with Files

+ **What is printing**

+ **What is file sharing**

+ **Why save files**

3. Double click *What is printing*.

4. Review and close the content.

5. Open, review and close *What is file sharing*.

6. Open, review and close *Why save files*.

7. Select DITA > Build FM Document from DITA Map.

8. Select the folder *c:\tutorials\fm8dita\tutorial_23\concept_map*.

9. Name the file **ConceptFile.fm**.

10. Click [Select] .

11. Review the file that is generated.

12. Close the generated file.

13. Close the map.

Publish an existing map to a book

The following steps outline how to convert a map to a FrameMaker book.

1. Select DITA > Build FM DITABook from DITA Map file.

2. Select the file *c:\tutorials\fm8dita\tutorial_23\concept_map\Concepts.ditamap*.

3. Click [Select].

    The Save Book dialog displays.

4. Name the book **Concepts.book**

5. Click [Save].

    FrameMaker converts the map and its topicrefs into a FrameMaker book and files.

6. From within the book double click *c_PrintingFiles.xml.fm* and review the content.

7. Close the file.

8. From within the book double click *c_SharingFiles.xml.fm* and review the content.

9. Close the file.

10. Review and close the last file.

11. Close the book.

Create a map

1. Select DITA > New DITA File > New <map>.

2. Save the map as *c:\tutorials\fm8dita\tutorial_23\SavingFiles.ditamap*.

3. Click [Select].

4. Using the Structure View, expand the *map* element attributes.

5. Double click the *title* attribute.

6. Change the attribute value to **Saving Files**.

Saving Files

Add DITA topics to a map

1. Using the Element Catalog insert a *topicref* element.

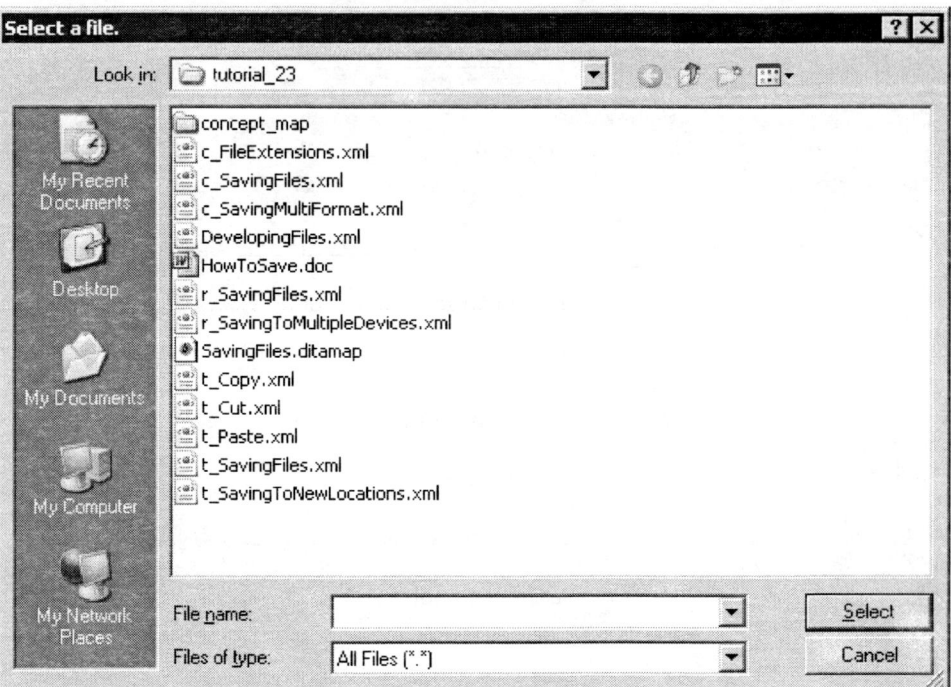

2. Select ..*tutorial_23\\c_SavingFiles.xml*.

3. Click Select.

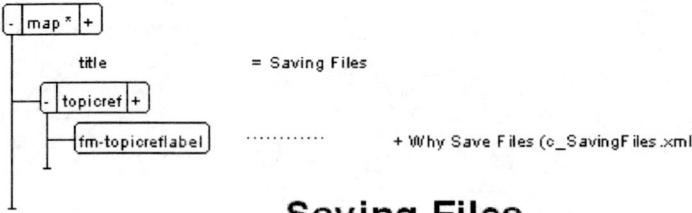

4. Collapse the *topicref* element.

5. Add another *topicref* element below the previous *topicref* element.

6. Select ..*tutorial_23\\c_SavingMultiFormat.xml*.

7.   Click [Select].

8.   Add the files *t_SavingFiles.xml* and *t_SavingToNewLocations.xml*.

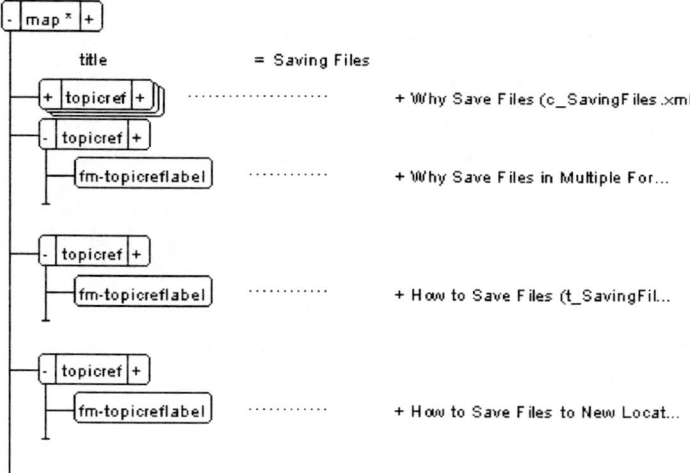

Saving Files

+ **Why Save Files (c_SavingFiles.xml)**

+ **Why Save Files in Multiple Formats (c_SavingMultiFormat.xml)**

+ **How to Save Files (t_SavingFiles.xml)**

+ **How to Save Files to New Locations (t_SavingToNewLocations.xml)**

9.   Save the map.

10. Convert the map to a single FM file using the DITA > Build FM Document From DITA Map menu and name the file **SavingTopics.fm**.

11. Review and close the generated file.

12. Collapse all *topicref* elements in the map.

Adding non-DITA content to a map

1.   Using the Element Catalog insert a *topicref* element.

2.   Select *..\tutorial_23\HowToSave.doc*.

3. Click **Select**.

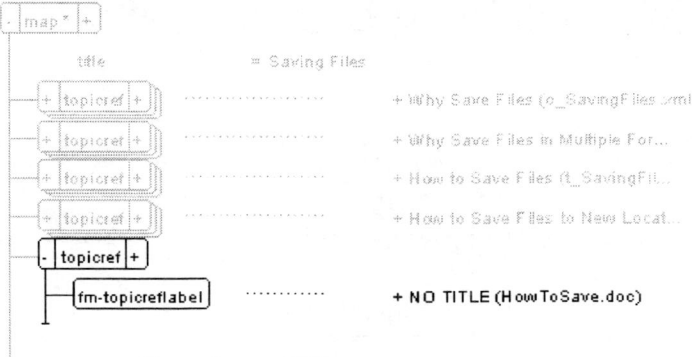

4. Using the Structure View, expand the *topicref* element attributes related to the .doc file.

5. Double click the *navtitle* attribute.

6. Change the attribute value to **Quick Guide to Saving (MS Word File)**.

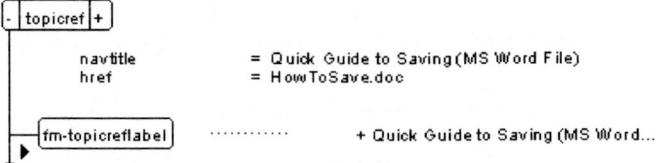

7. Convert the map to a single FM file using the DITA > Build FM Document From DITA Map menu and name the file **SavingTopicsWithDoc.fm**.

8. Review the generated file noting that the content on the last page is formatted poorly.

    FrameMaker added the content and converted it from Word automatically. Not all processing tools do this with topicrefs.

9. Close the generated file.

10. Collapse all *topicref* elements in the map.

Reorganize map content

1. Expand all *topicref* elements.

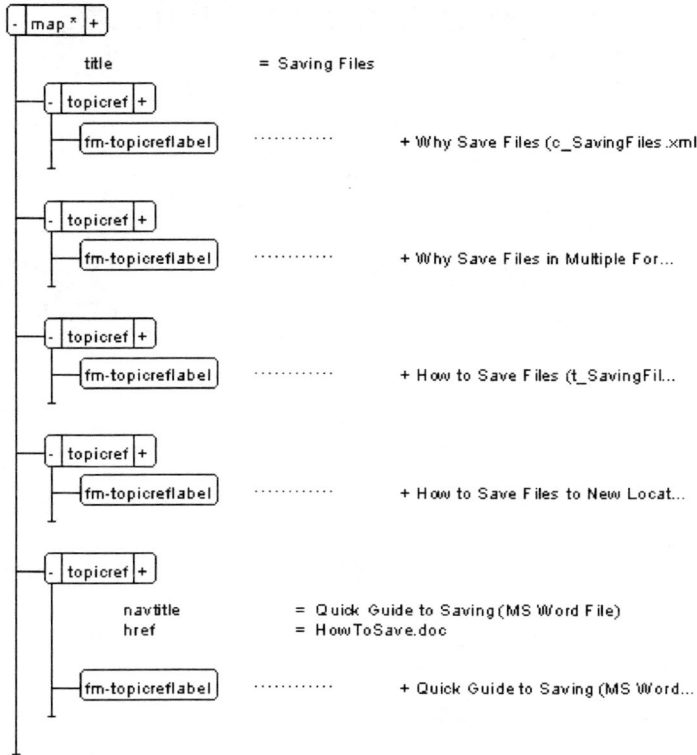

2. Move the *topicref* element for the .doc file to the beginning of the *topicref* elements.

3. Nest the topic *How to Save Files to New Locations*, as a child of *How to Save Files*.

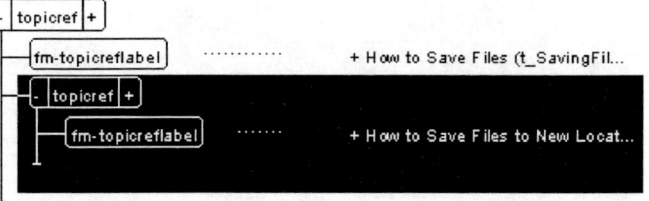

4. Convert the map to a single FM file using the DITA > Build FM Document From DITA Map menu and name the file **SavingTopicsWithNesting.fm**.

5. Review the generated file noting that the content on the first page is structured and formatted poorly. Additionally, the topic titled How to Save Files to New Locations is nested as a subordinate entry.

How to Save Files

TASK

1. Click the **Save** icon.

ADDITIONAL INFORMATION: The file can be managed using the Windows Explorer or the Macintosh Finder.

How to Save Files to New Locations

Files can be saved to a different location for use in other documents.

PREREQUISITE

6. Close the generated file.

7. Delete the *topicref* element referencing the .doc file.

8. Collapse all *topicref* elements except the last *topicref* element.

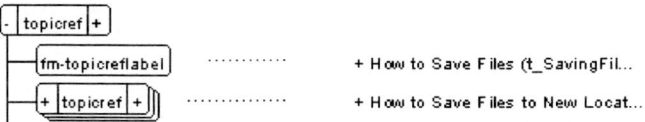

9. Unnest the topicref related to *How to Save Files to New Locations*.

10. Reorganize the content to appear as seen below.

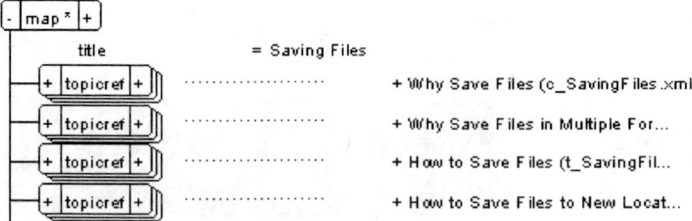

Saving Files

+ **Why Save Files (c_SavingFiles.xml)**
+ **Why Save Files in Multiple Formats (c_SavingMultiFormat.xml)**
+ **How to Save Files (t_SavingFiles.xml)**
+ **How to Save Files to New Locations (t_SavingToNewLocations.xml)**

11. Save the map.

Group map content

1. Click between the second and third *topicref* element.

2. Using the Element Catalog insert a *topichead* element.

3. Set the attribute value for the navtitle to **Tasks**.

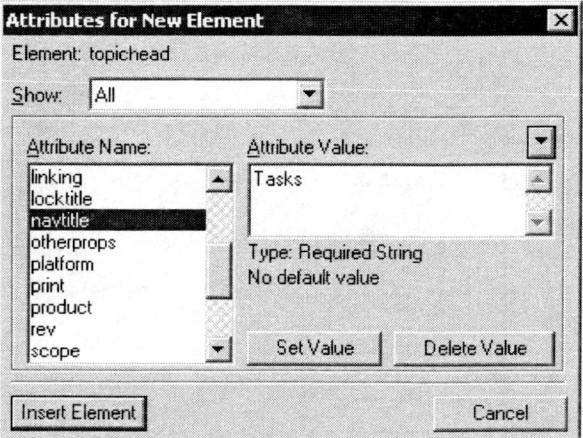

4. Click Insert Element .

5. Nudge the first *topicref* element below the *topichead* element to the right.

That is, click and drag it about the width of a character to the right. Note that the mouse cursor appears as a small arrow pointing right when properly executed.

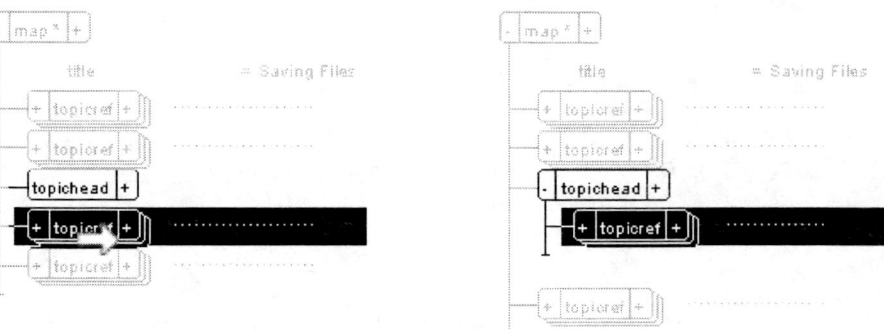

6. Reorganize the structure as seen below by adding another *topichead* element with an attribute *navtitle* set to **Concepts** and nesting the remaining three *topicref* elements as needed.

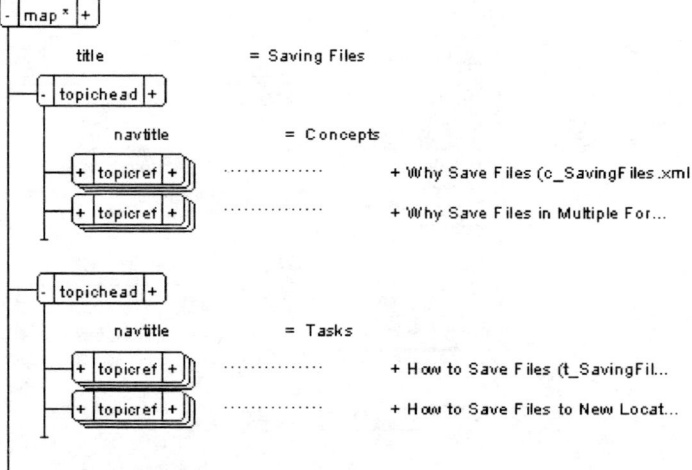

7. Save and close the map.

Inserting maps within maps

In this section you create a new map that includes a reference to both topics and to other maps.

1. Select DITA > New DITA File > New <map>.

2. Save the map as *c:\tutorials\fm8dita\tutorial_23\WorkingWithFiles.ditamap*.

3. Click [Select].

4. Using the Structure View, expand the *map* element attributes.

    title   = MAP TITLE

5. Double click the *title* attribute.

6. Change the attribute value to **Working with Files**.

7. Using the Element Catalog insert a *topicref* element.

8. Select *..\tutorial_23\DevelopingFiles.xml*.

9. Click [Select].

    [- [map * +]]

           title   = Working with Files

       [- [topicref +]]

           [fm-topicreflabel] ....   + Developing and modifying files...

10. Collapse the *topicref* element.

11. Add another *topicref* element below the previous *topicref* element.

12. Select *..\tutorial_23\EditingFileContent.ditamap*.

13. Click .

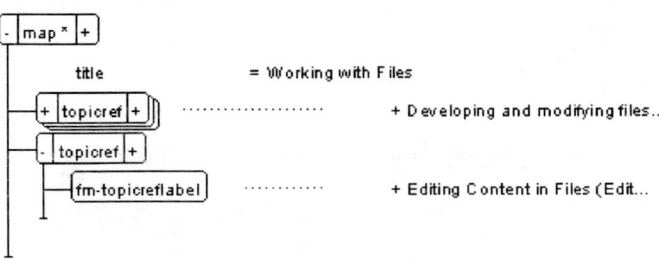

14. Collapse the *topicref* element.

15. Add another *topicref* element below the previous *topicref* element.

16. Select ..*tutorial_23\\SavingFiles.ditamap*.

17. Click 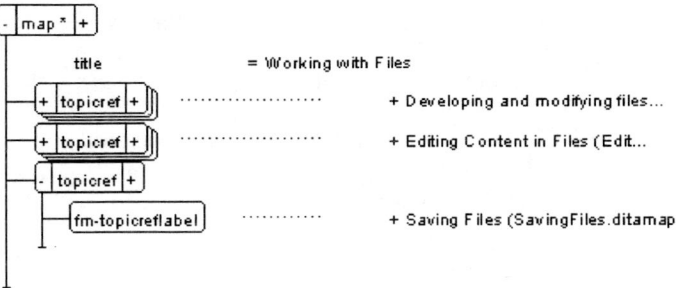.

18. Convert the map to a single FM file using the DITA > Build FM Document From DITA Map menu and name the file **WorkingWithFilesMap.fm**.

19. Review the generated file noting that the content of two maps is published and nested according to the hierarchy of the content.

20. Save and close the generated file.

Implement multiple changes to a ditamap

In this section you make multiple changes to a nested map, test the output that is generated, and update a map that contains the modified nested submap.

1. Double-click *Saving Files*.

The nested ditamap opens.

2. Collapse both *topichead* elements.

Saving Files
Concepts
+ **Why Save Files (c_SavingFiles.xml)**
+ **Why Save Files in Multiple Formats (c_SavingMultiFormat.xml)**
Tasks
+ **How to Save Files (t_SavingFiles.xml)**
+ **How to Save Files to New Locations (t_SavingToNewLocations.xml)**

3. Add a topic heading (*References*) and two topic references (*r_SavingFiles.xml* and *r_SavingToMultipleDevices.xml*) as seen below.

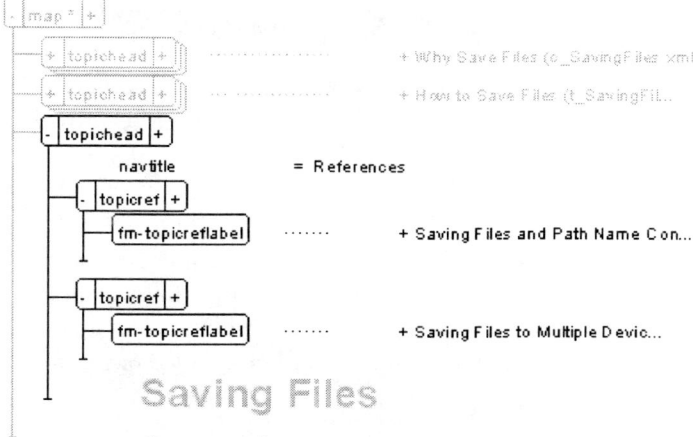

Saving Files
Concepts
+ Why Save Files (c_SavingFiles.xml)
+ Why Save Files in Multiple Formats (c_SavingMultiFormat.xml)
Tasks
+ How to Save Files (t_SavingFiles.xml)
+ How to Save Files to New Locations (t_SavingToNewLocations.xml)

References
+ **Saving Files and Path Name Conventions (r_SavingFiles.xml)**
+ **Saving Files to Multiple Devices (r_SavingToMultipleDevices.xml)**

4. Convert the map to a single FM file using the DITA > Build FM Document From DITA Map menu and name the file **SavingTopicsWithReferences.fm**.

5. Review the generated file noting the map is published and nested according to the hierarchy of the content with the content of the *reference* elements appearing last.

   These are titled *Saving Files and Path Name Conventions* and *Saving Files to Multiple Devices*. The page numbers for this content should be page 3 and page 4. In the next steps a larger map which contains the *Saving Files* map is generated.

6. Save and close the generated file.

7. Save and close the map.

   The *WorkingWithFiles.ditamap* displays.

Working with Files

+ Developing and modifying files and content (DevelopingFiles.xml)

+ Editing Content in Files (EditingFileContent.ditamap)

+ Saving Files (SavingFiles.ditamap)

8. Convert the map to a single FM file using the DITA > Build FM Document From DITA Map menu and name the file **SavingTopicsWithReferences.fm**.

9. Review the generated file noting the map is published and nested according to the hierarchy of the content with the content of the *reference* elements appearing last.

   These are titled *Saving Files and Path Name Conventions* and *Saving Files to Multiple Devices*. The page numbers for this content should now be page 5 and page 6, rather than 4 and 5 as there are additional topics in the map for *Working With Files* which did not get included when only the *Saving Files* map was published.

10. Close the generated file.

11. Save and close the map.

Tutorial 24

Work with relationship tables

Overview

This tutorial teaches you the basics of creating and publishing maps that have relationship tables in them. The relationship table is not used by FrameMaker, but is available for processing of content using the DITA Open Toolkit.

This section contains the following topics:

- *Tutorial overview*
- *Open and publish an existing map*
- *Insert a basic relationship table*
- *Add content to a relationship table*
- *Nest entries in a relationship tables*
- *Working with topicref attributes and reltables*
- *Create a collection-type*

Tutorial overview

This tutorial guides you through working with Adobe FrameMaker 8.0 to develop relationship tables in maps and ensure compliance with the DITA specification.

The tutorial assumes a default installation of FrameMaker. If your product has been customized, some of the default options may not be available.

Most of the step-by-step information in earlier tutorials is not detailed and procedures are simplified in the way they are written.

Open and publish an existing map

1. Launch FrameMaker.

2. Open the file *c:\tutorials\fm8dita\tutorial_24\SavingFiles.ditamap* using the DITA-Map-FM application.

Saving Files

Concepts

+ Why Save Files (c_SavingFiles.xml)
+ Why Save Files in Multiple Formats (c_SavingMultiFormat.xml)

Tasks

+ How to Save Files (t_SavingFiles.xml)
+ How to Save Files to New Locations (t_SavingToNewLocations.xml)

References

+ Saving Files and Path Name Conventions (r_SavingFiles.xml)
+ Saving Files to Multiple Devices (r_SavingToMultipleDevices.xml)

3. Compare the map with the following samples of a *.chm file created using the DITA Open Toolkit.

   Notice that by default there are no related links in any of the samples.

Insert a basic relationship table

1. In the Structure View, collapse all three *topichead* elements and click just before the end of the map.

2. Using the Element Catalog insert a *reltable* element with the following settings.

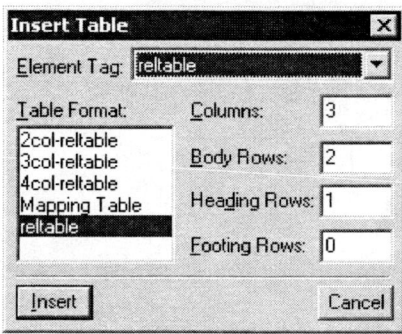

3. In the *relheader* element, set the *type* attribute of the *relcolspec* elements to *task*, *concept*, and *reference*.

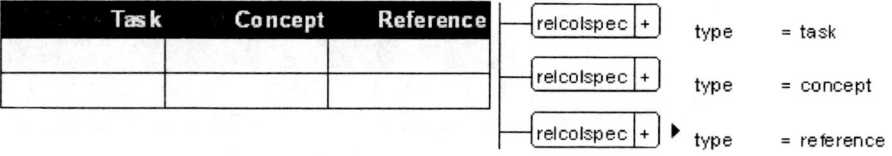

Add content to a relationship table

1. In the relationship table, click in the first empty cell below the *Task*.

2. Using the Element Catalog insert a *topicref* to ..*tutorial_24\t_SavingFiles.xml*.

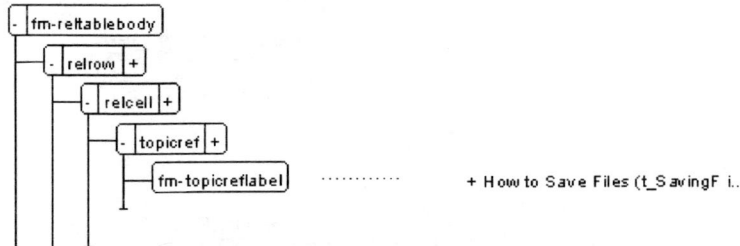

3. Select the entire table and choose Table > Resize Columns.

4. Under To Width, type **1.75"** and click Resize .

5. In the relationship table, click in the first empty cell below the *Concept*.

6. Using the Element Catalog insert a *topicref* to ..*tutorial_24\c_SavingFiles.xml*.

Task	Concept	Reference
+ How to Save Files (t_SavingFiles.xml)	+ Why Save Files (c_SavingFiles.xml)	

7. In the relationship table, click in the first empty cell below the *Reference*.

8. Using the Element Catalog insert a *topicref* to ..*tutorial_24\r_SavingFiles.xml*.

9. Compare the map with the following samples of a *.chm file created using the DITA Open Toolkit.

There are related links in the samples due to the use of the relationship table.

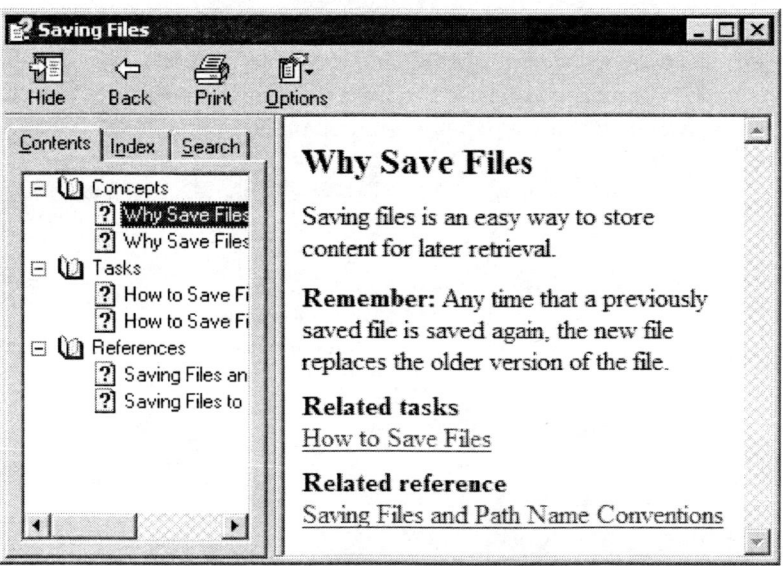

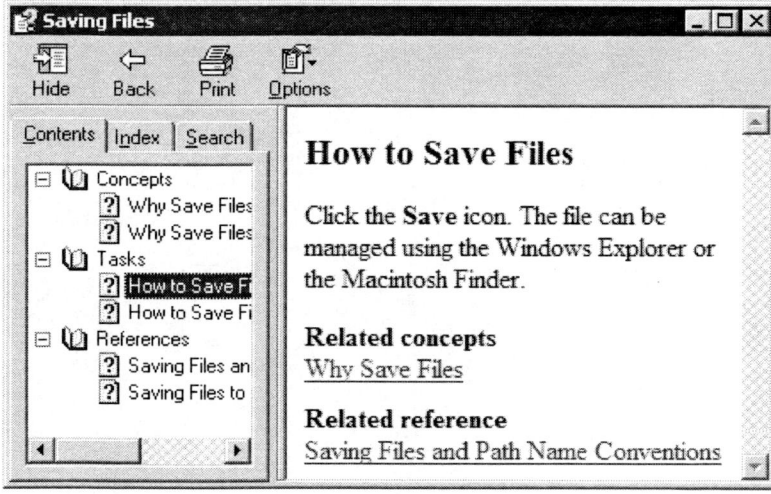

Nest entries in a relationship tables

1. Develop the relationship table to appear as follows by adding a second *topicref* element in the cell for the concept column.

   There are related links in the samples due to the use of the relationship table. The related concepts will have two links (as opposed to the previous output which had only one link) because of the addition of the sibling *topicref* element.

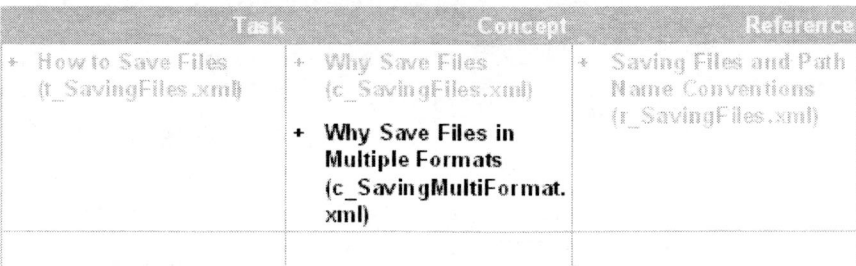

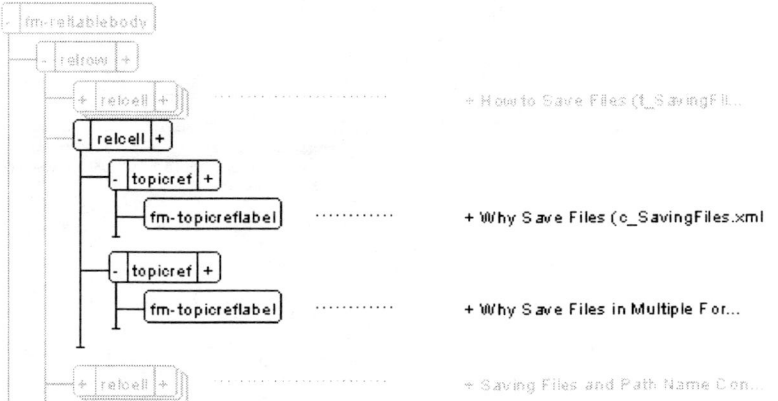

2. Compare the map with the following samples of a *.chm file created using the DITA Open Toolkit.

Note the difference in the new output compared with the old output.

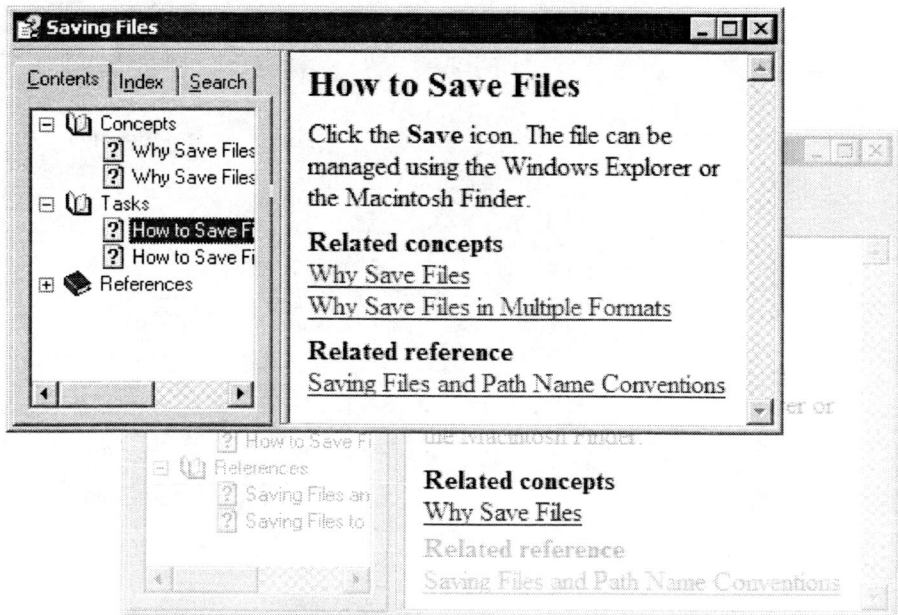

3. Reorganize the relationship table to nest the second *topicref* element as seen below:

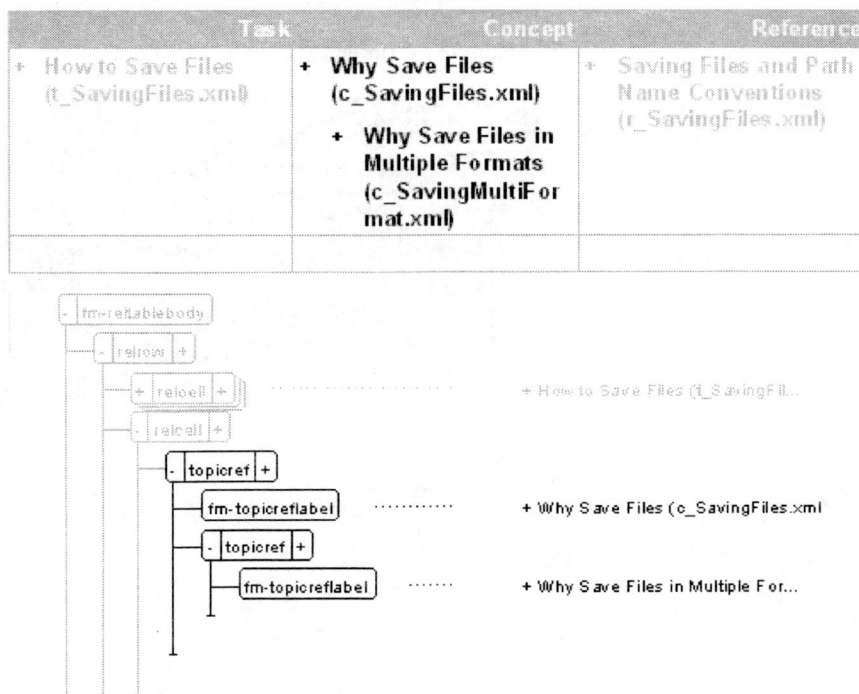

Task	Concept	Reference
+ How to Save Files (t_SavingFiles.xml)	+ Why Save Files (c_SavingFiles.xml) + Why Save Files in Multiple Formats (c_SavingMultiFormat.xml)	+ Saving Files and Path Name Conventions (r_SavingFiles.xml)

4. Compare the map with the following sample of a *.chm file created using the DITA Open Toolkit.

Note

Due to the relationship table nesting, the second topic is linked as a child. The title and short description are displayed. The TOC is not changed. Only the relationship between elements has been modified. The original map hierarchy is unchanged.

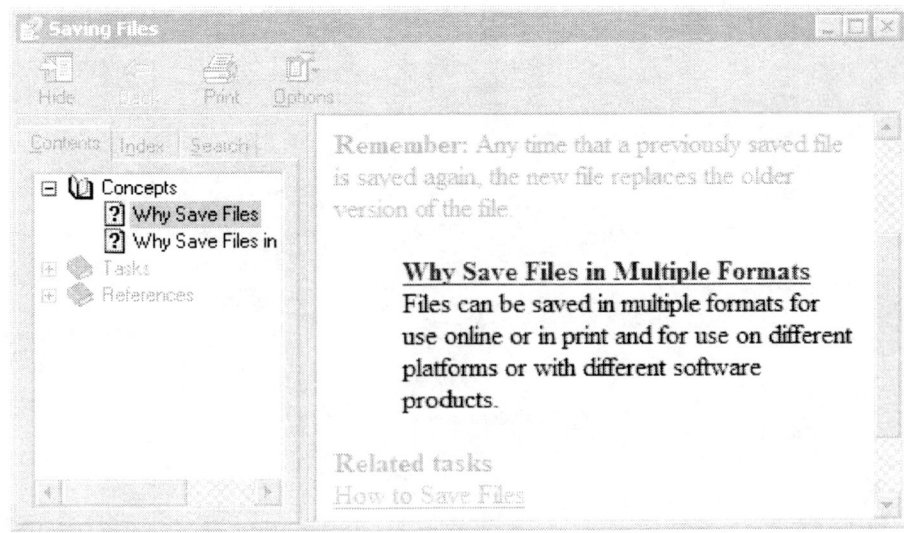

Remember: Any time that a previously saved file is saved again, the new file replaces the older version of the file.

Why Save Files in Multiple Formats
Files can be saved in multiple formats for use online or in print and for use on different platforms or with different software products.

Related tasks
How to Save Files

5. Compare the map with the following sample of the next topic in the *.chm file created using the DITA Open Toolkit.

Due to the relationship table nesting a link to the parent topic is inserted.

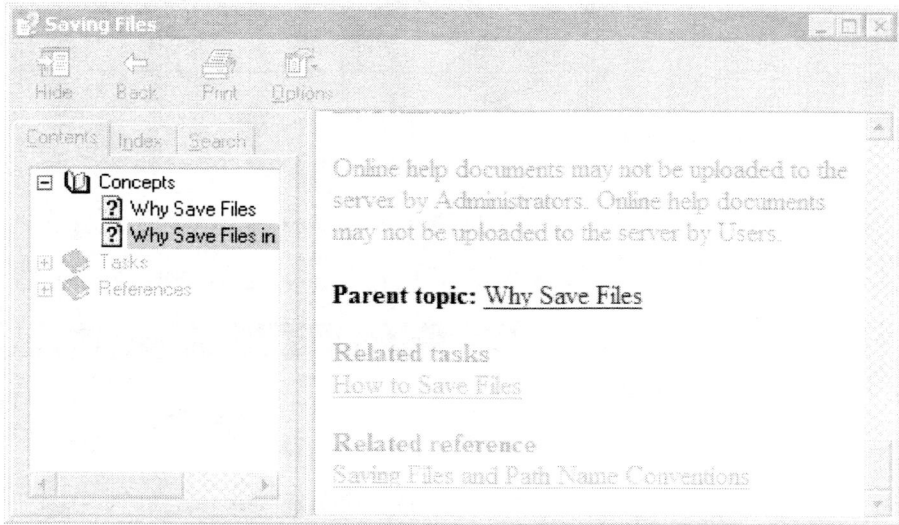

6. Delete the relationship table from the map.

Working with topicref attributes and reltables

Attributes related to rows, columns, cells or topicrefs allow relationships to be further defined.

1. In the Structure View, click just before the end of the map.

2. Insert a *reltable* element with three columns, two body rows, and 1 heading row.

3. In the *relheader* element, set the *type* attribute of the *relcolspec* elements to *task*, *concept*, and *reference*.

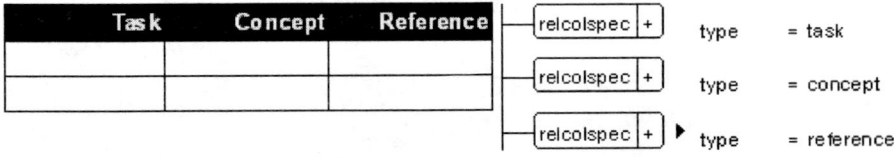

4. Select the entire table and choose Table > Resize Columns.

5. Under To Width, type **1.75"** and click Resize .

6. Develop the following relationship table using files in ..*tutorial_24*.

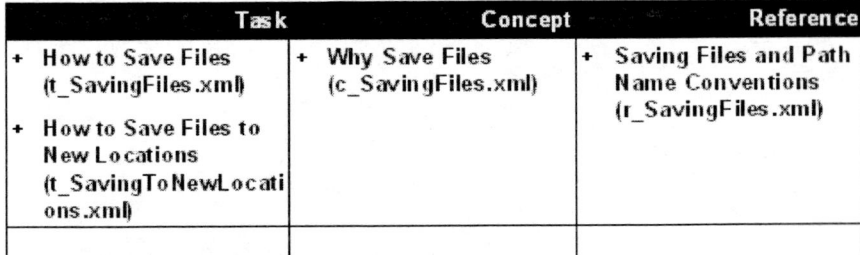

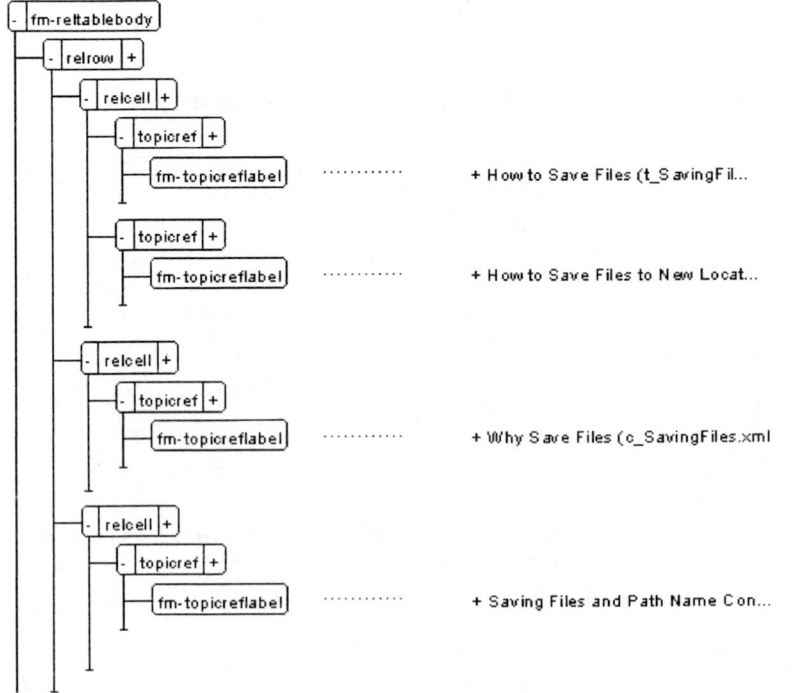

7. Compare the map with the following sample of the first concept in the *.chm file created using the DITA Open Toolkit.

Due to the relationship table configuration the concept references both tasks and the reference.

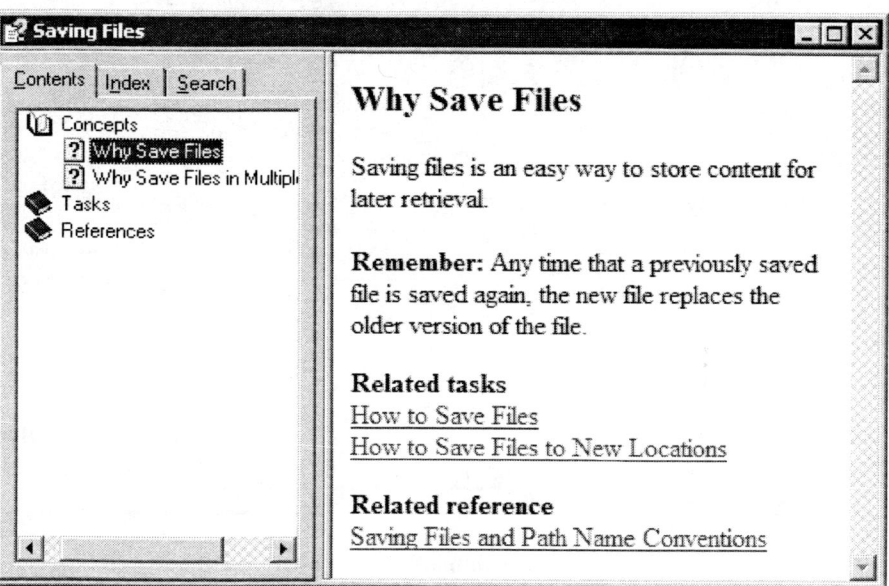

8. Compare the map with the following sample of the first task in the *.chm file created using the DITA Open Toolkit.

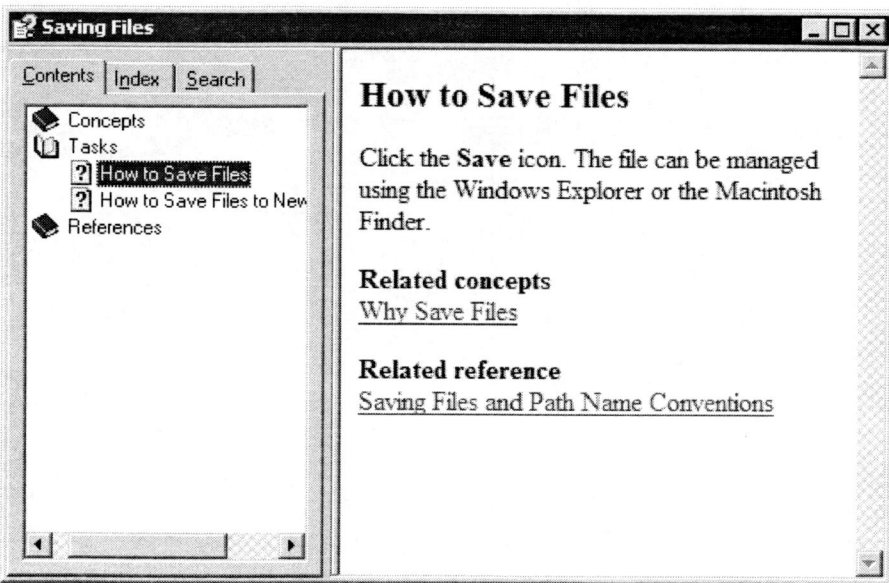

9. Compare the map with the following sample of the end of the second task in the *.chm file created using the DITA Open Toolkit.

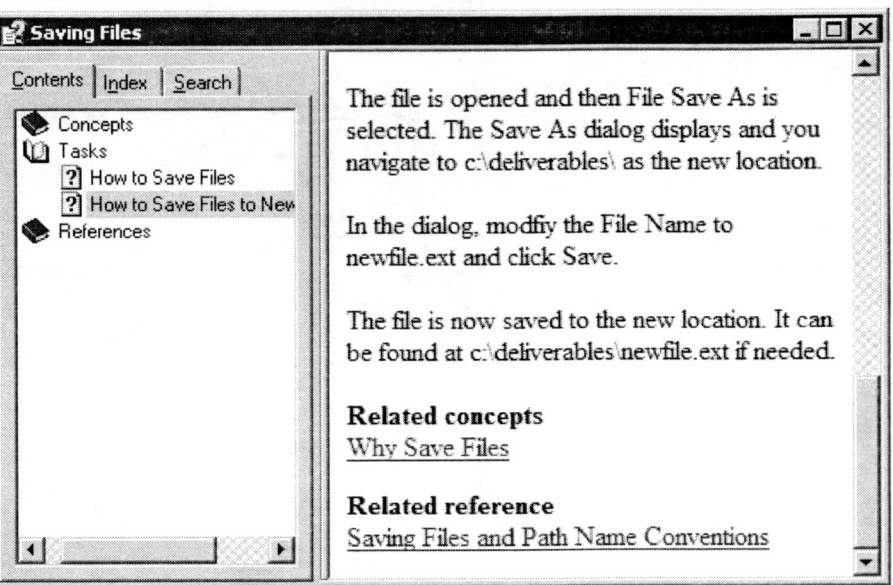

10. Compare the map with the following sample of the first reference in the *.chm file created using the DITA Open Toolkit.

Due to the relationship table configuration the reference references both tasks and the concept.

Note

Review this example of the last reference element in a default relationship table. Note that the reference links to both related concepts and related tasks. The links exist because default values were initially used. In the next steps the relationship table will be modified and the links disabled. This is done externally to the topic and only applies when the topic is used as part of the ditamap with the specific relationship table.

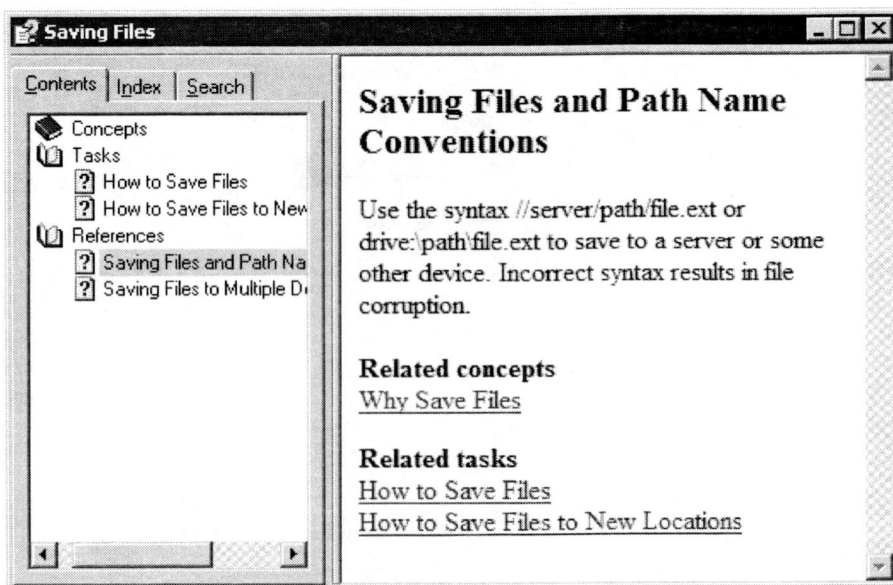

11.   In the Structure View, display the attributes for the *topicref* element *Why Save Files*.

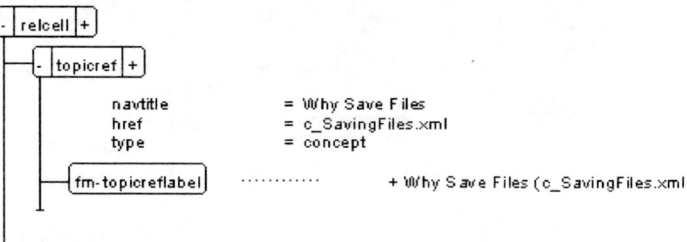

Task	Concept	Reference
+ How to Save Files (t_SavingFiles.xml) + How to Save Files to New Locations (t_SavingToNewLocati ons.xml)	+ **Why Save Files (c_SavingFiles.xml)**	+ Saving Files and Path Name Conventions (r_SavingFiles.xml)

```
.  relcell  +
   .  topicref  +
              navtitle          = Why Save Files
              href              = c_SavingFiles.xml
              type              = concept
       fm-topicreflabel   ···········   + Why Save Files (c_SavingFiles.xml
```

12.   Click the plus sign next to *topicref* element a second time to expand and display all attributes.

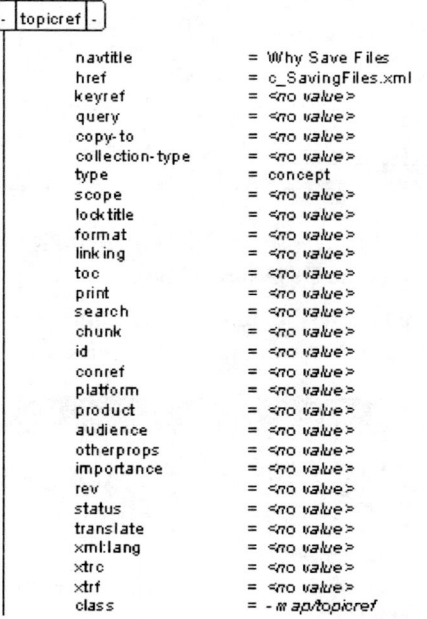

```
.  topicref  -
              navtitle          = Why Save Files
              href              = c_SavingFiles.xml
              keyref            = <no value>
              query             = <no value>
              copy-to           = <no value>
              collection-type   = <no value>
              type              = concept
              scope             = <no value>
              locktitle         = <no value>
              format            = <no value>
              linking           = <no value>
              toc               = <no value>
              print             = <no value>
              search            = <no value>
              chunk             = <no value>
              id                = <no value>
              conref            = <no value>
              platform          = <no value>
              product           = <no value>
              audience          = <no value>
              otherprops        = <no value>
              importance        = <no value>
              rev               = <no value>
              status            = <no value>
              translate         = <no value>
              xml:lang          = <no value>
              xtrc              = <no value>
              xtrf              = <no value>
              class             = - map/topicref
```

13.   Double click the *linking* attribute and modify the value to *sourceonly*.

      This ensures the element will only be used as a source in generated content such as a *.chm file.

14. In the Structure View, display the attributes for the *topicref* element *Saving Files and Path Name Conventions* and modify the *linking* attribute value to *targetonly*.

    This ensures the element will only be used as a target in generated content such as a *.chm file.

15. Compare the map with the following sample of the first concept in the *.chm file created using the DITA Open Toolkit.

    Due to the relationship table configuration the concept references both tasks and the reference. Note that related links to the task and the reference are maintained.

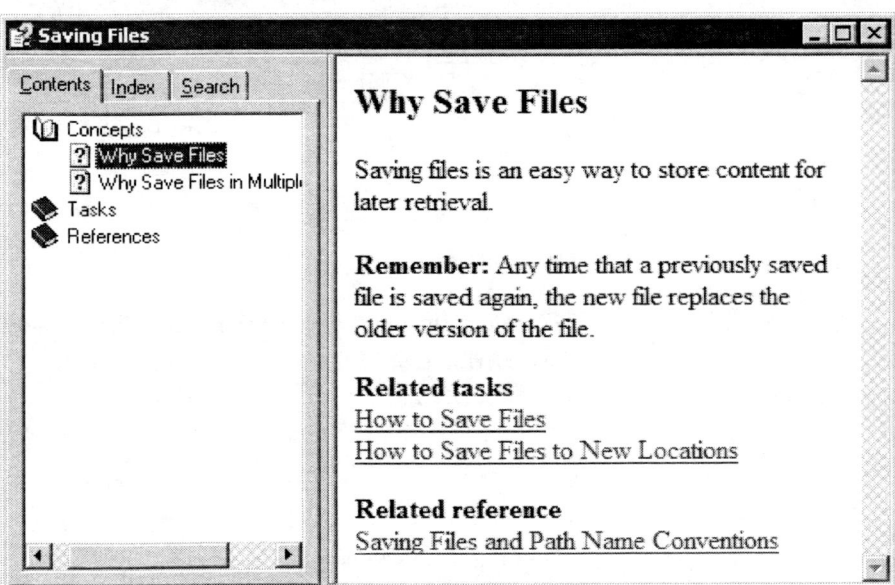

16. Compare the map with the following sample of the first reference in the *.chm file created using the DITA Open Toolkit.

    Due to the relationship table configuration the reference links to no other files (it is a targetonly and may not link to other topics).

Create a collection-type

1. In the Structure View, display the attributes for the *relcell* element in the first *relrow* element of the *fm-reltablebody* element.

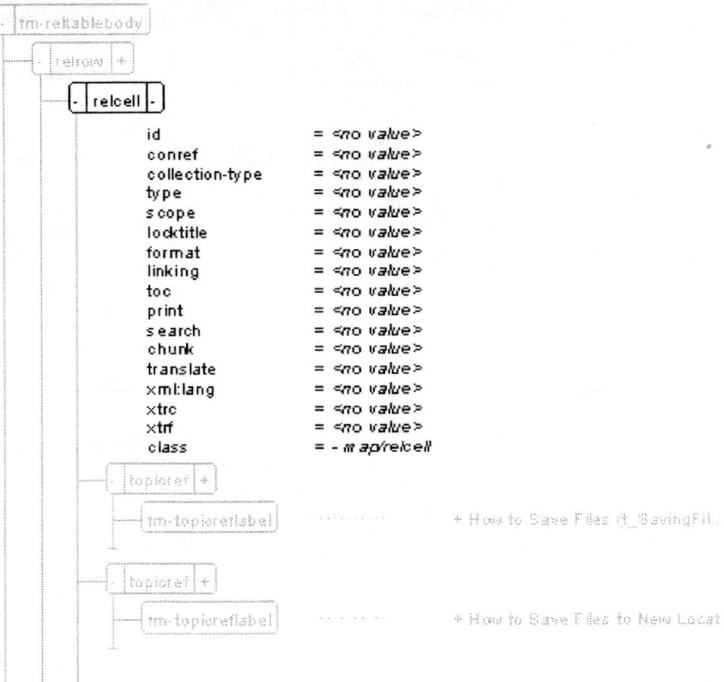

2. Modify the *collection-type* value to *family*.

3. Compare the map with the following sample of the tasks in the *.chm file created using the DITA Open Toolkit.

Due to the relationship table configuration the tasks references each other as part of a family. Note that related links to the reference are maintained as well.

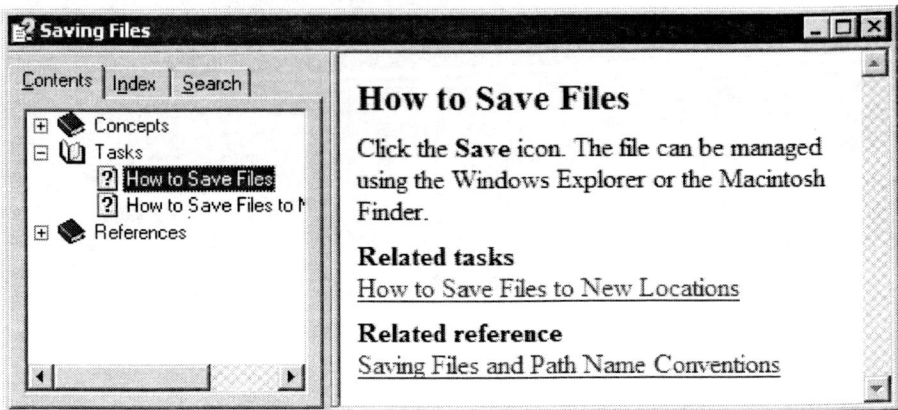

4. Delete the relationship table from the map and save and close the file.